Livelihood in Colonial Lagos

Livelihood in Colonial Lagos

Monsuru Muritala

LEXINGTON BOOKS
Lanham • Boulder • New York • London

Published by Lexington Books
An imprint of The Rowman & Littlefield Publishing Group, Inc.
4501 Forbes Boulevard, Suite 200, Lanham, Maryland 20706
www.rowman.com

6 Tinworth Street, London SE11 5AL, United Kingdom

Copyright © 2019 by The Rowman & Littlefield Publishing Group, Inc.

All rights reserved. No part of this book may be reproduced in any form or by any electronic or mechanical means, including information storage and retrieval systems, without written permission from the publisher, except by a reviewer who may quote passages in a review.

British Library Cataloguing in Publication Information Available

Library of Congress Control Number: 2019949926
ISBN 978-1-4985-8214-8 (cloth)
ISBN 978-1-4985-8215-5 (electronic)

Contents

Acknowledgments	vii
List of Abbreviations	ix
Introduction	xi
1 An Overview of the Pre-Colonial Economy and Society of Lagos	1
2 Colonial Infrastructure and the Modern Economy, 1861–1960	9
3 Waged Employment, the Extended Family, and Urban Culture, 1900–1960	27
4 Women and Urban Experience, 1900–1960	71
5 Neighborhood Cultures and the Redefinition of Social Values, 1861–1960	99
Conclusion	135
Bibliography	143
Index	153
About the Author	161

Acknowledgments

My research for this book started with my interest in urban and livelihood studies, which was shaped by my childhood experience on the streets of Lagos. Most sincerely, I wish to express my joy and gratitude to Professor Olutayo Adesina, whose mentorship, comments, corrections, and encouragement made this book a reality. He identified in me the inherent academic potentials and has been mentoring me for over two decades. My interest in livelihood studies was further enhanced by my interaction with Professor Ayodeji Olukoju, who offered useful professional advice and guidance at the early stage of my research.

I wish to also express my appreciation to my colleagues in the Department of History, University of Ibadan for their encouragement—Professors Sofela Babatude, Ajayi Ademola, C.B.N Ogbogbo, Victor Edo, Drs. Olaniyi Rasheed, Olisa Muojama, Oladejo Mutiat, Ajayi Olayinka, and Abolorunde Ayodele.

My sincere gratitude also goes to the members of staff at the National Archives Ibadan (NAI), particularly Messer Mark Ehumadu, Abraham Olayemi, and Adelowo Adegboyega. Same goes to Mrs. Babalola Victoria Modupe, Mrs. Ologunmeta Olayemi, Mrs. Oluwafemi Victoria, and Mrs. Omisore for their assistance and unflinching support throughout the period of my search for documents at the archives. I must not forget those who assisted me in the course of my search for other materials and field work—Mr. Adeyanju (formerly of Jade Trust), Dr. (Mrs.) Adesina Oluwakemi, Messrs Seriki Kazeem, Oderinde Ayobami, and Ogundare Nurudeen. I am also grateful to the editorial board of the *Journal of the Social Sciences*, University of Faisalabad, for granting me permission to reprint in this book my article, which had earlier been published in volume 5 number 1 of this journal. Similarly, I wish to record a debt of gratitude to the editorial board of *Afrika Zamani*: an annual journal of African history and CODESRIA for also granting me permission to reprint in this book my article, which had earlier been published in volume 22 & 23, 2014–2015.

I am also grateful to the Department of African Studies and Anthropology (DASA), University of Birmingham, United Kingdom for the award of Cadbury Fellowship in 2015, which provided the platform to discuss my research output at seminars.

I must not fail to acknowledge my teachers, friends, and colleagues in the academics for their concern and moral support: Professors Adebayo Akanmu, Oloyede Abdurahman, and James Ilevbare; Drs. Kareem Idowu, Adebiyi Adelabu, Akinboye Goke, Alade idowu, and Leslie James of Queen Mary University, London. Also, my gratitude goes to Dr. Aderinto Saheed for his encouragement and useful comments on the final manuscript. I want to specially thank Mr. Raji Ololade Ahmed whose residential apartment I turned to second home during my field work in Lagos between 2010 and 2013. To my family and friends: Dr. Kadiri Aremu Jasiliu, Mr. and Mrs. Ajibola: Messrs Shittu Ganiu, Oladele Femi, Adedire Adegboyega, and Odunlami Monsurat. I also thank Alhaji and Alhaja Ayoola, for their moral support. You are all cherished more than you can imagine. I appreciate every other person not mentioned but has been supportive to me.

I am particularly grateful to my mother, Alhaja Isiwatu Muritala, for the inspiration and financial and moral support she gave me throughout my educational career. You are indeed a "sweet mother." My gratitude also goes to my siblings: Ogundare Fatimah, Muritala Akeem, Adedapo Monsurat, and Oguntoyinbo Lukmon.

My special thanks to my darling wife, Abimbola Balqis, for her love, understanding, and encouragement. Words are not enough to express my appreciation for your steadfastness, support, and inspiration. I love you. To my children, Abdulrahaman, Habeedah, and Halimah, I say, you are all cherished.

List of Abbreviations

AAT	Anglo African Times
AG	Action Group
AM	African Mirror
COLA	Cost of Living Allowance
DO	Daily Observer
DR	Daily Record
DS	Daily service
ECN	Electricity Corporation of Nigeria
HMP	Herbert Macaulay Papers
LEDB	Lagos Executive Development Board
LMWA	Lagos Market Women's Association
LSDPC	Lagos State Property Development Company
LWR	Lagos Weekly Record
LWL	Lagos Women League
MOH	Medical officer of Health
NAI	National Archives Ibadan
NCNC	National Council of Nigerian and Cameroon
NDT	Nigerian Daily Times
NNDP	Nigerian National Democratic Party
NP	Nigerian Pioneer
NM	Nigerian Magazine
NYM	Nigerian Youth Movement
UAC	United African Company
WAP	West African Pilot
WAR	West African Review
YN	Yoruba News

Introduction

LIVELIHOOD, URBANIZATION, AND LAGOS IN CONTEXT

Historically, cities have developed and evolved as vehicles for socioeconomic interaction, growth, and social change. The lives and livelihoods of millions of people are constructed, affected, and modified by what is done in cities. "Urbanization" is a term that refers to at least four sets of phenomena at the same time.[1] First, urbanization refers to the rural out-migration to cities or population centers of at least 20,000.[2] This is the familiar rural-urban migration. Second, it relates to an increasing proportion of a country's population that lives in large population centers.[3] Third, it refers to the transition of a country's population from rural society to an urban-industrial one. This focuses on the increasing proportion of the people that are engaged in non-agricultural activities.[4] Fourth, urbanization may also point to the growth of cities or development of settlements of 20,000 or more inhabitants, which provide a level of variety of services that are not available in rural areas.[5] Such urban settlements have provided the critical nexus between human existence and livelihood. Thus, urbanization and city growth are germane to the study of urban livelihood and development.

Urbanization or city creation predates colonialism in many African countries.[6] Apart from Egypt, where urban civilization is as old as 5,000 years, several cities in other African regions have centuries old histories.[7] In Nigeria, powerful local rulers promoted the evolution of these early cities into effective nodes of human development and as engines of economic and social growth. Prominent among these pre-colonial urban formations spread across the different geographical zones now known as Nigeria are Benin, Oyo,

Ile-Ife, Ilorin, Sokoto, Kano, Abeokuta, Nguru, Bonny, Calabar, Onitsha, and Maiduguri.

By the early twentieth century, a second generation of cities started to emerge in Africa. These were urban formations that can be categorized as colonial cities. Such cities either began as pre-colonial formations before being transformed into colonial cities or were established by colonial officials. Either way, the character and the contexts of such cities became defined by Western parameters. The construction of railways and roads, coupled with new economic activities and improvements in agricultural methodologies introduced by colonial administrations, helped to create many new urban centers that served as administrative, commercial, industrial, and mining and transport nodes.[8] Examples of these second-generation cities include colonial Lagos, Jos, Port Harcourt, Kaduna, Jebba, Lokoja, Dakar, Conakry, Accra, and Niamey. The European objectives of using them as administrative and economic hubs and expanding export production and distribution of their manufactured goods facilitated the urbanization process in such cities. Abdoumaliq Simone has distinguished the role of colonialism in this regard:

> The long period in which different versions of colonialism were in operation was, of course, critical to the shaping and present day capacities of most African cities. But the importance of colonialism is not that it gave rise to cities in what was for the most part rural continent, rather, the crucial move was to shape urbanization so cities would act instrumentally on African bodies and social formations. They would act on them in ways that made various endogenous forms of, and proclivities toward, urbanization possible within the context of an enforced engagement with the European world.[9]

Simone, no doubt, has captured an important aspect of the growth and development of colonial cities. His explanation seeks to locate the consequences of colonialism, modernization, and urbanization in a peripheral state. Corroborating Simone's assertion is Lewis Munford who claims that the city is at once "a container and transmitter of culture."[10] Also, in the context of Africa, Thomas Hodgkin has invoked the same theme to depict the dual role of the African city in modern times—as a solvent, "weakening traditional social ties and loosening the traditional beliefs and values" and as promoter of new associations, new ideas, and a new economic and social ethos.[11] It is within this framework that this study tries to understand livelihood in the city of Lagos between 1861 and 1960. It examines the experiences of the peoples of Lagos by analyzing and synthesizing the livelihood of the people in order to reconstruct aspects of the social and economic history of Lagos. This book explores the nexus between urbanization and socioeconomic change that accompanied the modernization process initiated by the British during the period of study. Thus, one of the main objectives of this book is to articulate the specific character of urbanization under British rule. For the city of Lagos, that predates the arrival of British colonialists, the study examines the outcome of British economic and urbanization policies on the lives of the people. It focuses on the general coping and survival strategies adopted by the masses.

By the late nineteenth century, in the aftermath of the annexation of Lagos, the colonial administration had introduced some measures that fostered the process of urbanization, which diverged significantly from traditional practice and processes. In spite of this, these measures were not universally adopted in modern cities that came under British influences. In some instances, change was represented by the selective development of transport infrastructure such as seaport, river ports, and rail terminals.[12] These ultimately culminated in the rise and expansion of towns and cities as well as modern infrastructure. Consequently, some major towns grew as colonial administrative headquarters as a result of massive spending and development of social and physical infrastructure. These centers included Lagos, Enugu, Ibadan, and Kaduna. Further implications of this were increases in population and size, as workers of all types and the unemployed flocked into the towns for anticipated economic opportunities.[13] Thus, a key feature of these colonial towns and cities was the phenomenon of rural-urban migration.

Although a reasonable degree of scholarly attention has been paid to the African cities in terms of their infrastructure, demography, politics, economy, ethnography, and social structures, there is a gap to be filled in how all these affected livelihood in an emerging modern milieu characterized by strong adherence to traditional values and norms. Therefore, of great importance to this study are not only those who oiled the wheel of colonial progress in the city of Lagos through their contributions as civil servants, traders, and merchants, but also the livelihood of those that existed at the fringe of the so-called modern society. This study presents historical explanations regarding the functioning of the "modernized" spaces in which human subjects lived their lives within, between and against the dominant colonial structures and official bureaucracies. This has been largely ignored in the existing literature on Lagos. Based on this, the following questions were addressed:

1. What were the impact of colonial economy and infrastructure on the lives of the people of Lagos between 1861 and 1960?
2. How did informal sector serve as economic strategy of livelihood?
3. What benefits did income, family structure, and the flow of social capital have in mitigating the challenges faced by both migrants and indigenes of Lagos between 1861 and 1960?
4. Beyond domestic service, what sociopolitical and economic roles did women play in the alleviation of hardship in the city of Lagos?

5. Did crime provide livelihood in Lagos?
6. Why was the need for urban slum clearance and its impact on settlement and livelihood patterns in Lagos?
7. Of what significance was the evolution of urban and neighborhood cultures for the movement of people and ideas across social and geographic boundaries?

URBANIZATION AND LIVELIHOOD CONCEPTUALIZED

For the purpose of clarity, this section provides the conceptual analysis of urbanization and livelihood. It also provides the methodological framework for highlighting and understanding the dynamics of colonialism and urban livelihood within the context of modernization, urbanization, dispossession, culture, and change. Urbanization in the colonial history of Lagos, brought with it life-altering urban policies and programs, prominent among which was the 1955 slum clearance exercise in central Lagos. This exercise became a paradox for the residents of Lagos. While the city gained in terms of physical planning, environmental sanitation, and urban improvement, the experiences were different for the displaced and dispossessed residents of Lagos. Thus, the study concerns itself with the political economy of the slum clearance exercise in colonial Lagos in order to shed light on the controversy surrounding the reasons for the exercise, and particularly, to examine both the negative and positive impacts it had on the peoples' livelihood.

Urbanization entails spatial, social, and temporal phenomena, and thus, requires an interdisciplinary approach.[14] There have been many attempts to arrive at a theoretical definition of the city and city life. Marx and Engels, Durkheim, and Weber dealt in detail with the issue of what it were that characterized their modern, increasingly urban, societies.[15] Louis Wirth describes density and heterogeneity in permanent settlement as the core of the criteria to be used in the definition of urbanism. Gideon Sjoberg on the other hand, accepts Wirth's criteria but goes on to say that these are insufficient. There is a need to add the requirement of a significant number of full time specialists, including a literate group, and those engaged in a relatively wide range of nonagricultural activities.[16]

In tune with the above arguments is Falola and Heaton's position that agriculture remains the way of life in rural areas, where communities remain largely homogenous, while in urban areas lifestyles and economic activities are more heterogeneous.[17] Viewed from the criterion of Loius Wirth earlier, pre-colonial cities of Yorubaland contained such large numbers of farmers but the buildings were so village-like that to the foreign eye they seemed no more than dense rural settlements. In terms of population, by the 1850s Yoruba towns of Ibadan, Abeokuta, and Oyo had already recorded populations of 100,000, 60,000 and 25,000 respectively.[18] However, those accustomed to the character of urban areas in Europe and America has questioned the urban status of these pre-colonial Yoruba towns. In comparison with the British model, the lineage argument has been used until now to deny Yoruba cities their character of true cities. Lloyd posits that although Yoruba towns were large and densely populated, they were but settlements of agricultural people.[19] This lend credence to the assertion that one of the dramatic consequences of the impact of Western capitalism on those countries to which it had turned for materials and markets for its products is the spectacular growth of cities.[20] Colonialism transformed towns in Africa into cities as a result of infrastructural facilities and economic improvement, especially those towns designated as administrative headquarters.

The conception of urbanization is different as it applies to different areas of the world. Mabogunje defines it as a process whereby human beings congregate in relatively large numbers at one particular spot of the earth's surface.[21] Buchanan and Pugh point out the difficulty of trying to apply Western concepts of urbanization to Nigeria. "The difficulty arises from the deficiencies of the statistical material . . . in part from the character of the 'towns' themselves."[22] Many of these lack the basic services and functions which constitute the criteria of an urban area.[23] Besides, Hugh Smythe reinforces this position, arguing that population and heterogeneity is not an enough criterion for a place to be called a city. According to him, Nigerian cities do not provide in kind and degree many of the services and facilities associated with Western cities.[24] He cites Nigerian cities with high population without amenities in 1952: Akure (38,853) without electricity; Benin (53,753) without street light; Kano (130,173) with no public library.[25] This assertion by Smythe does not necessarily define urbanity, especially within the context of Africa's condition.

In the view of Anthony King, urban processes, whether community organization or class and ethnic politics, have to be understood in terms of their structural bases or how they are conditioned by the larger economic, political, and socioeconomic milieu.[26] He posits further that it has become increasingly impossible to ignore the overwhelming importance of the historical, cultural, and political significance (Europeans) as a major contributing factor in the making of the culture and space of many contemporary cities.[27] This is because the Europeans conceptualized a city as any settlement where the majority of occupants are engaged in occupations other than agricultural activities.[28] This view compared urbanity in America and Europe of the period to Africa of the period under study.

Louis Wirth warns of the danger of confusing urbanism with industrialism and modern capitalism. He contends that the rise of cities in the modern world is undoubtedly not independent of modern power-driven machine technology, mass production, and capitalistic enterprises. Cities are places where people from many different ethnic, religious, and socioeconomic backgrounds interact on a regular basis.[29] In this way, mutual understanding and respect between people can be fostered. Cities also tend to be places where ethnic, religious, and class tensions often erupt.[30]

Considering the various views of scholars on urbanization and cities, there is no doubt that urbanization has been difficult to define in a universal or precise way. This study in its usage and interpretation situates the concept within Rose Hum Lee's definition that cities are basically population aggregates which are large, heterogeneous, and densely settled within a limited land area.[31] The Lagos of the colonial period was populated with indigenes, liberated returnees from Sierra Leone and Brazil, and immigrants from the hinterlands and neighboring countries.

The concept of livelihood is dynamic as the conditions and composition of people's livelihood changes, sometimes rapidly and also over time. Livelihood is complex with households in the developing world undertaking a wide range of activities, as they are not just farmers, or laborers, or factory workers, or fisher folk but they engage in self-sustaining activities formally and informally.[32] Livelihood has been discussed extensively among scholars and development practitioners, but there is an assumption that livelihood is about the ways and means of "making a living." However, the most widely accepted definition of livelihood is that given by Robert Chambers and Gordon Conway. They aver that "a livelihood comprises the capabilities, assets (including both material and social resources) and activities required for a means of living."[33] To Wallman, an anthropologist, livelihood is an umbrella concept which suggests that social life is layered and that these layers overlap (both in the way people talk about them and the way they should be analyzed). Thus, livelihood is more than just a matter of finding or making shelter, transacting money, and preparing food to put on the table or exchange in the market place.[34] It is a matter of ownership and circulation of information, management of social relationships, affirmation of personal significance and group identity, and the inter- relation of each of these task to the other.

Livelihood is also about creating and embracing new opportunities. While gaining livelihood, or attempting to do so, people may, at the same time, have to cope with risks and uncertainties, such as a wide range of forces, social, economic, political, legal, environmental and institutional, both within and outside the locality in which they live, which are beyond the family control.[35] The binding feature of these definitions and interpretations is that "livelihood" deals with people, their resources, and what they do with these. Therefore, livelihoods, essentially, revolve around resources, but these resources cannot be disconnected from the issues and problems of access and changing political, economic, and sociocultural circumstances. It is, therefore, within this context that this book historicizes livelihood in colonial Lagos by analyzing the strategies of survival adopted by the people (indigenes and immigrants) in order to explore the available physical, financial, human, social, economic, and natural assets or capital for the reconstruction of their general well-being.

NOTES

1. Nimi Wariboko, "Urbanization and Cities in Africa," in *Africa: Contemporary Africa*, Vol. 5, ed. Toyin Falola (NC: Carolina Academic Press, 2003), 633.
2. Ibid.
3. This is referred to as the rate of urbanization, and it is defined as "the average annual rate of change of the proportion of urban and its equivalent to the difference between urban and global rate of growth of the population under consideration." See United Nations, *World Urbanization Prospects* (New York, NY: United Nations, 1998), 3.
4. Ibid.
5. Wariboko, "Urbanization and Cities in Africa," 633.
6. United Nations Human Settlement (UN-HABITAT), *The State of African Cities 2008: A framework for Addressing Urban Challenges in Africa*, Nairobi, 81.
7. Ibid.
8. Ibid.
9. Abdoumaliq Simone, "On the Worlding of African Cities," *African Studies Review* 44, no.2 (2008): 19.
10. Mumford Lewis, "The City in History, Cited in Adewoye, O. Legal Practice in Ibadan, 1904–1960." *Journal of Legal Pluralism* no.24 (1986): 57.
11. Thomas Hodgkin, *Nationalism in Colonial Africa* (New York, NY, 1962), 63.
12. Ayodeji Olukoju, "Nigerian Cities in Historical Perspective," in *Nigerian Cities*, eds. Toyin Falola and Steven Salm (Trenton, NJ: African World Press, 2003), 11–46.
13. Ayodeji Olukoju, "Population Pressure, Housing and Sanitation in West Africa's Premier Port City: Lagos 1900–1939." *Journal of Australian Association of Maritime History* 15, no.2 (1993): 91–106.
14. Catherine Conquery Vidrovitch, "The Process of Urbanization in Africa: From the Origins to the Beginning of Independence." *African Studies Review* 34, no.1 (April, 1991): 1–98.
15. Williams Flanagan and Josef Gugler, eds., *Urbanization and Social Change in West Africa* (Cambridge: Cambridge University Press, 1978), 19.
16. Gideon Sjoberg, "The Pre-industrial City," *American Journal of Sociology* 60, (1955): 438–45.
17. Toyin Falola and Mathew Heaton, eds., *A History of Nigeria* (Cambridge: Cambridge University Press, 2010), 5.

18. Flanagan and Gugler, *Urbanization and Social Change*, 19.
19. Peter Cutt Lloyd, "The Yoruba: An Urban People?" in *Southhall, An Urban Anthropology*, ed. A. Southhall (Oxford: Oxford University Press, 1973), 107–23.
20. Clyde Mitchell, *Cities, Society and Social Perception: A Central African Perspective* (Oxford: Clarendon Press, 1987), 1.
21. Akinlawon Mabogunje, *Urbanization in Nigeria* (London: University of London Press, 1968), 331.
22. Keith Buchanan and John Charles Pugh, *Land and People in Nigeria* (London: University of London Press, 1955), 63.
23. Ibid.
24. Smythe Hugh, "Urbanization in Nigeria." *Anthropological Quarterly* 33, no.3 (1960): 144.
25. See for details *Nigerian Year Book*, 1958.
26. Anthony King, *Cities as Texts: Paradigms as Representation* (London: Macmillan Press, 1986), 1.
27. Ibid.
28. Egon Ernest Bergel, *Urban Sociology* (New York, NY: McGraw-Hill, 1955), 8.
29. Falola and Heaton, *A History of Nigeria*, 5.
30. Ibid.
31. Hum Lee, *The City* (New York, NY: Lippincott Cited in Weber Max, 1958), *The City* (New York, NY: Macmillan Publishing, 1955), 28.
32. Frank Ellis, "Household Strategies and Rural Livelihood Diversification." *Journal of Development Studies* 35, no.1 (1998): 1–38.
33. Robert Chambers and Gordon Conway, *Sustainable Rural Livelihoods: Practical Concepts for the 21st Century* (Brighton: Institute of Development Studies, 1992), 9.
34. Sandra Wallman, *Eight London Households* (London: Tavistock, 1984), 6.
35. Adedamola Ademola, *Factors Affecting Livelihood Activities in Ileogbo Commuity of Aiyedire Local Government Area, Osun State, Nigeria* (MSc diss., University of Ibadan, 2010), 13.

Chapter 1

An Overview of the Pre-Colonial Economy and Society of Lagos

Deriving its modern name from early Portuguese contacts probably in the seventeenth century, Lagos has grown from a small Yoruba farming settlement to become the most populous metropolis in black Africa. Topographically, the capital of the pre-colonial kingdom of Lagos, as well as the pulsing, crowded, and constricted heart of the modern city that has grown from it, lies on a sandy, swampy island of only about two square miles in size, which is located around a large lagoon that opens onto West Africa's Bight of Benin.[1] The island forms part of the southern border of a region that stretches from the Volta River in the west to the River Nun in the east and was inhabited historically by a number of peoples whose polities waxed and waned and who interacted with one another culturally.[2] These inhabitants included Gbe speakers (Aja, Fon, and Gun) in the west, Yoruba speakers in the center, and Edo speakers in the east.[3] Besides, a vast network of lagoons, creeks, and estuaries, fed by sometimes navigable rivers flowing in from the north, runs parallel to the coast between the Volta and the Nun, constituting a 400-mile inland waterway that facilitated movement and exchange.[4] Subsequently, the island became a center where peoples and cultures intermingled well before the contact with the Europeans.

Its traditional name *Eko* is said to be a corruption of the Yoruba word *Oko* which means a farm, and properly refers to the oldest part of the city on Lagos Island.[5] Another point worthy of note is the assertion of Bini source that Lagos derived its name Eko from Orogbua's camp.[6] Nevertheless, this claim should not be interpreted as contradicting the claim of the Yoruba sources that the Olofin and his subjects regarded Lagos Island as an *Oko* or farm. Indeed, "Oko" and "Eko" mark two distinct periods of Lagos history—periods of Awori rule and of Bini hegemony.[7] Lagos spreads across four islands: Lagos, Iddo, Ikoyi, and Victoria Island and considerable area of the mainland.

But today, the city, in order to accommodate population growth, witnessed several suburban expansions into the countryside from its central core, an area of 70 km^2, encroaching and absorbing other fringe settlements.[8]

The pre-colonial period in Lagos represented the time when the economy of Lagos was dynamic and self-sustaining. This is evident when we consider the traditions of origins or the peopling of Lagos Island.[9] It is a popular tradition that Ogunfunminire, a hunter from the royal family of Ile-Ife, founded the first of the series of settlements to the north of the island.[10] This shows that hunting can be considered as one of the occupations of early Lagosians. Another area of tradition of origin of Lagos that can be used as a pointer to the economy of Lagos is the present palace of the Oba of Lagos which was, according to tradition, used by one Aromire for planting pepper and other vegetables.[11] This was an indication that early Lagosians might have engaged in some subsistence form of farming. The fact that the "sons" of the legendary Ogunfunminire were referred to as the *Idejo*[12] fishermen co-operative, also point to the fact many early Lagosians were fishermen. The early settlers in Lagos were not only professionals, but also traders who engaged in long-distance trade with their neighbors. This is evident in the established markets by neighbors, such as Obun Eko markets in Lagos, which was made popular by the Ijebu traders in Lagos.[13] Besides, markets like Ebute-Ero and ItaFaji served as centers of commerce and exchange during this period. In these markets, various articles could be found, ranging from yam, fish, pepper, vegetables, and cloth.[14] This partly supports the argument that "Lagosians" have always traded in legitimate articles before the Europeans introduced trade in human beings. Until the era of the Atlantic slave trade, slavery existed in Lagos only on a limited scale.

By the end of the nineteenth century, a picture of the economic organization and commercial activities of Lagos had become clear and noticeable. Broadly, these included fishing, farming, hunting, smithing, salt making, palmwine tapping, and a wide and intricate network of trading systems that involved not only daily and periodic market activities, but also short- and long-distance trading practices.[15] However, it should be noted that at the twilight of the eighteenth and nineteenth centuries, the phenomenon of slave trade had become a significant feature of Lagos commerce. "Lagosians" participated fully by acting as middlemen between the Europeans on the coast and the indigenous Africans in the hinterland. According to Aderibigbe, traditions affirm that Lagos had its first experience of the slave trade in the reign of Akinsemoyin, who made friends with some Portuguese slave traders whom he invited to Lagos on his ascension to the throne.[16]

The geography and the location of the city of Lagos also played a significant role in its phenomenal growth as a flourishing slave port before 1900. Kristin Mann posits that the foreign slave trade at Lagos developed as part of a broader Atlantic and regional commercial networks. That is, the regular, direct export of slaves from the town began as a consequence of political and economic changes to the west along the Slave Coast and in the interior of the Bight of Benin.[17] So important was the wealth and prosperity that accompanied the trade in slaves especially between the period 1760 and 1850 that one would not but conclude that it was the most important feature of the economic set up of the society. In fact, direct export of slaves which began slowly with 269 in 1761 had risen to 37,715 slaves in 1850.[18] Consequently, by the middle of the nineteenth century, the town became the leading slave port in the Bight of Benin and also developed into the largest exporter of slaves north of the Equator.[19] This explains the affluence and sophistication of the wealth from trading in slaves brought upon the foreign slave partners as well as the powerful and the ruling classes whose positions in the society became greatly enhanced. In fact, the interior and exterior decorations of Oba Akinsemoyin's palace during the period lend credence to the assertion that he benefited from the trade enormously.[20]

In spite of the fame and prosperity associated with the trade in human beings, Lagos was also popular for its trading activities both as a center of domestic and foreign trade and the land of traders. At the domestic level, daily markets were operated by Lagosians where articles of daily need were exchanged. The mode of exchange was generally assumed to be by barter until cowries, European goods, and later currency notes were introduced.[21] Although on the eve of annexation of Lagos, the slave trade had almost eclipsed other forms of commercial activities, later on, legitimate trade in commodities was introduced to replace the trade in human beings.

The social development of Lagos, like many African societies, had witnessed remarkable transformation resulting from both internal and external influences. It is not easy to demarcate between religion and social development in Lagos like many African societies. The performance of *etutu* is common religious phenomenon among the Yoruba. This was also practiced in pre-colonial Lagos. For instance, the various chieftaincy houses (like other Yoruba societies) had their different religious practices. A few examples will suffice. The Oniru was in charge of the propitiations to the goddess of the ocean, Olokun, for whom an annual elaborate festival was performed to avoid flooding in the ocean bank.[22] The Onitana performed sacrifices during the raining season to the Onita in order to avoid calamity. The Oloto performed the Agba ritual, which usually lasted some seven days in order to bring prosperity to the people.[23] Besides, various forms of traditional festivals had firm roots in religious practices. For instance, Eyo—The Adamu Orisa festival of Lagos—started over 300 years ago as an Ijebu Ibefun fertility ritual introduced into Lagos on account of Queen Olugabani, wife of Ado, the first Oba of Lagos, has now become the nucleus of the activities marking the obsequies of a Lagos *Oba*, chief or prominent citizens.[24] Igunnuko, the tall imposing masquerade connected with soil fertility and witchcraft rituals, was introduced by the Nupe to Lagos, while the Awori of the southwest introduced *AlagbadaAlabala* and *Erudi*.[25]

Apart from traditional religion, Islam and Christianity had been in existence before the British annexation of Lagos. Although no specific date has been assigned to when Islam got to Lagos, Gbadamosi has suggested that Islam reached Lagos through its northern neighbors such as the Ijebu, Ibadan, and farther still, Ilorin.[26] Balogun suggests that the first mosque was built at Idoluwo in 1776.[27] This lends credence to the assertion that Lagos had witnessed the practice of Islam as far back as about the mid-eighteenth century. In fact, by the reign of Adele Ajosun (1805) Islam had become popular with some members of royalty openly embracing it. The embrace of Islam by the chiefs and some members of the royalty had implications for the politics of Lagos in the colonial period.

Christianity, unlike Islam, at the initial stage, did not enjoy patronage as the citizenry were perhaps, suspicious and skeptical of the intentions of the missionaries who were mostly seen as the successor to the slave traders. The growth of Christianity took place much after it was introduced into Badagry in 1842 when the first set of Christian missionaries landed in Badagry.[28] But significantly, its growth on the Lagos Island was engendered by the succor it offered to the deviants and those persecuted by the monarch. Missionary houses and a refugee camp where the occupants were readily and sympathetically disposed to their problems were founded.[29] Christianity subsequently made its journey to other parts of the Yoruba hinterland from Lagos, Badagry, and Abeokuta.

SOURCES AND METHODOLOGY

This book adopts the subaltern approach in its analysis. This is done in order to shift from the elitist historiography in which the dominant groups and the colonial authorities are studied to the neglect of the lower class and groups which constitute the mass of the laboring population. Thus, the thematic study of urban livelihood in Lagos from below is employed to study the means of livelihood in the informal sector of the society: focusing on the general subject of livelihood with special reference to the colonial period. This approach becomes necessary because livelihood deals with people, their resources, what they do with them, and how these affect their welfare. This approach will add to the knowledge and understanding of the nature and the relationship between the economy and livelihood involving different social classes in the urban centers.

The historical approach is used to explain the pre-colonial situation in Lagos as well as the early European activities in the city following the annexation of 1861. Also, this approach is also used to explain the effects of the demographic pattern occasioned by the attractiveness of the city as a result of its modern outlook. Thus, it enables us to understand the demand of the modern city within the context of the new social institutions that emerged over time.

Interviews were conducted with purposively selected key informants from Lagos Island, Ebute-Meta, Surulere, Mushin, and Agege. They comprised former employees of colonial administration, academics, railway pensioners, artisans, clerics and small-scale traders whose age ranged from 60 to 88 years. Archival materials, which included documents from Chief Secretary's Office (CSO), Commissioner of Colony (COMCOL), Department of Commerce and Industry (DCI), and annual reports, were obtained from the National Archives, Ibadan; Lagos State Records and Archives Bureau; and the Nigerian Railway Corporation Archives in Lagos. The data were subjected to historical analysis.

CHAPTER PRÉCIS

Chapter 1 provides an insight to the aim of this book, particularly the gap to be filled in the existing literature on Lagos. It highlights the pre-colonial economic organization, social structure, and the political structure of the city with the aim to provide readers with an overview of what was obtained socially, economically, and politically in pre-colonial Lagos. Thus, it provides the foundation for understanding the subsequent chapters, which focuses on the changes urbanization brought on the livelihood of the people of Lagos between 1861 and 1960.

Chapter 2 examines the advantageous nature of the city's location on its growth as a trading center, which enhanced the expansion of its infrastructural facilities. It indeed emphasizes that the transformation of Lagos from a small compact fishing, farming, and coastal settlement to a modern city of pride and envy had its foundation in colonial rule.

In chapter 3, the livelihood strategies adopted by the residents of Lagos and government reactions remain the concern of this section. It examines the impact of waged employment opportunities, social capital, roles of kinship ties, and extended family relations in mitigating the burden of unemployment and housing on indigenes and migrants during the period of study. Besides, the political economy of the slum clearance scheme of 1955 in Lagos was analyzed and interpreted within the context of urbanization, dispossession and sociocultural and economic changes.

Chapter 4 is dedicated to the study of women and their experience in colonial Lagos. It examines the livelihood and political experience of women in the wake of modernization and urbanization policies of the British in colonial Lagos, especially from the eve of the World War II up to independence in 1960.

Chapter 5 focuses on popular and neighborhood cultures in Lagos. Themes such as urban life and identity in colonial Lagos, crime and criminality, begging culture, destitution, juvenile delinquency, and the growth of informal economic sector were adequately discussed.

NOTES

1. Kristin Mann, *Slavery and the Birth of an African City: Lagos, 1760–1900* (IN, USA: Indiana University Press, 2007), 24.
2. Ibid.
3. Ibid.
4. Ibid.
5. Akinlawon Mabogunje, *Cities and African Development* (London: Oxford University Press, 1976), 31.
6. Adeyemi Bamidele Aderibigbe, "Early History of Lagos to About 1850," in *Lagos: The Birth of an African City*, ed. Adeyemi Bamidele Aderibigbe (Lagos: Longman, 1975), 5–6.
7. Ibid., 5.
8. *State of the Lagos Megacity and Other Nigerian Cities Report 2004*, A Publication of the Lagos State Ministry of Economic Planning and Budget, 37.
9. Hakeem Ibikunle Tijani and Saidi Ologunro, "Stages in the Economic History of Lagos," in *Fundamentals of General Studies*, ed. A.O.K. Noah (Lagos State University: Rex Charles, 1997), 146.
10. Aderibigbe, "Early History of Lagos," 1.
11. Ibid., 3.
12. Ibid.
13. Tijani and Ologunro, "Stages in the Economic History," 46.
14. Ibid.
15. Olakunle Lawal, "Background to Urbanization: Lagos Society before 1900," in *Urban Transition in Africa: Aspects of Urbanization and Change in Lagos*, ed. Olakunle Lawal (Lagos: Longman, 2004), 13.
16. Aderibigbe, "Early History of Lagos," 36.
17. Toyin, *Slavery and the Birth*, 31.
18. Ibid., 39.
19. Ibid., 40.
20. Aderibigbe, "Early History of Lagos," 12.
21. Lawal, "Background to Urbanization," 15.
22. Ibid.

23. Ibid.
24. Jacob Festus Ade Ajayi, *Christian Missions in Nigeria 1841–1891: The Making of a New Elite* (London: Longman, 1965).
25. Tajudeen Gbadamosi, "Aspects of Socio-Religious History of Lagos," in *Lagos: The Development of an African City*, ed. Bamidele Adeyemi Aderibigbe (Lagos: Longman, 1975), 176.
26. Tajudeen Gbadamosi, *The Growth of Islam among the Yoruba: 1847–1908* (London: Longman, 1979).
27. I.A. Balogun, *Excellence for Lagos State University*, Send-off Lecture delivered at Lagos State University, 1988, 2.
28. Jide Osuntokun, "Introduction of Christianity and Islam in Lagos State," in *History of the Peoples of Lagos State*, eds. Ade Adefuye, Babatunde Agiri, and Jide Osuntokun (Ikeja: Literamed, 1987), 127.
29. Lawal, "Background to Urbanization," 17.

Chapter 2

Colonial Infrastructure and the Modern Economy, 1861–1960

Modernization, both as a process and as an ideology, seems to manifest itself in a vastly increased range of new choices confronting individuals, and in the chance to sever old relations and forge new ones. David Apter suggests that modernization in nonindustrial societies might be analyzed as the "transposition of certain roles . . . and the transposition of institutions supporting these roles."[1] But one question that becomes relevant is: What factors attend the transition of a traditional society to a modern one? The immediate answer to this question is that the range of agents, both internally and externally generated, are so vast that no single factor could ever provide a satisfactory explanation of an inherently very complex set of process and events. Clearly, much depends on who the modernizers are, what their position is in the total fabric of the national life, what their ideology of modernization is, and how they expect to affect change.[2]

British imperialists, in their bid to "open up" Nigeria to British trade, began the process of modernization by promoting a highly monetized economy, improved transport and communication systems, and banking facilities. These facilities changed the economy of the territories affected. But it has been argued that these infrastructural facilities were used to promote British economic exploitation of Nigeria during the colonial period.[3] In contrast to this position, colonial apologists refer to the creation of social infrastructural facilities as a concrete step taken by the British colonial administration in Nigeria to bring about rapid economic development.[4] It is in view of this debate that this book examines the impact of British infrastructural development and urbanization policies in colonial Lagos.

INFRASTRUCTURAL DEVELOPMENT AND
URBANIZATION IN COLONIAL LAGOS, 1861–1960

There are different schools of thought on why the British annexed Lagos in 1861. Prominent of them are the colonial and the African schools. Robert Smith traced the process of annexing Lagos to the British bombardment of 1851. He argued that the intervention of the British in the affairs of Lagos in 1851 is explicable in terms of three separate but interlocking causal consequences.[5] He identifies politics of the island; British humanitarian drive to abolish the slave trade; and the desire to extend political, commercial, and religious interests.[6] However, the contemporary official explanation, accepted by the "colonial" school, which ascribes intervention to Britain's humanitarian concern to eradicate the obstinately lingering slave trade, has much force. The abolition of slave trade had called for a tremendous effort by those who supported the movement. However, closely aligned with the negative aim of abolition was the positive aim of its substitution by legitimate trade. Once it had been accepted in London that the fulfillment of these aims required action at Lagos, it became the role of those on the coast to translate the general permission given Whitehall into an appropriate form. Thus, the Royal Navy, missionaries, and the traders all sprang to action to extend their activities beyond the coast. The summary of this process is that, by 1851, Britain bombarded Lagos, forced Oba Kosoko to flee the country, and placed Oba Akitoye on the throne.[7] This was done on the excuse that Kosoko was a notorious slave trader who constituted an anathema to the Britain's aim of abolishing trade in slaves. In the 1860s, the British administrator cleared the:

> Filthy beach of the wretched native tenements and for a considerable distance back from the Lagoon border destroyed them and formed a wide promenade ... he also pulled down hundred of huts behind the promenade and constructed wide streets for the sea-breeze to blow through. The consequence is that, on the promenade fronting the lagoon, merchants have erected brick stores, with comfortable luxurious dwelling above, fronting the glorious life sustaining sea-breeze ... markets have been regulated ... soldiers and a police force organized, a race-course established, schools, courthouses, Government House and barracks built and lastly a cemetery (which drives a brisk trade).[8]

The above describes the process by which the natives were dispossessed of their lands, with their property destroyed, the beginning of change in values, and the introduction of a different system of administration. The African's view of British annexation of Lagos, as represented by J.F. Ade Ajayi, is that: "The anxiety of Britain to intervene in Lagos was not just philanthropic desire to destroy the slave trading activities of the Portuguese and Brazilian there, but also the economic desire to control the trade of Lagos from which they had hitherto been excluded."[9]

The period of colonial rule in Nigeria, which began in 1861 following the British annexation of Lagos, witnessed considerable investment of resources in the development of modern infrastructure. Infrastructure can be divided into two: social infrastructural services and economic infrastructural facilities. Social infrastructures are those provided by government or society at large for the benefit of all. It is generally assumed that the provision of social services is the responsibility of government and is seen as an indicator of development. Social infrastructure covers matters such as recreation and tourist services, personal welfare, health services, housing, and education.[10] Economic infrastructural facilities concern the overall development of an organization or a country, such as the provision of water, electricity, roads, railways, seaports, and airports.

The rapid growth of population had very significant effects on the development of the neighborhood and also over-stretched urban facilities. Consequently, from 1861 to 1960, colonial authorities fashioned out infrastructure to accommodate the population, which rose from 25,083 persons in 1866 to 73,766 in 1911.[11] This figure and the trading propensity earned Lagos the appellation "Liverpool of West Africa."[12] By 1931, the aerial extent of the city had further increased to 24.4 square miles and Lagos had come to assume "a more commercial role and its presence began to be felt in the neighborhood."[13] The urbanization process of Lagos was greatly enhanced by the influx of the freed slaves, Sierra Leonean and Brazilian repatriates the cessation of civil wars in the Yoruba hinterland, the subsequent expansion of the British rule to the area, the development of the port and the growth of local commerce and overseas trade. But the most spectacular growth during this period was recorded in the second half of the century: 400,000 people were added to the population of the city itself between 1950 and 1963, while its suburbs gained some 390,000 inhabitants.[14] By 1960, Lagos and its suburbs had a total population of over one million persons, the first city in West Africa to attain that mark.[15] Before the annexation of Lagos by the British in 1861, the dawn of history could be traced to the earliest settlers of modern Iddo Island (formerly called as Ile Olofin and known by the colonial officials as Bruce Island) where a sedentary settlement was established by a group of Awori-speaking peoples who probably migrated from Ile-Ife, the "ancestral" home of the Yoruba.[16] They were later joined by another group with its leader, the Olofin, playing the legendary role of the most civilized because it appeared that the leader and his group enhanced farming and fishing ideas in this area, especially with their forming the "Aladejo" or fishermen co-operative society under the leadership of the Olofin (Ile Olofin).[17] It was one of these that first led a settlement party to the island across the lagoon to the present Lagos

Island. Much later, around the late fifteenth century, the Benin people successfully invaded this settlement and established a military camp or post on a land not far away from the pepper and vegetable farm of the earlier Awori settlers.[18] Thus, Lagos settlement before the advent of the British comprised the settlements that had their roots linked to Ile Olofin as well as those of the Benin hegemony of between the fifteenth and seventeenth century. In the nineteenth century Lagos, however, the heterogeneity of the population which comprised the indigenes, liberated slaves, the Europeans as well as the people from the hinterland played significant roles in the settlement pattern of the city. This settlement pattern was the determinant of the implementation of the infrastructure in colonial Lagos, especially social infrastructure.

Spatial segregation was a remarkable feature of the settlement since the nineteenth century. By 1890, the city consisted of four distinct quarters inhabited by different racial and social groups. The Europeans inhabited Marina, described as "the most important street"[19]; the Brazilian repatriates lived at Portuguese Town or PopoAguda; Saro or SierraLeonians repatriates lived at Olowogbowo; and indigenous Lagosians occupied the rest of the Island. Echeruo remarked that "for all practical purpose the sophisticated and expanding parts of the town were Faji and Portuguese town."[20] The implication of this was that residential pattern of Lagos was divided along the racial lines. By 1929, on the one side of the Macgregor Canal was the densely populated African settlement and on the other hand, the European residential area at Ikoyi, with the police and army barracks and a few indigenous villages.[21] Consequently, urban facilities were concentrated in the European residential areas and the areas where public offices were located. During this period there was also a rapid transformation of transport facilities especially in railways, roads, and seaports.[22] Such improvement in infrastructure in the colonial period was in line with the philosophy of European imperialist powers which saw transport development as the key to colonial economic exploitation. This was corroborated by King Leopold who was credited with the second famous dictum "colonizer cest transporter,"[23] and by Lord Lugard's famous invocation: "the material development of Africa can be summed up in one word 'transport.'"[24] This confirms the assumption that infrastructural facilities were improved in order to facilitate trading activities and exploitation of their colonies.

The infrastructure of trade provided by the colonial government included railways, roads, currency and banking as well as port facilities. Port development was pivotal to colonial transport development and to the expansion of the colonial "rubber" economy which emphasized production of export commodities.[25] Until the advent of the railway, the port city of Lagos was totally dependent on the river and lagoon system that linked it with the Yoruba hinterland.[26] The constraints of river transport in terms of distance covered and capacity of vessels, as well as the seasonality of Ogun River, made railway construction inevitable. The construction of the railway started in the late nineteenth century with a line extending a north-easterly direction from Lagos.[27] This was a period when there were no roads except those within the townships. By 1901, the line had reached Ibadan, a distance of 93 kilometers. By 1909, railway lines totaling 486 kilometers and extending to the banks of River Niger at Jebba had been constructed.[28] The pattern of railway construction revealed the British motives of exploitation at all stages. For instance, the government was apparently more interested in the extension of railway to Abeokuta, "that part of the interior from which the largest amount of produce comes" to Lagos.[29] In fact, Engineer Bryne once proposed the extension of railway to Ifo-Ilaro on the premise that "the area was considered a large market source for palm oil and kernels, cocoa as well as timber because the area is heavily wooded."[30] The traffic grew as the railway was extended till it reached Kano in 1911. This extension, according to Olukoju, gave to Lagos a vast, diverse, and rich hinterland from which it tapped oil and kernels, cotton, groundnuts, and later cocoa. The economic importance of railway to the commercial enterprise of the British was so significant that, by 1912, railway authorities admitted that "the effect of linking up with the Northern section has not been felt in any appreciable degree . . . we are only beginning to tap the trade of the hinterland."[31]

Railway construction was complemented by the provision of feeder roads in the hinterland. Governor Walter Egerton, an exponent of road construction, promoted road development such that, by 1905, metaled roads were introduced in Lagos and work had begun on the 35 mile Ibadan-Oyo Road. Within two years, Lagos had about eight miles of fifteen to thirty-foot metaled roads while the twenty-foot wide Ibadan-Oyo Road had been completed and partially metaled.[32] Also, inland tramway was introduced to complement the railway transport system in 1901. The colonial administration built a 2ft. 6 in. gauge line tramway over the Carter Bridge and commissioned the Lagos steam tramway on May 23, 1902.[33] In spite of the success of the improved inland transport services in Lagos, the government decided to close down the tramway passenger service in 1914 due to the deficit of only £248 recorded in 1913 as well as the refusal to renew the original rolling stock.[34]

The combination of railway, the seaport facilities, and roads network facilitated onward movement of produce and raw materials to the metropolis. The point being made here is that the modern economy introduced by the British following the abolition of the slave trade was facilitated by the infrastructure of trade in which transportation played a significant role.

Monetization is an essential feature of a "modern economy." This explains the reason why the British improved the existing exchange system and indigenous currencies by introducing a "modern currency" as a new medium of exchange. Long before the trade of Nigeria and its hinterland came to be dominated by the mercantile houses from Liverpool, Glasgow, and London, the people possessed a well-established currency system which consisted of brass rods, manilas, copper wires, and cowries.[35] The existing form of currency became prohibited and was replaced with the British currency. The implication of this was that the economy became monetized. And as Walter Rodney argues, "It was on this very issue of currency that the colonial government did most manipulations to ensure that Africa's wealth was stashed away in the coffers of the metropolitan state."[36]

The effectiveness of monetization policy of the British became entrenched with the establishment of foreign and indigenous financial institutions in replacement of the traditional institutions. The first bank in Nigeria—the Bank of British West Africa—was established in 1894 with the objective of providing banking services for the British trading enterprises and the British colonial administration. This bank was owned by Alfred Jones, a shipping magnate, whose shipping line had monopolized the shipping trade of the British West Africa until 1926 when Barclays Bank was established.[37] These two British banks dominated banking operations in Nigeria up to the early 1930s. Their operations in Lagos enhanced trading activities as well as consolidated the path to modern economy. These banks were predominantly concerned with meeting the needs of the expatriate enterprises and government. They did not encourage local entrepreneurship, and since they provided few or no loans to the local people, most borrowers acceptable to the banks were expatriates.[38] This deprivation partly explains why efforts were made in the 1930s by some Nigerians to break through the duopolistic hold of the credit of the economy by the two British banks. Unfortunately, the established indigenous banks failed during the great depression period.

By 1933, the establishment of the National Bank of Nigeria in Lagos set the pace for the creation of more indigenous banks. The Agbonmagbe Bank was established in 1945, the Nigerian Farmers and Commercial Bank in 1947, the African Continental Bank in 1948, and a host of others were all attracted into the banking field by both the general boom of the post-war economic condition, and the evident success of the National Bank of Nigeria.[39] In spite of the adverse effects of the Banking Ordinance of 1952, which required for minimum paid-up capital of £12,500, the indigenous bank found strength in the government of the Western Region in the late 1950s. The establishment of the Central Bank of Nigeria in 1959 finally marked the end of the old colonial monetary system.

MODERN LAGOS: SOCIOECONOMIC INFRASTRUCTURE AND URBAN CHARACTERISTICS

The foundation for the choice of Lagos as a place to seek for livelihood and a residential abode was laid by the colonial authority when social infrastructure was put in place after the annexation of the colony. As noted by Olukoju, water supply and electricity were the earliest infrastructural facilities envisaged for the city since the nineteenth century but neither materialized till the late 1890s and early 1900s.[40] Prior to this period, Lagos was poorly illuminated; gas lanterns using kerosene fuel were placed at certain points on the island for illumination.[41] The dangers associated with darkness on the streets of Lagos, especially persistent increase of burglaries, heightened the tension of the residents that both the expatriate merchants and the Western-educated elite pressurized the colonial government for illumination of Lagos.

By 1891, the call for lighting in Lagos received the sympathy and attention of acting governor George Denton, who drew the attention of the Secretary of State for the Colonies to "the very inferior manner in which the streets in Lagos are lighted."[42] After several exchanges between Lagos and London, electricity was finally introduced in 1898. However, it was limited at the beginning to few strategic buildings: the hospital, Europeans residential area and Government House.[43] This was the situation until 1923, when the Ijora Power Station was formally commissioned and became the source of electricity supply to Lagos and its environs during the colonial period.[44] This shows that the rationing of electricity experienced in the country today had been in existence from the colonial period. This is evident in the fact that, in spite of the complaints over the cost and the electricity ordinance introduced during the period, electricity supply was subjected to restrictions and rationing. The explanation for this was the demand for electricity that exceeded supply. Besides, as reported by a senior electrical engineer to the district officer, a delay in the delivery of materials from United Kingdom incapacitated electricity supply.[45] Consequently, consumers were placed on restrictions on the use of appliances. These restrictions were made public using all available media of communication including town criers in order to reach out to illiterate members of the public. The above account clearly indicates that before the establishment of the Electricity Corporation of Nigeria (ECN), in 1950, the energy sector had a faulty foundation, especially when, in the 1890s, wrong equipment was imported from England.[46]

The supply of potable water to the teeming population of Lagos was of great concern to the colonial government in the nineteenth and early twentieth century. Most of the inhabitants of the city relied on the supply of water from springs and streams until when Sir John Glover, an early colonial Governor of Lagos, introduced public wells to the city.[47] But on health grounds, especially possibility of contamination of well water with sewage water, the well water was condemned. In fact, the colonial surgeon recommended that samples of water be tested regularly.

The colonial governor reacted differently by emphasizing that something should be done to improve the quality of well water rather than discontinuing its usage.[48] After several attempts to find suitable sources of good water supply in the island had failed, the colonial authority relocated their search to the mainland, and the most appropriate place was Iju, to the north of Lagos.[49] From the outset, the colonial governor envisaged that the water rate would generate negative reactions from the Lagosians, but was convinced that the objection would be overcome. This is because the colonial authority did not want to bear the cost of this infrastructure from the colonial coffers. Subsequently, the Iju water works was completed in 1910 and formally commissioned in July 1915 by Nigerian Governor General Sir Frederick Lugard. Located some 1000 feet below the confluence of the Adiyan River and the Iju Stream, the water scheme cost a little over £300,000, and it had an initial capacity of about two and a half million gallons per day, sufficient for 115,000 people.[50] Like electricity, potable water from the waterworks, from the beginning, was intended for the European residential area at Ikoyi, but supply was gradually extended to the African community on the island. In fact, a Lagos newspaper remarked in 1915 in its feature article that potable water and "fine houses" were the key changes taking place in the city during this period.[51] By the end of 1915, it was claimed that improved water supplies had begun to reduce mortality rates in Lagos.[52]

The supply of potable water did not stabilize without its own crisis. This is evident in the struggle occasioned by the introduction of water rate in Lagos. By an order under the water works ordinance of March 30, 1933, payment of water rate was to be in advance by equal half yearly payments on the first day of April and the first day of October.[53] Tenements exempted from payment included those on which buildings had not been erected, cemeteries, government premises, places of worship, public recreation grounds, and tenements with a value lower than £6.[54] The generality of the people of Lagos vehemently opposed this levy. This opposition is graphically captured in a popular song by the people during this period:

Kasanwoina, kasanwooju eta

(Should we continue to use all our meager resources to paylevies and rates (for light and now water) we will have nothing left to improve ourselves).[55]

The issue of the introduction of water rate levy created the first polarization of Lagos society since it came under British control. The society was divided into two mutually opposing camps, the pro- and anti-water rate factions.[56] The two groups were led by prominent leaders of the Lagos community who were the political and social elites of the period. In fact, this division was said to have continued on almost every point at issue within the Lagos society until well into the 1940s.[57]

The uniqueness of any city lies in the specific arrangements, forms, and functions of its spaces and the intersection between the spaces and individual and collective experiences.[58] This buttresses the fact that what makes a city distinctive is beyond aesthetic architecture and urban design. It also includes the demographic pattern, economic features, and social institutions. By the end of colonial rule in 1960, the city of Lagos had evolved unique characteristics that distinguished it from other cities in Nigeria, not only as a capital city, but also as a land of opportunities for all and sundry.

The demographic characteristic of this city between the periods of study (1861–1960) remains a paradox. Initially, its primary role as a center of trade and transformation underlies its attraction for ever-increasing migrants from rural areas and the hinterland. For these people, the relative poverty resulting from their subsistence agriculture stood in sharp contrast to the wealth and glamour of the city. By moving to the city, most of them hoped to improve their skills, earn more money, and raise their social standing. However, the reverse was the case because the colonial white-collar jobs could only cater for a few. In fact, as early as 1915, a Lagos newspaper had to decry the ease with which people migrated into the city and forewarned of its consequences. Noting that many of these people were "indigent persons . . . without feasible means of support and without friends," the newspaper declared that if some means are not devised to stem the flow of these undesirables, a serious problem will confront the administration, which will entail a good deal of handling, careful handling.[59] Several years later, the same newspaper observed that Lagos had "outgrown herself"[60]; while in 1927 it described the city as the "dumping ground for all sorts and conditions of the poor, the maimed (sic) and halt from everywhere, even from the neighboring Colony of Dahomey."[61] The uncontrolled movement of the in-migration is attributable to the loose transport system of the period especially the railway system. For instance, Alhaji Sherifdeen Abubakar Namama narrated his experience in 1947 when he traveled by rail on board a passenger train from Nguru (Northern Nigeria) in company of his kinsmen numbering fifteen, aged between ten and twenty years to Lagos, without any job and definitely with no plan on what to do. He added that, on getting to Iddo, he took the job of a porter loading and offloading goods into the train for ten years before relocating to Agege in 1957.[62] For two years, he slept at the railway terminus in the absence of any worthwhile accommodation.

However, the in-migration also served as a saving grace during the declining birth rate period in Lagos. This decline resulted from the influenza epidemic of 1918. In fact, a newspaper reported that "Lagos has ceased to increase her population by the number of children born, and were it not for the influx of people from the hinterland, the situation would be serious."[63] The seriousness of the situation is captured by Olukoju, when he compared

Table 2.1   Lagos 'Corrected' Birth and Death Rates, 1926–1938

Year	Birth Rate	Death Rate	Year	Birth Rate	Death Rate	Year	Birth Rate	Death Rate
1926	24.1	34.0	1931	22.3	17.8	1936	23.7	18.9
1927	23.4	25.0	1932	24.6	17.9	1937	22.9	23.3
1928	23.0	26.1	1933	22.1	18.9	1938	24.1	21.6
1929	23.3	22.3	1934	27.8	13.05			
1930	NA	NA	1935	26.4	18.9			

the births and deaths rate in Lagos between 1917 and 1922. The census of the birth rate in 1917 showed a figure of 2,846 and by 1922, it had increased to 3,263, while the death rate census revealed 2,167 for 1917 and 2,628 for 1922.[64]

From the forgoing analysis, it could be seen that the population of Lagos did not record any significant increase as a result of procreation. However, the statistics for the period 1926–1938, as shown in table 2.1 indicates that but for the steady in- migration, the situation would have been disastrous. In 1931, it was reported that 58 percent of the inhabitants of the township had been born outside the municipal area.[65] Besides, as shown in table 2.1, there was a noticeable increase in recorded birth, as opposed to death rates in the city after 1928. The only exception recorded in 1937 was as a result of an upsurge in the diseases of the respiratory systems which reflected in increase in the death rate.[66]

The point here is that Lagos attracted a sizable proportion of its inhabitants from the hinterland as a result of assumed economic opportunities it aroused in their minds. Consequently, this increase in population put a lot of pressure on housing and food supplies in the city. Hence, the emergence of slums and the slum clearance policies that followed as well as the food supply scheme of the British. The implications of this for the citizenry shall be examined in subsequent chapters.

THE BUSINESS COMMUNITY IN LAGOS

The business community in Lagos consisted of expatriate and indigenous merchants and traders. The former comprised Europeans (mainly British, Germans, and French) and later, Levantines (Greeks, Lebanese, and Syrians), while the indigenous elements comprised mainly Lagosians, both Christian and Muslim indigenes, and Saro.[67] The economic characteristic of Lagos during the period of study became notable for its phenomenal growth. At the beginning, trade and trading activities in the city showed some rather peculiar characteristics. Trade was carried on at what may be described as three levels. The highest of these was virtually monopolized by large-scale

European trading companies.[68] Their big departmental stores, as well as other specialized wholesale and retailing establishments, formed the nucleus of the modern central business districts in Lagos. Below them were numerous smaller firms owned by Asian companies and Levantine families.[69] The stores of most of these people are no more than a room affair, but the real importance, however, is that they represented the last in the chain of distribution to the final consumers distributing cattle, cooking utensils, and cotton goods.[70] One of them, the Lebanese Michael Elias dominated the cattle trade in Lagos during this period, such that by 1920, he was sending from Kano 15,000 herd of cattle to Lagos annually, and was thus "the first Levantine to achieve commercial prominence in Lagos."[71]

For the period up to World War I, three classes of European businessmen could be identified: those who imported and sold goods for cash and also bought produce for export; specialists in import trade only, mainly British and French; and the commission agents, mainly Germans and Austrians, who dealt in imported goods.[72] European firms in the produce and import trade were G. L. Gaiser; Witt and Busch; Compagnie Francaise; John Holt and Company Ltd; MacIver and Company Ltd; Lagos Stores Ltd; Paterson Zochonis and Company; Miller Brothers; and H.B Russell and Co; and Lever Brothers (now Unilever).[73]

The German firm G. L. Gaiser alone controlled about a quarter of the palm kernel and palm oil export trade and a large proportion of the import trade. Seven Manchester firms—John Walkeden and Co; Pickering and Berthoud; G. Gottschalk and Co; Rylands and Sons Ltd; Ashton and Kinder and Co; G. B. Ollivant and Co; and Blackstock and Co—were prominent in the import trade, their specialty being cotton goods. The French firms H. Deputy and J. Gros imported manufactured and retailed spirits, while the German firm Sachse and Co specialized in the bead trade.[74]

The Africans participated in the new colonial economy at different levels. There were those who imported and sold goods in Lagos. They usually patronized the Levantine and Syrian merchants who stationed their ships at Ehinigbeti, now Marina.[75] This was one way of participating in import trade through the representatives of the foreigners. Before World War I, an increasing number of Syrians and Lebanese had been participating in the foreign trade of Nigeria.[76] Most of them began as retailers of imported goods and middlemen in the marketing of the export crops, and a few prospected for alluvial gold and tin. The most significant feature of the participation of Syrians in the Nigerian trade was the strong spirit of togetherness which existed among them.[77] The rich Syrian assisted his less fortunate brothers to obtain funds and make the right trade contacts. They made efforts to study local languages and customs in order to be more acceptable to the people than the Europeans.

Among the Africans, there were those who bought goods in wholesale quantities from Europeans for retailing in the hinterland and returned with produce for sale to European firms. Unlike the import trade, few of them specialized in export trade. P.J.C. Thomas, S.H. Pearse and J.K. Coker exported produce by 1914. Braimah Igbo was said to be the most prominent kola merchant.[78] The main point is that trading as part of the colonial economy provided means of livelihood for the residents of Lagos: Europeans, Levantines, indigenes, returnees, and migrants from the hinterland and neighboring states as wholesalers, retailers, petty traders as well as service providers.

THE FORMAL SECTOR OF LAGOS ECONOMY

The formal sector during the period of study was synonymous with wage employment. This wage employment was created by the modernization drive of the British. The modernization drive resulted in the development of infrastructure of trade, urbanization, as well as the monetization of the economy. It was in the year 1895 that the Nigerian railway labor force came into being, initially very humbly, when Shelford and his team of engineers employed a few indigenous people to assist in tropical bush clearing and exploratory equipment carrying as they conducted the first expert survey to determine the course of railway construction from the coast to the hinterland.[79] Railway laborers were recruited through the Nigerian head chiefs and political officers who passed them on to the engineers. The chiefs were remunerated on the basis of the number of workers they recruited, while the laborers were themselves paid a shilling a day, which was two pence more than what their counterparts in Sierra Leone got and three pence less than what was paid on the Gold Coast.[80] Railway employment was probably most attractive after the opening up of the Lagos-Ibadan line on March 1901. This date marked the beginning of railway operation, which also opened greater opportunities for indigenous railway workers. Those of them who learned fast on the job had become semi-skilled and skilled and eventually got placed on the permanent establishment, leaving others behind to care for the track. Nigerians started to become carpenters, masons, and blacksmiths on the railway, while a few mastered locomotive engine driving and telegraph operation.[81] Railway clerical posts were filled by school leavers from Lagos and Abeokuta for a start.[82] Indeed, the railway employees were harbingers of the currency revolution in Nigeria in the first two decades of the twentieth century.[83]

The railway employees received their wages in coins and notes and ultimately created far greater credit than the face value of what they earned. Since their wages were regularly paid, it was convenient for needy railway employees to buy consumer goods on credit and promise the vendor that the bill would be settled on pay-day. The vendor could, in turn, take other articles from some market women with a similar promise of settlement on the railway workers pay-day. They, in turn, could acquire other goods from various sellers on the promise of settlement on the railway worker's day. In effect, a unit of payment has in its potentiality commanded purchasing power in chained reactions in much the same way as commercial banks created and still create liquidity through checks and advances in more developed economies.[84] Ayoola Tijani observes that working for the railway corporation before independence was a thing of pride. He likens it to working with an oil company in contemporary Nigeria. For him, as an assistant proof-reader in the printing division, his salary was £220 per annum as far back as 1950, but that kind of top level job, according to him, was meant for the few educated ones.[85]

Some Lagos residents were also employed as civil servants in colonial administration, some as shopkeepers for European merchants, reporters in the newspaper outfits, and cashiers in the banks. The larger percentage of the population found their means of livelihood in the informal sector. This buttresses the fact that majority of the illiterates that came into Lagos were either unemployed or they found succor in the informal sector.

However, the city of Lagos did not witness industrial growth until toward the period between 1950 and 1960. Although the federal government, in 1958, introduced a "model" industrial estate in Lagos, it was in 1960 that hundreds of factories began to spring up in the various towns throughout Nigeria.[86] This introduced fundamental and, in some cases, complex changes into the burgeoning urban centers.

CONCLUSION

From the forgoing analysis, it is clear that the transformation of Lagos from a small compact fishing, farming, and coastal settlement to a modern city of pride and envy had its roots in colonial rule, and several other important factors. Prominent among these were the advantageous location of the city and its phenomenal growth as a trading center which necessitated the expansion of its infrastructural facilities. However, this modern economy, which was premised on selective infrastructural facilities also, had serious implications on the standard of living of the people not only in the colonial period, but also in the contemporary period.

Lagos, especially Lagos Island, became truly cosmopolitan as it became the habitat for many and different peoples from the various continents of the world. This had its roots in the colonial period and, as emphasized by Kunle Lawal, Lagos has been an *El-dorado* right from the pre-colonial period. By that time, the city witnessed influx of migrants and population increase of significant proportion. The glamour of the city was such that no matter one's economic plight in the course of living, a migrant to Lagos can never dream of returning home. This of course lends credence to the saying that *Eko gbo'le o gba'ole* (Lagos is home to all, the thief and the indolent ones). It is in the light of this that this book examines in the next chapter, the role of waged employment and the concept of social capital in relation to extended family roles in the economic and social strategies of livelihood in colonial Lagos.

NOTES

1. David Apter, *The Politics of Modernization* (Chicago, IL: Chicago University Press, 1995), 42.
2. Peter Gutkind, "Tradition, Migration, Urbanization, Modernity, and Unemployment in Africa: The Roots of Instability." *Canadian Journal of African Studies* 2, Special Issue (1965): 350.
3. Stephen Adegoke Olanrewaju, "The Infrastructure of Exploitation: Transport, Monetary Changes and Banking," in *Britain and Nigeria: Exploitation or Development?* ed. Toyin Falola (London: Zed Books, 1987), 60.
4. Allan Macphe, *Economic Revolution in British West Africa* (London: Routledge, 1926), 41.
5. Robert Smith, *The Lagos Consulate, 1851–1861* (London: Macmillan Press Ltd., 1978), 31.
6. Ibid.
7. Patrick Dele Cole, "Lagos Society in the Nineteenth Century," in *Lagos: The Development of an African City*, ed. Bamidele Aderibigbe (Lagos: Longman, 1975), 33.
8. John Whitford, *Trading Life in Western and Central Africa*, 2nd edition (London, Liverpool: Porcupine Office, 1967), 86.
9. Jacob Festus Ajayi, "The British Occupation of Lagos, 1851–1861," *Nigerian Magazine* (NM) 69, (1961): 96.
10. Ayodeji Olukoju, *Infrastructure Development and Urban Facilities in Lagos, 1861–2000* (Ibadan: Institute of African Studies, 2003), 1.
11. Danladi Ali, "Environmental Influence and Crime in Lagos Metropolis 1850–1999," in *Technology, Knowledge and Environment in Africa: A Perspective from Nigeria*, eds. Akinwunmi Olayemi et al. (Zaria: Keffi International, 2009), 345.
12. Olukoju, *Infrastructure Development*, 7.
13. Ayinde Adalemo, "The Physical Growth of Metropolitan Lagos and Associated Planning Problems," in *Spatial Expansion and Concomitant Problems in the Lagos Metropolitan Area*, ed. D. Oyeleye (Lagos: Department of Geography, University of Lagos, 1981), 9.
14. Olukoju, *Infrastructure Development*, 8.
15. Pius Sada and Ayo Adefolalu, "Urbanization and Problems of Urban Development," in *Lagos: The Development of an African City*, ed. Adeyemi B. Aderibigbe (Lagos: Longman, 1975), 79.

16. Lawal, "Background to Urbanization," 4.
17. Ibid., 5.
18. Ibid.
19. Michael Echeruo, *Victorian Lagos: Aspects of Nineteenth Century Lagos Life* (London: Macmillan, 1977), 19.
20. Echeruo, *Victorian Lagos*, 18.
21. Cole, "Lagos Society," 42–43.
22. Babafemi Ogundana, "Seaport Development in Colonial Nigeria," in *Topics on Nigerian Economic and Social History*, eds. Adeagbo Akinjogbin and Segun Osoba (Ile-Ife: University of Ife Press, 1980), 159.
23. Hailey Lord, *An African Survey* (London, 1957), 1535.
24. Fredrick Lugard, *The Dual Mandate in Tropical Africa* (Edinburgh: William Blackwood & Son, 1922), 5.
25. Ogundana, "Seaport Development," 159.
26. Ayodeji Olukoju, *The Liverpool of West Africa: The Dynamics and Impact of Maritime Trade in Lagos, 1900–1950* (Trenton, NJ: Africa World Press, 2003), 14.
27. Olanrewaju, "The Infrastructure of Exploitation," 67.
28. Stephen Adegoke Olanrewaju, *The Economics of Rail Transport in Nigeria: A Case Study in Transport, Cost Analysis* (MSC diss., University of Ibadan, 1974), 4.
29. NAI, CSO/1/16 261 of December 1896, a Correspondence from Denton to Chamberlin.
30. NAI, CSO 19/2/file 2634 Proposal to Extend Branch of Railway from Ifo to Ilaro, 1914, 3.
31. NAI, CSO1/32/2 Lugard to Harcourt, May 29th, 1913. Acting GMR's Memo, 3.
32. Olukoju, *The Liverpool of West Africa*, 18.
33. Nevile Miller, "Nigerian Island Tramway: Erstwhile Lagos Steam Tramway and Its Unique Locomotives." *The Railway Magazine* (1966), 103–106.
34. Features story in, *The Railway Magazine* (July 1964), 581.
35. Olanrewaju, "The Infrastructure of Exploitation," 75.
36. Walter Rodney, *How Europe Underdeveloped Africa* (Nigeria: Panaf Press, 1972), 60.
37. Olanrewaju, "The Infrastructure of Exploitation," 75.
38. Ibid.
39. Ibid.
40. Olukoju, *Infrastructure Development*, 22.
41. Ibid.
42. NAI, CSO 1/1/13, Denton to Knutsford, Correspondence on Poor Lighting in Lagos, June 8, 1891.
43. Olukoju, *Infrastructure Development*, 23.
44. Ibid., 25.
45. NAI, Comcol 1 1170, Correspondence from Senior Electrical Engineer to DO, February 16, 1948.
46. NAI, CSO1/1/22, Governor, Lagos to Chamberlain, July 23, 1897, Enquiry for Report on Mistakes made by DPW and Two Others, Dated July 20th, 1897.
47. NAI, CSO 1/1/8, Rowe to Kimberley, "Introduction of Public Wells in Lagos," April 17, 1882.

48. Ibid.
49. NAI, CSO 1/1/28, Governor to Chamberlain, December 11, 1899.
50. Olukoju, *Infrastructure Development*, 50.
51. Editorial, *Nigerian Pioneer* (NP), January 8, 1915, 1.
52. Editorial, *NP*, October, 22, 1922, 1.
53. NAI, Comcol 1 File 1505, "The Waterworks Ordinance," 1933.
54. Ibid.
55. Interview with H.A. Sanni quoted in Olakunle Lawal, "Politics in an Emergent Urban Settlement: The Eleko Affair 1915–1950," in *Urban Transition in Africa: Aspects of Urbanization and Change in Lagos*, ed. Olakunle Lawal, New Edition (Lagos: Longman, 2004), 5.
56. Ibid.
57. Ibid.
58. Deborah Stevenson, *Cities and Urban Cultures* (Philadephia, PA: Open University Press, 2003), 72.
59. "Random Notes and News," *NP*, July 1, 1955, 2.
60. Editorial, *NP*, December 2, 1921.
61. *NP*, June 24, 1927, "Random Notes and News."
62. Personal communication with Sheriffdeen Abubakar Namama. Age 74 years, September 26, 2009.
63. For details see *NP*, November 8, 1918.
64. Olukoju, "Population Pressure," 36.
65. Ibid.
66. Nigeria: Annual Report, 1938, 13.
67. Olukoju, *The Liverpool of West Africa*, 12.
68. Mabogunje, *Cities and African Development*, 25.
69. Ibid.
70. Ibid.
71. Anthony Hopkins, *An Economic History of Lagos, 1880–1914* (PhD diss., University of London, 1964), cited in, Olukoju, *The Liverpool of West Africa*, 13.
72. Ibid.
73. Olukoju, *The Liverpool of West Africa*, 13–15.
74. Ibid.
75. Personal Communication with Kudirat Mabinuori, 68 years, August 1, 2012.
76. Michael Crowder, *West Africa under Colonial Rule* (London: Hutchinson, 1968), 345.
77. Olufemi Ekundare, *An Economic History of West Africa, 1860–1960* (London: Methuen & Co, 1972), 218.
78. Olukoju, *The Liverpool of West Africa*, 13–15.
79. Wale Oyemakinde, "The Railway Workers and Modernization in Colonial Nigeria." *Journal of the Historical Society of Nigeria* 10, no.1 (1979): 113.
80. Ibid., 114.
81. Ibid., 115.
82. Ibid.

83. Anthony Hopkins, "The Currency Revolution in Southwest Nigeria in the late 19th Century." *Journal of Historical Society of Nigeria* 3, no.3 (December 1966): 471–83.

84. Oyemakinde, "The Railway Workers," 114–116.

85. Personal Communication with Ayoola Tijani, 77 years, September 27, 2009.

86. Adebayo Ayinla Lawal, "Industrialisation as Tokenism," in *Britain and Nigeria: Exploitation or Development?* ed. Toyin Falola (London: Zed Books, 1987), 121.

Chapter 3

Waged Employment, the Extended Family, and Urban Culture, 1900–1960

The British annexation of Lagos opened a new chapter in the existence and livelihood of the peoples of Lagos. The infrastructural development and the modernization drive in the city attracted migrants from the neighboring towns and villages as well as from the hinterland. Although it is generally agreed that the search for economic betterment plays a major role in rural-urban migration, the impact of what are frequently identified as social factors has gained little attention. Thus, the relationships between economic and noneconomic factors are examined in this chapter in order to analyze the coping and survival strategies of the heterogeneous populace in the city of Lagos. The factors examined range from waged employment opportunities to the roles of extended family and social capital, urban culture, urban poverty, family and social change, and the political economy of slum clearance scheme in colonial Lagos.

MIGRATION, POPULATION EXPLOSION, AND THE LABOR MARKET IN COLONIAL LAGOS

Population movements have always been a major feature of African history.[1] Peoples have sought better hunting grounds, new grazing lands for their cattle, and better soils for farming. They have fled before the onslaught of stronger neighbors or the tsetse fly. Men, women, and children have been carried off from their homes into slavery. However, with the development of the money economy and the opening up of employment opportunities, a new pattern of migration was introduced.[2] In the case of Lagos, the city had always been an *Eldorado*[3] for the residents, traders, and travelers, especially the people of the coastal areas before the advent of British annexation. The city enjoyed an advantageous position as a coastal settlement which invariably translated to trading opportunities with neighbors from far and near. A natural concomitant of the growth of Lagos trade was the steady rise in urban population.[4] The population of the city, which covered a mere 1.55 square miles on the Island of Lagos, was 25,083 in 1866, 25,518 in 1871 and 37,452 in 1881.[5] There was an inexplicable drop in the population in 1891, but there was an appreciable increase to 41,487 in 1901. By 1911 when the population had risen to 73,766, the Lagos metropolitan area had expanded beyond the island to encompass Iddo Island, as well as Ebute-Meta and Apapa on the mainland, a total area of 18 square miles[6] The population of Lagos rose by 70 percent within a decade, largely on account of the growth of trade, which had drawn a steady stream of migrants from the hinterland. By the opening decade of the twentieth century, Lagos had become "by far the largest commercial coast town in British West Africa if not in the whole of the West African seaboard."[7]

In addition, the area was further increased to 20 square miles in 1921, 24 square miles in 1927 and, by 1950, a total of 27 square miles had been demarcated and delimited.[8] The changes in the extent of the city resulted from its growing urban population such that it recorded a steady growth of 98,303 in 1921, 126,474 in 1931, 230,256 in 1950 and 655,246 in 1963.[9] By 1960, Lagos had extended to the mainland and suburbs covering Yaba, Apapa, Ebute-Meta, Surulere, Mushin, Ajeromi, Ikeja, Oshodi, and Agege.[10]

An important feature of Lagos society was the spatial segregation of the settlement since the nineteenth century. By 1890, the city (then limited to the island) consisted of four distinct quarters inhabited by different racial or social groups.[11] The Europeans inhabited the Marina, described as the "most important street of Lagos"[12]; the Brazilian repatriates lived at Portuguese Town or Popo Aguda; the *Saro* or "Sierra Leonians" (recaptives or liberated slaves from Sierra Leone) lived at Olowogbowo; while the indigenous Lagosians occupied Pashi, Agarawu, Isale Ofin, Bamgbose, Ita Faji, and Oke Aarin. At that period, the Lagosians were classified into two groups, the first were the Lagosians who did not have any other place to call their homes, such as the Brazillian descendants, the Sierra Leonean descendants, and most importantly the Awori who lived in Isale Eko, who constituted the majority of the population of Lagos.[13] In the second category were the contemporary migrants who came to Lagos in search of livelihood, most especially people that came from the hinterland, particularly Oyo, Ilorin, Ilesha, and Ogbomoso who resided mostly at Oke Popo, Oko Awo, and Oke Aarin area of Lagos.[14] There were also migrants from eastern Nigeria: Onitsha, Awka, Abakaliki and the Delta area such as Isoko, Warri, Calabar, and Sapele. Also from Northern Nigeria were the Hausa, the Nupe, and the Fulani. Besides, there were the migrants from the neighboring countries of Ivory Coast, Liberia, Togoland,

Gold Coast, and Dahomey popularly referred to as the Aganyin, Ajase, and Kurumo. They resided mostly at Araromi and Lafiaji area of Lagos.[15] *The Koras*, Syrians, and Lebanese also lived along Ereko, Tinubu Square, and Idumota area of Lagos, while the British colonialists occupied Ikoyi as their home, but worked in the colonial civil service offices at Onikan, Broad Street, and Race Course.[16] Echeruo, however, remarks that "for all practical purposes the sophisticated and expanding parts of the town excluding Ikoyi were Faji and Portuguese Town."[17]

Among the natives of Nigeria, the most important ethnic groups represented in Lagos were the Ibo, the Ijo, the Edo, and the Hausa. Their contribution to the population from 1911 to 1950 revealed that out of the 54,085 non-Yoruba native immigrants in Lagos, the percentage representation showed 47 percent for Ibo, 6 percent for Ijo, 13 percent for Edo, 7 percent for Hausa, and the remaining 27 percent for other ethnic groups.[18] The most striking fact from the figures according to Mabogunje is the phenomenal increase of Ibo, from less than 300 in 1911 to nearly 26,000 by 1950.[19] This demographic characteristic of Lagos during the period confirms the heterogeneous status of the city. Also, of non-Nigerians, four countries on the west coast provided the bulk of African immigrants. They were Ghana-Togoland, Sierra Leone, Liberia, and Dahomey.[20]

By 1950, Dahomeans in Lagos were estimated at 3,873, followed by the Ghanians and Togolese with a combined population of 1,736 and Sierra Leone recorded 631, while the rest of West Africans recorded 283 of the 6,523 West Africans in Lagos. Among the Europeans the major groups represented were the British, French, and German. Their demographic composition between 1911 and 1950 revealed a steady increase such that by 1950, out of the Europeans and Asians, Britain recorded the highest number with 2,044, while Syrians and Lebanese recorded the least with 288 out of the 2,510 figures for Europeans and Asians.[21]

Lagos had evolved heterogeneous characteristics as early as the beginning of colonialism. The British were in the majority of the nonimmigrants in the European and Asian categories because up till 1950 Lagos was still a colony of the British, and the civil service was dominated by the British. For the Germans, it was a downward trend because a boom in the trade in palm kernels before the World War I attracted them to Lagos, but following the sack of the German merchants after the war, the Germans had no choice but to leave the colony of one of their enemies. In the case of the Syrians and the Lebanese, they dominated the commercial activity, especially trade in textiles.[22] This partly explains their appreciable numbers during the period under consideration.

The occupational distribution of the Lagos population between 1891 and 1911 revealed that the larger percentages of the population were traders, while artisans of various types were prominent in the population. In 1891, out of the 32,508 employed residents, 12,041 were traders, the 1901 census returned 15,687 for traders out of the 41,847 employed populations, while in 1911, and the number of traders had increased to 21,293 out of the 73,766 employed populations.[23] This attests to a largely nonclerical character of the population. The artisans were predominantly bakers, blacksmiths, bricklayers, canoemen, carpenters, dressmakers and seamstress, fishermen, painters, printers, shoemakers, and weavers.[24]

It is evident that between 1891 and 1911, a greater percentage of the populations of Lagos were traders. This stemmed from the expansion of British power into the hinterland of Lagos in the 1890s which brought about a shift in political power and subsequently weakened the hold of the indigenous ruling class over its dependent labor force.[25] In the nineteenth century Lagos, the dominant occupation was trade, and most traders were slaves whose business activities were directed by their masters.[26] The position of such slaves was described in 1881 by Brimah Apatira, who was a prominent trader and slave owner:

> The boys live with their masters in the house, receiving food, clothing, and being treated as one of the family. But no wages are paid. If they need money they are dashed some. If they conduct themselves well the master gets them wives and gives them money to start for themselves. The boys work for their masters and go to market for them. If they don't behave they are sent away with nothing.[27]

Clearly, this was a state of dependency which could be interpreted to mean either the full exploitation of the slave as a unit of production or the operation of a more lenient system of apprenticeship.[28] However, in drawing attention to the variety and flexibility of slavery as an institution, care must be taken not to obliterate the essential features of the labor force as it existed toward the close of the nineteenth century. In Lagos and its hinterland, production and exchange depended not only on a multiplicity of small producers, who used mainly family labor, but also on a relatively small number of important entrepreneurs, who controlled a large labor force consisting mainly of slaves.[29] While it was possible for some slaves to improve their position in society, the great majority remained bound to their employers by a contract which had not been negotiated freely, and which benefited the masters to the extent that they were unwilling to encourage the development of a competitive labor market.[30] Thus, the question may be asked, when did labor begin to attract wages in Lagos?

Labor did not attract wages in the traditional economy in Nigeria in the pre-colonial period. The household provided the bulk of the labor supply. If a man had many wives and children, he had that size of labor under his control.[31] Also, mutual labor transaction provided additional hands as might be needed. It involved the farmer associating with his age mates to provide labor force for the farms of individual members of the group, on a rotational basis, until everybody would have its due. But when the entire local community needed to work on a common project, like constructing a building to house the village shrine or clearing the road leading to the central marketplace, the able-bodied men would rise as one man.[32] Rather than expect to be paid for their services, men would consider it enough for the head chief to feed them on their return from the assignment if he had the means to do so. Other labor recruitment forms that featured had to do with slavery and the slave trade. Slavery could take the form of pledging or pawning the services of one's children to one's creditors till such a time that the debts would have been paid. Or it could be that the rich man procured slaves from their vendors so as to engage them for his productive endeavors. Valiant war chiefs kept slaves as retainers around themselves to assist with farm work, carry merchandize from place to place, and function generally as household labor force.[33]

It was with the coming of the colonial economy that labor regularly attracted wages. The colonial authorities in Nigeria wasted no time in establishing an administration that had to be manned at the lower level by indigenous workers. Products of missionary education were at hand for this purpose and when later the imperial rulers participated in the provision of educational facilities, the products of such institutions also joined.[34]

Mercantile houses similarly recruited workmen to operate their shops, factories, and warehouses in the country. But by far the single largest employer of labor was the Nigerian railway. Beginning with 1895 when the construction of the permanent way started, through to 1901 when the Lagos-Ibadan line commenced operation, down to 1912 when the Lagos Railway linked with the Baro-Kano line to form the national network, haulage and mobility by the iron horse required more than a handful of men.[35] For instance, the unskilled labor cut the bush, leveled the ground, and carried rails, sleepers, and ballasts for erection of the lines, and trained hands were engaged for setting and gauging.[36] It is important to re-emphasize that it was the deliberate policy of the colonial government to employ indigenous workers to fill the positions for which they had competence. This was to ensure that the services would be cheaply run since expatriate staff earned a lot higher than their local counterparts. It was also to secure operational stability since foreign staff, whether from Europe or the West Indies, tended to be birds of passage.[37]

The expansion in the Public Works Department (PWD) provided a platform through which more Nigerians were progressively drawn into wage employment. The teaching services also needed additional men from time to time. It, thus, became fashionable to try and secure wage employment and to train to become employable. Labor hire no longer carried the stigma of slavery, as the band of workmen rippled into wider circles. Lagos became an element of attraction to the rural population. Most of the migration to Lagos has been from relatively nearby villages and towns.[38] According to the census of 1953, nearly three-fourths of the inhabitants of Lagos were from the contiguous Western Region of Nigeria. (However, over a twenty-year period, people who had come to Lagos from the Eastern Region increased five times as compared with the doubling of those from Western Region.)[39] Thus, as heterogeneous as Lagos was, so was the labor market during the colonial period. It comprised unskilled, semi-skilled, and skilled labor spread across the formal and informal sectors.

URBAN POVERTY: ECONOMIC AND SOCIAL STRATEGIES OF EXISTENCE IN COLONIAL LAGOS

One of the controversies in the study of poverty is whether it is a social, an economic, or a political problem or a composite of all three.[40] Walton conceptualizes poverty as having many dimensions: inadequate incomes, malnutrition, lack of access to social services, and lack of social and political status.[41] Besides, poverty is a historical phenomenon and the poor have lived in Africa from pre-colonial period till now.[42] In pre-colonial Africa, poverty varied with time and place. Hunger was a typical feature of poverty. In clothing, demeanor, and sometimes, food, noblemen distinguished themselves sharply from commoners, whose poverty was emphasized by most observers.[43] A traveler wrote of Issiny (in modern Ivory Coast) early in the eighteenth century:

> The remainder of the Negroes of this kingdom are very wretched and impoverished, having not a cloth to cover themselves, nor rightly anything but what the Brembis (nobles) choose that they should have. Most of the time they die of hunger, which obliges them to work every day, and often even to engage themselves as perpetual slaves to the nobles in order to have the means of life.[44]

Apart from the above description, a typical African began his life through birth into a particular social class and grew to learn the language, skills, and vocation of his people or the profession of his parents.[45] Then he became integrated into the processes that ensured his admission or initiation into certain age grades. Wealth was in form of land, chieftaincy titles, livestock, skill and vocation, age, wisdom, spirituality, kingship and membership of royalty, and so on.[46] Poverty often existed on an individual level when the individual was not able to assess most of the above or if his ability to assess them was hindered by disability, through being born into what was regarded as a degrading social class.[47] Thus, poverty measurement and determination in pre-colonial Africa was not essentially monetary. The monetary yardstick for poverty became popularized in Africa with the advent of colonialism, which came with monetization of the economy.

Rapid urban growth in the absence of strong urban economies and urban livelihood generation tends to generate urban inequalities which are defined by individual or group status.[48] This was characteristic of the nineteenth and twentieth century Lagos where urban, social, and physical fragmentation created two cities within the city. The urban poor lived in high urban densities, with unplanned urban spatial layout and mostly deprived of access to adequate housing, residential land, municipal services, and other urban benefits. The spatial segregation practiced in Lagos reinforces Wilson's view that the concentration of poverty results in the isolation of the poor from the middle class and its corresponding model resources and job network. More generally, he argues that being poor in a mixed-income neighborhood is less damaging than being poor in a high poverty neighborhood and that concentration effects increase the livelihood of being unemployed and taking up crime.[49] Thus, this study argues that modernization and monetization of Lagos economy attracted migrants from far and near in the absence of strong urban economies and planning, which degenerated to "urbanization of poverty." This implies that poverty is not limited to inaccessibility to income or social amenities, it includes high cost of living, unemployment, poor housing and settlement pattern, poor health facilities, and low literacy level.

Unemployment in the city of Lagos became acute in the depression period, which started in 1929 but became prevalent after World War II. According to a survey carried out by the colonial authorities, 74 percent of the unemployed are non-Lagosians, being men from the provinces (mostly Yoruba) or from Dahomey, Togoland, or the Gold Coast.[50] Colonial authorities succinctly described them as follows:

> Of the men from the provinces 52 per cent are people who have arrived in Lagos in the 1920s, either to learn a trade or to find work, leaving behind them homes to which they might without difficulty return.[51]

Investigation by the chief secretary of state revealed that most of those unemployed were illiterates. Also, there were large numbers of artisans: carpenters, bricklayers, and painters who had engaged on "a daily wage, having more or less continuous work for the past seven or eight years, but lost their jobs because the operations of the PWD or Private Contractors had come to an end."[52] Indeed, the commercial dominance of Lagos over other cities and towns made it a place of succor for the immigrants. This manifested in the way and manner infrastructure of trade attracted immigrants into the city throughout the period under investigation. According to the employment data of September 1956, out of the 97,556 people employed by Federal government, Local Government Council, Public Corporations, and the private sectors, 54,237 were employed in the informal sector in the colony of Lagos in the late 1950s. Besides, the three regions of the East, West, and North combined recorded 113,827 in the commercial and informal sectors against 54,237 recorded by the colony of Lagos alone.

From the forgoing, it is evident that in the colony of Lagos, a large percentage of the population was employed by informal sectors. This shows the superiority of Lagos over any other urban center in Nigeria. However, this made Lagos to attract the rural poor (persons lacking both assets and urban skills).[53]

A vivid description of the economic life and attitudes of the people toward wealth and work in Lagos would enhance our understanding of the nature and types of unemployment experienced in the colony during the period under investigation. A desire to make money, particularly through trade, seemed to be an integral part of the Yoruba personality.[54] For the liberated African in Sierra Leone and those who returned to Lagos, the desire to make money was accentuated by the need to compete with the white man on his terms.[55] Thus, both the indigenes and the Sierra Leonean returnees emulated the Europeans, who refrained from manual labor, and so ventured into commercial activities as well as investment in land sales and speculations in order to become wealthy. Spencer claims that the indigenes' aversion to work derived from the traditional native social structure which allocated manual labor primarily to the women and to the domestic slaves.[56] The men helped only in the initial clearing of the farmland. The man's job was to help govern, to be able at all times to defend the community, and to occasionally supplement the family larder by hunting and fishing.[57] This assertion cannot be true because there was a level of division of labor between men and women in pre-colonial Lagos such that the men would do the fishing, while their women counterparts would see to the marketing of the surplus to those who were in need.

A position similar to Spencer's argument on the attitude of the indigenes to work, especially manual labor, was by Raji Risikat, who recounted the stories narrated to her by her mother. She asserted that a typical Lagosian, preferred fishing and trading, and when he was out of work, had usually his own house or that of his father or mother in which to live. His mother or his wife would provide a meal; his friends would generally give him something. He was not faced with the possibility of death from hunger or deprivation.[58] The inference here is that besides trading and fishing, Lagosians hardly engaged in manual labor.

In the colony of Lagos, the most common business activity in the society was trading. The indigenes were active traders, and the first generation of the

Sierra Leoneans to return to Lagos had been taught to consider independent trading, even if on the smallest scales, as respected way to make money.[59] On the other hand, the Brazilian repatriates were mostly craftsmen and artisans who engaged in manual labor with few of them in business ventures. While they were only a small minority, these Afro-Brazilians made an important contribution to the city's architecture.[60] In the case of the strangers from the provinces and the hinterland, the acting administrator of the colony in 1929 described their situation thus:

> The stranger from the provinces appears to live in Lagos even when he is not earning anything. He can always find lodging with his brother or countryman and food as well. If he is out of work after a spell of employment his landlord will allow him to remain on credit. He has no expenses and 3d will buy him a meal enough to keep him going for a day.[61]

Further, he described the case of the stewards and houseboys, who were for the most part from Warri or Onitsha province as those in the habit of an employed houseboy keeping one who was looking for work.[62] The state of unemployment in colonial Lagos between 1929 and 1945 (Great Depression and World War II periods) worried the colonial administrators so much that they devised means of addressing the situation. In fact, the chief secretary to government wrote on the situation as follows:

> There is no doubt that the larger proportion of persons unemployed in Lagos are casual laborers who have drifted from the provinces to this town for many and various reasons. Persons unemployed in Lagos may be divided into three: skilled labor, semi-skilled labor and unskilled labor. For the skilled labor, they includes clerks and skilled mechanics who are Lagosians or whose families had settled permanently in the town who can only wait for a demand for their services or try to seek employment in provincial towns. The semi-skilled labor comprised of large quantities that have been apprenticed to but never mastered such trades as carpentry, tailoring, blacksmith, bricklaying etc. These are persons for whose services are in little demand and yet who are unwilling to work as laborers. So long as they can exist on the food supplied them by their womenfolk or on the charity of their friends or the sale of property acquired in more prosperous time, they are content to remain in Lagos. The greater number of persons unemployed in Lagos will be found to be laborers from the provinces. Of 100 cases of unemployment into which detailed enquiry were recently made, 74% were non-Lagosians.[63]

Corroborating the observation by the chief secretary to government, Oluwole Akinsanya opined that the city of Lagos witnessed phenomenal drift of labor from the provinces acting on tips of possible employment from agencies at such places as Ibadan, Ilorin, and Kaaba in order to avail themselves to the opportunities for casual labor jobs at the docks, railway termini, merchant stores, or customs warehouses.[64] Besides, such men are usually only temporarily employed because most of them were unskilled, but many of them preferred to remain in Lagos at the end of their contract and seek their fortune there rather than return to agricultural pursuits in their own country. This was because they found the city of Lagos to be a land of opportunities with all the infrastructure of trade and possibility of making money there unlike what obtained in the hinterland.

Apart from the skilled, semi-skilled, and unskilled labor categorizations of the unemployed in Lagos, mention must also be made of the beggars, paupers, and ex-servicemen who also constituted the bulk of the unemployed residents of Lagos. The influx of the beggars to Lagos received the attention of the colonial authorities in 1944. The Colony Welfare Officer to the Commissioner of Police and the Director of Medical Services, in a letter, drew attention to the large number of beggars on the street of Lagos and emphasized that there was the need not only to control the influx of crippled beggars into Lagos, but also to contain those that were already living in the city.[65] He stated further that of the 153 beggars investigated, there were two classes: those who begged because it was the easiest way of making a livelihood and those who begged because it was the only way of subsisting themselves.[66] Although these beggars, by their activities, had devised a strategy of survival, they were still regarded as the unemployed that constituted a nuisance to the city during the period.

In addition to the above, the city of Lagos between 1943 and 1945 witnessed large number of destitute laborers and paupers. This was similar to what was experienced between 1930 and 1935 as a result of the "slump" that put an end to the very building and construction program which had been in progress in Lagos.[67] Consequently, the large number of laborers that had been attracted to Lagos by military works refused to leave in spite of the large demand for farm labor in the provinces. The reason for this was because the farmer could not pay the high wages paid by government since the introduction of Cost of Living Allowance (COLA) and a laborer who had been receiving 2/- or 1/6 would be very reluctant to accept 10d or 9d.[68] In addition, it could be argued that some of them had become accustomed to the city life such that village life was not fascinating to them any longer.

The colonial authorities and the residents of Lagos adopted both social and economic strategies in responding to the hardship occasioned by the Depression and the World War II. They had foreseen the outbreak of unemployment as early as 1935. Then it was observed that very large numbers of laborers had been attracted to Lagos by the military works which had been undertaken in or near Lagos.[69] The chief secretary noted that because much of the public works was nearing completion, he anticipated a considerable amount of unemployment in the comparatively near future. In response to this observation, a committee was appointed in 1935 to tackle the problem of dealing with the Lagos' unemployed. The report was forwarded to the COMCOL under cover of the chief secretary's confidential letter no 24243/206 of the January 13, 1935.[70] Its main recommendations were:

a. Compulsory repatriation,
b. Land settlement,
c. A Lagos Labor Bureau.[71]

Repatriation expressed the determination of the colonial authorities in Lagos to maintain "certain approved standards and practices by the inhabitants,[72] and most of those repatriated were labeled "undesirable," whom, the authorities considered a nuisance to the new urban environment. During this period, however, no action was taken on land settlement, and only fifty-five persons were repatriated under the Township Ordinance. A Labor Bureau was opened on January 6, 1936 by the Youth Movement, assisted by the government.[73] The Labor Bureau closed down operation the following year, precisely March 31, 1937, because the government's financial support ceased. The failure of this 1935 committee to achieve much in the alleviation of the conditions of the unemployed made the colonial authorities to revisit the repatriation strategy along with other measures during the war years.

The "undesirables" to be repatriated were classified as the temporary floating population from the province, who had no visible means of support (to be given free transport back to where they came from) and any person from the province who had not had work for a period of six months. This policy was to be carried out with the condition that anyone could be allowed to visit Lagos for two weeks each in six months to look for work but if not successful by that time to clear out.[74] These included the sick and destitute laborers, able- and non-able-bodied beggars, as well as the juveniles of non-Lagos origin. A survey was carried out to determine the number of beggars in Lagos. Particulars of 153 beggars comprising eleven cripples were taken. The colonial authorities accepted the figure but still believed that the beggars were more than the number given by the investigating officers.[75]

Further classification also included old people, residents of Lagos for many years who had no means of supporting themselves, and therefore took to begging. A newspaper in Lagos, *Lagos Standard* described their situations thus:

> Some practiced the Yoruba tradition of religious begging, others travel from house to house on Saturdays, or stand at the corners of streets and in the market places begging alms, and . . . in the majority of cases are maimed or infirm,

while by the end of the century Hausa professional beggars had arrived Lagos. The town simply inundated with begging impostors, mostly from the interior-stout, hale, hearty fellows who feigning blindness or pretending to suffer from some imaginary malady tramp from street to street and from house to house, chanting some doleful ballad.[76]

The beggars were so numerous in the twentieth century Lagos. The colonial authorities discovered from their survey that large numbers of these professional beggars invaded Lagos from the northern part of Nigeria.[77]

By April 26, 1945, the acting town clerk of the Lagos Town Council forwarded to the superintendent of police names of thirty non-able-bodied people to be repatriated under section 79(1) and (2) of the Township Ordinance, chapter 57, to leave the township of Lagos within fourteen days. They were:

1. Mesanmari Kumasi,
2. Danladi Kano,
3. Seibu Katsina,
4. Amodu Jebba,
5. Waziri Kano,
6. Dankaro Sokoto,
7. Sunmonukano,
8. Garuba Kano,
9. Adamu Kano,
10. Karimu Mueri,
11. Aliu Madandi,
12. Momo Dende,
13. Adamu Mala,
14. Amodu Alumalo,
15. Wano Sebarumo,
16. Dambalam Lamgaran,
17. Awudu Sokoto,
18. Waziri Kano,
19. Yauri Kano,
20. Mohammadu Yaruwa,
21. Abudu Raimi,
22. Gogobiri Kano,
23. Chiroma Yola,
24. Ibrahim Zaharma,
25. Ladi Kano,
26. Amadu Agege,
27. Yinusa Katango,
28. Jimmai Kano,

29. Masalati Kano,
30. Mallam Garuba.[78]

Also, by November 1 of the same year, another set of beggars numbering thirty-three were also repatriated under section 79(1) and (2) of the Township Ordinance, chapter 57. In a letter sent to the superintendent of police, they were also asked to leave the colony within fourteen days of service. They were:

1. Zandalma Maiduguri,
2. Mohammed Mustafa,
3. Umaru Bornu,
4. Momodu Kanike,
5. MomoYaruwa,
6. Asabe Baramutum,
7. Garuba Kano,
8. Adamu Kano,
9. Ramatu Kano,
10. Zakari Yawu,
11. Garuba Hadeija,
12. Salihu Kano,
13. Lawani Egba,
14. Umaru Zabarma,
15. Garuba Sokoto,
16. Hawawu Almigra,
17. Talefi Binta,
18. Oke Ibadan,
19. Salawu Atanda,
20. Amusa Ajadi,
21. Adeshiyan Oyo,
22. Audu Zabarma,
23. Idie Dosso,
24. Adamu Lafungu,
25. Umaru Zabarma,
26. Bayo Aremu,
27. Momodu Alao,
28. Momodu Tijani,
29. Musa Iyanda,
30. Hassan Doso,
31. Danladi Ikpo,
32. Abdulai Sabarumo,
33. Garuba Sokoto.[79]

Apart from the paupers that were repatriated, the colonial government also became embarrassed with the increasing number of juveniles seeking employment in the colony. A committee named Advisory Committee on Juvenile Employment and After Care was established. And the colonial administration, in order to forestall the influx of child laborers into Lagos from other provinces, issued the Lagos Township Young Persons Ordinance No.51 of 1946. This regulation specified that only those children who had attended a bonafide primary school in Lagos and colony for a period of three years were as being qualified and were without further formalities eligible for what was considered "blue card," that is to be registered at the Lagos employment exchange as juveniles seeking employment.[80] Details of the impact of this scheme on juvenile delinquency in the city of Lagos shall be examined in chapter five of this book.

The most important factor that stimulated immigration into Lagos during the period 1901–1950 was the widening gap in employment opportunities between Lagos and the rest of the country. This gap became more pronounced with the World War II, when, owing to shortage of supplies, many employers in the country had to dismiss most of their staff.[81] So great was the influx of the unemployed people at this time that, in order to ensure that many of those resident in Lagos had a chance of securing employment, the registration of workers in Lagos (currently employed) and (unemployed) was closed to people from the provinces by a series of orders, nos. 202, 234, 271 of 1944, and nos. 6 and 7 of 1945.[82]

After 1945 the number of the unemployed in Lagos swelled by a fresh stream of immigrants, namely, ex-servicemen. This was as a result of the general demobilization of troops serving overseas, which began in October 1945. In response to this, the colonial authorities enacted an ordinance named, The Employment of Ex-servicemen ordinance, No.48 of 1945. This made it incumbent on all employers of not less than ten Africans to register and then to employ ex-servicemen, until ten percent of their normal establishment consisted of ex-servicemen.[83] By 1948, a record of the number of ex-servicemen absorbed by such employers shows the positions as follows: (see table 3.1)

Table 3.1 Employment of Ex-Servicemen by Regions, 1948

Regions	Ex-Servicemen Employed	Civilians Employed	Total
Northern Region	9,474	71,444	80,918
Eastern Region	7,883	54,112	61,995
Western Region	4,074	46,987	51,061
Lagos	6,001	47,102	53,103
Total	27,432	219,645	247,077

What is most striking from the above figures is that, compared with the regions, each of which had a population of over five million, Lagos, with its population of only about 200,000 was easily the most important employment center in the country.[84] This socioeconomic strategy of alleviating the conditions of the poor in Lagos helped as far as the survival of the war returnees both able and disabled were concerned.

Having examined the strategies employed by the colonial authorities to combat poverty and unemployment condition, it is important to examine the various strategies adopted by the immigrants as well as the residents to survive Lagos. The majority of Lagos residents at that period found succor largely in the informal sector of the economy. This study has dedicated a subsection to the role of the informal sector in urban livelihood in chapter 5. A summary of the general employment pattern revealed, on the surface, the available means of livelihood of the citizenry in Lagos. For instance, the 1950 Census showed that of the 202,000 persons in Lagos, 119,000 (59 percent) was gainfully occupied. There was employment for both males and females, even though at a ratio of 2 to 1.[85]

The census officer, however, commented that this proportion of gainfully occupied males and females was due, on the one hand, to the employment in various undertakings of large numbers of young person's less than fifteen years of age and, on the other, to the fact that many housewives combined, with their duties as home makers some gainful occupation, usually trading.[86] Child labor was also practiced in colonial Lagos during that period. Besides, three out of every four women gainfully occupied were employed in trading, while 70 percent of the males were employed in four occupations, namely craftsmen and production process workers (30 percent), clerical and related workers (14 percent), laborers (14 percent), and domestic and personal service workers (12 percent).[87] It is obvious from this analysis that a larger percentage of the residents in Lagos found their livelihood means in the informal sectors. An in-depth analysis of this sector is undertaken in chapter 5.

HOUSING AND STANDARD OF LIVING IN COLONIAL LAGOS

Like cities everywhere, West African cities harbor a range of conditions and living standards and styles.[88] The cities boast of modern buildings and facilities occupied and utilized by national and expatriate elites, but they also contain the range of places of residence and work of the rest of the urban population.[89] A major proportion of this large remainder of homes and businesses accommodating unemployed migrants, factory workers, clerks, and even skilled workers consisted of overcrowded tenements and shacks. These are the slums and shanty towns found throughout the Third World. Colonial Lagos was not an exception because the urbanization process of the British in Lagos segregated the indigenes, migrants, and the Europeans from one another in terms of housing and development. An analysis of the British urban policy and settlement pattern will shed light on the standard of living of the poor natives and immigrants in Lagos.

One of the major problems of environmental management in the coastal areas was how to provide more land space with improved physical conditions, to meet the ever-increasing demand.[90] An influx of immigrants from the hinterland and the existing settlement of the Brazilian and Sierra Leonean returnees in Lagos put great pressure on available land in Lagos, especially the island. The quickening tempo of commercial activities that accompanied it also compelled the urban population to use the poorly drained, swampy and marshy sandy terrain for housing and settlement. The early settlers of the Island of Lagos (excluding Ikoyi) occupied the patches of sandy ridges and mounds of limited area extent found on the Island.[91] Abegunde emphasizes that about three-quarters of the surface area of the island were then occupied by lagoon inlets, mangrove swamps and creeks. The widespread nature of the lagoon inlets and swamps was a major obstacle to a systematic expansion of settlements on the island. The northern front of the lagoon, for instance, was broken into several lagoon inlets which included extensive ones as the Idumagbo and Isaleigangan lagoons and the inlet north of Epetedo.[92] The Idumagbo lagoon, being the largest, occupied an area of about sixteen hectares. On the western front of the island, there were also the Elegbata and Alakoro creeks. Within the island, the largest areas of swamps were found in the north and south of Ikoyi, Okesuna, and behind Marina.[93]

The Europeans took the existence of these creeks and swamps as excuse to segregate the settlement pattern in Lagos. By 1929, it was noted in a report that the city was divided into two parts by the Macgregor canal. On the one side was the densely populated African settlement and, on the other, the European residential area, Ikoyi, with police and military barracks and a few indigenous villages.[94] Also, the colonial administrators and foreign commercial agents built their administrative offices, residential houses, and warehouses along Marina, in order to take the advantage of the constant breeze from the lagoon and the sea. They cut drainage channels through Marina and reclaimed the swamps there. But unfortunately, they did not consider it essential to organize a similar systematic planning and improvement of the poorly drained and congested areas occupied by the indigenous people.[95] In fact, as earlier as 1893, there existed large stretches of swamps that separated the Whiteman's built-up areas of Marina from the northern and central sectors of the island occupied by local people. And as noted by Olukoju, a high density of the population resided in the indigenous part of the island. The congestion associated with it had adverse effects on the living conditions of the people.[96] Sada also avers that "a major part of the problems of planning and administration of the Lagos Metropolis can be traced directly and indirectly to the rapid growth or misdistribution of the population."[97] In this connection, the bulk of the population resided on the island. Indeed, up to 1950, 65.4% of the population of Lagos lived there.[98] The desire to reside as near as possible to the center of economic activities, and the infrastructure of railway and metaled roads further facilitated the movement of the people from the mainland and the hinterland to Lagos, especially the island.

As mentioned earlier, larger proportions of the island were swampy or waterlogged. But owning to the enormous pressure on land, many people resorted to erecting buildings even in such areas as Elegbata, Alakoro, Anikantanmo, Oko Awo, and Sangrouse, which were ordinarily uninhabitable. It was observed in 1919, for instance, that the floors of buildings in these areas were constantly damp and during the rainy season the yards and outhouses were mostly under water.[99] In fact, Oko Awo was a basin standing below the 1.5-meter contour, which formed the margin of the Idumagbo inlet.[100] It was a permanently waterlogged area, yet highly occupied by residents. The standard of housing in Lagos was very low. This was evident in the type of houses built. Most houses had neither piped water nor a sewage system. The only bathroom or lavatory might be a rough shelter of corrugated iron with a bucket, knocked together in a corner of the yard.[101] Water had to be collected from a stand pipe in the street, and latrine buckets collected by the Town Council, complemented by the night soil men otherwise popularly referred to as *agbepo*.[102] Every part of Lagos was congested. In central Lagos (*Isale Eko*) an area of narrow winding streets, it was common to see some places with open drains running through living areas, densely populated and indigenous in essence and character.[103] The living condition was such that the rooms were usually crowded and most of these rooms were small, poorly illuminated, and without cross ventilation.[104] Because of the poor habitation in such places, epidemics were imminent, and it eventually happened with the outbreak of tuberculosis and the bubonic plague in 1919 and 1924, respectively.

As an aftermath of the population increase without corresponding housing and urban planning scheme, the standard of living in Lagos between 1919 and 1930 had deteriorated unlike what was obtained in the pre-colonial period. A leading newspaper succinctly describes the situation thus:

> The virility of the African is generally conceded, but nowhere has the ability to exist anywhere and anyhow apparently impervious to bad surroundings been demonstrated by our people than the denizens of this most unhealthy and pestiferous district... Such a place as Oko-Awo should not be allowed to continue in

the middle of the municipal Area of Lagos to the danger of lives in surrounding areas and the detriment of trade.[105]

The above remark by the *Nigerian Pioneer* (NP)—a foremost newspaper of the period—on the impending danger of disease epidemics was not yielded to on time both by the residents and the colonial administrators. These bad living conditions and the public health negligence associated with the incomplete modernization of the colonial cities, such as Lagos, snowballed into the outbreak of tuberculosis in the city in 1919, owing to overcrowding and defective ventilation.[106] Within a short period, tuberculosis had become prevalent in the city. The major reasons adduced for its fast spread was "overcrowding in the city." The medical officer of health claimed that, in one instance, fifteen persons slept in one room measuring nine feet by ten feet square. He contended that "overcrowding approximating to this is not uncommon."[107] The medical officer also attributed the steady rise in death and infant mortality rate over the preceding years to poor conditions of living and overcrowding.[108] A survey of certified deaths of Africans from tuberculosis and lungs combined between 1912 and 1922, recorded 332 and 1196 respectively lends credence to the prevalence of respiratory diseases in the city.[109]

The prevalence of tuberculosis attracted the reactions and protest of the elite in Lagos. By 1922, representatives of the Lagos community, comprising four white cap chiefs, professionals, such as lawyers and newspaper editors and businessmen, presented an address to the governor on "a very vital question," which deserved "close attention."[110] The signatories to the address lamented that the development of the European residential area at Ikoyi had "disappointed the sanguine expectations of the native community who are thus compelled to huddle themselves together under insanitary conditions and are also faced with perplexing problem of discovering some other outlets for expansion." They, therefore, asked the colonial government to grant the people access to a large area of Ikoyi plains.[111] The Governor, in his response, claimed that Ikoyi and its surrounding villages had been underutilized even by the Lagosians before the establishment of European settlements and that the presence of the European settlements at Ikoyi did not impede the natural expansion of Lagos. He assured them that Africans could settle at Ikoyi at a later date if they desired to do so.[112]

It is important to state also that Oko Awo, Anikantanmo, and Sangrouse area of Lagos were filthy, swampy, overcrowded, and infested with rats. This partly explains why the bubonic plague that began in 1924 and ravaged Lagos into the 1930s started from these areas. Within three months of its outbreak, 318 people were reported dead, while over 60,000 persons were inoculated.[113] The plague got worse in 1926, when 476 deaths resulted from 490 reported cases. There was a drop to 163 cases and 159 deaths in 1927, but the respective figures rose to 514 and 504 in 1928.[114]

The severity of the plague eventually generated response from the colonial authorities. Sir Thorton flagged off an anti-plague campaign which included the physical destruction of rats and the cleaning and disinfection of infested premises. Initially, it worked positively, and it was reported that as many as 400 rats per day were brought to the offices of the Town Council up to November 12, 1924 after which the figures dropped to eighty-five and then to sixty per day.[115] Subsequently, the anti-plague campaign seemed to have been inefficient in addressing the situation. *NP* suggested an alternative to Sir Thornton theories, when it "reported that the alarm being expressed in Lagos" not so much at the loss of life and the considerable harm being done to trade and shipping, but at the sad prospect of the plague becoming endemic in the country![116] The newspaper enjoined the colonial government to compulsorily evacuate the slums of Lagos under the Health Ordinance with adequate compensation paid to the evacuees. This was one of the reasons for the land reclamation and slum clearance exercise that was carried out in colonial Lagos.

POLITICAL ECONOMY OF THE SLUM CLEARANCE SCHEME IN COLONIAL LAGOS, 1900–1960

This study approaches the explanation of the utilization of spaces between colonial authorities and the rest of the residents of Lagos from the perspective of the political economy of environment, as espoused by J. K. Boyce. In his view, political economy of environment includes not only economics (the allocation of scarce resources among competing ends) but something more: it is about the allocation of scarce resources not only among competing ends, but also among competing people.[117] To this end, this study sheds light on the reasons behind the slum clearance schemes in colonial Lagos, especially the one executed in the late 1950s.

Nigeria had known urbanization long before colonialism. However, housing *per se* was not a concern in Nigeria until the advent of industrial economy pulled large number of workers into the urban areas in the twentieth century.[118] The colonial government, however, did little to meet the needs of a growing urban population. Unlike colonial cities in Australia or the Americas where a settling population developed planned cities, the built environment of Lagos was for the most part touched by colonialism only indirectly, through economic forces rather than direct legislation.[119] In fact, from early development as one of the leading centers of trade and commerce in West Africa, Lagos was imprinted with a persistent and striking disjuncture in living standards between European elites and African majority.[120] With the exception of William Macgregor who waged a most enlightened and successful campaign against malaria infestation in Lagos, all the British governments chose to concentrate on productive investment rather than on improving the general living conditions of their urban population.[121] Besides, Britain was not interested in the affairs of the interior economies in so far as trade flowed directly to the coast.[122] This made it easy for the European merchants at the coast to send raw products home for manufacture. This was because of the need to actualize their main aim of large markets for their produced goods and raw materials for their growing industries in the metropolis.

It was improvement in community health and general sanitary conditions for the white population who were resident agents of colonial capitalism that provided the rationale for undertaking limited planning of urban areas.[123] Following the annexation of Lagos in 1861, few efforts were made in this direction after those of Commander Glover who extended Marina, dug wells, and reclaimed swamps. For instance, in 1863, John Glover, in an attempt to cope with the fearful ravages which occurred every dry season in Lagos from fire, issued Ordinance 8 entitled "An ordinance for the better preservation of the town of Lagos from fire,"[124] This was enacted to improve the structure of houses and materials used for building them, because settlement pattern and overcrowding posed problems for those colonial officials and non-Africans who would have preferred a more dispersed settlement pattern and clear separation of residential areas marked out for various races. Apart from these efforts, conditions were allowed to deteriorate to the point where the Nigerian elite called for measures to broaden streets to reduce fire danger, ameliorate overcrowding in houses, provide street lighting to deter thieves, and construct more public wells.[125] In fact, Lagos according to Mathew Gandy became renowned as one of the most insalubrious cities in West Africa on account of its swampy setting and naturally nonexistent sewer system.[126]

Thus, there was the clarion call to Governor Egerton to salvage Lagos through town planning. This was, however, to be based on the principle of racial segregation. Citing medical reasons, Egerton decided to establish a European reservation around Race Course in Lagos by forcing Africans there to vacate their homes.[127] This segregation on the basis of racial and ethnic differences became a major element of urban planning in the early colonial period. In addition, in Nigeria, the Lugards Township Ordinance of 1917 gave rise to most urban centers showing a three-fold division, namely the native city, Non-European Township and the European reservation.[128] The native city remained traditional, a largely undifferentiated jumble of mud buildings with poor layouts, generally poor environmental conditions and hardly any infrastructural facilities. The non-European township was essentially planned, and the European reservation was also planned but was usually surrounded by a non-residential belt.[129] The consequences of this colonial urban policy were the emergence of what Zeynep Celik, Anthony King, and Anja Nevanlinnia depict in their works as a dual city. One part composed of quarantined government areas featuring European architecture and urban planning, and the other native quarters, which were either subject to heavily restrictive preservation law or else, as in the case of Lagos ignored entirely.[130]

Arising from the above, the following questions may be asked: at what point did the colonial authorities consider it necessary to embark on land reclamation and slum clearance? What factors were responsible for this urban policy? Is excuse for spatial expansion by the British acceptable or the political motives explanation by the educated elite and nationalists tenable? The analysis that follows handles on these posers. Land reclamation and urban slum clearance in Lagos can be divided into three phases: 1900–1929, 1930–1950, and 1951–1970. For the purpose of this study, concentration shall be on the period 1951–1970 specifically the slum clearance exercise of 1955.

URBAN SLUM CLEARANCE AND LIVELIHOOD IN LAGOS

Initially, the need to have more land space for urban expansion between 1900 and 1929 became evident to the colonial administration because of the rapid growth of commerce between the expanding port of Lagos and the interior of the country.[131] In 1900, swamps and lagoon inlets still covered more than 60 percent of Lagos Island. Ikoyi was not a separate Island then, and much of its northern and southern parts were covered by swamps and dense bush.[132] It was under Governor Macgregor that the first major large-scale land reclamation was carried out. By 1905, the north-south major canal otherwise known as Macgregor canal had been dredged.[133] It was this process that separated Lagos and Ikoyi into two detached islands. Following these reclamations, however, Lagos began to spread to Ikoyi and Ebute-Meta. So the need then arose to reclaim more swamps in these areas.

By 1929, the creation of the Lagos Executive Development Board (LEDB) marked the beginning of the second phase of land reclamation in Lagos. This body was saddled with the responsibility of land resource management with a bias for urban planning. The urban planning process of this board was tailored toward the segregation settlement pattern of the colonial authorities. This policy was in line with Bisola Falola's position on urban relations:

> Once created, spatial patterns condition how we live our lives, interact with one another, and perceive the world. The social and the spatial become mutually

constitutive, continuously interacting to structure possibilities and define boundaries based on social relations of power.[134]

Although saddled with the responsibility of reclaiming Elegbata, Idumagbo, and Isaleigangan areas, the body extended it by reclaiming Oko Awo as well as the remaining swamps at Ijora.[135] This was carried out by first embarking on the slum clearance in the areas surrounding the lagoon inlets at Idumagbo and Isale Igangan. By 1940, nearly all the lagoon inlets and swamps had been reclaimed for settlement and business expansion.

By the 1950s, the question of the status of Lagos in the era of transfer of power had become a contentious issue, especially during the 1953 constitutional talks in London.[136] The debate centered on whether Lagos should remain part of Western Region or be excised from it to form a federal territory which would be independent of the region.[137] The British administration, Northern and Eastern parties wanted Lagos to be the capital of Nigeria, but dissociated from Western Region.[138] The reason was mainly financial: the port and the growing industrialization of Lagos provided large resources for the state.[139] To abandon Lagos to Western Region included the risk of reinforcing the financial power of its dominant political party, the Action Group (AG). The AG, on the other hand, wanted to keep Lagos within Western Region for the opposite reason and suggested building a new capital in a central and neutral place.[140] At the end of the conference, it was decided that Lagos should be separated from the West as the Federal Capital Territory.[141] This decision, apart from being considered by Obafemi Awolowo as a fiscal and an economic suicide for Western Region, also had implications for the urban planning exercise as well as livelihood challenges for the residents of central Lagos during that period.

With the approach of independence, the people of Nigeria began to look more critically at their federal capital. From the point of view of authority or the public, the poorer sections constituted an embarrassment of substandard living.[142] These areas came about as a product of economic conditions and represented an adaptation to the low income of the urban masses.[143] In spite of this, the people saw in their proposed federal capital congested lanes of ramshackle houses, a poor reflection of their aspirations. The mind of the government about Lagos was summarized by Minister of Lagos Affairs Alhaji Musa YarAdua thus:

> It is the mirror through which foreigners make their initial appraisal of Nigeria and many regard it as an index of the progress of prosperity of Nigeria. The condition of central Lagos, was humiliating to any person with a sense of national pride.[144]

Besides, central Lagos had been described by *West African Review* (WAR) as "a notorious slum where some of the lean-to shelters occupied by large and poverty-stricken families in Lagos are not fit to house sheep and goats, much less human beings."[145]

It was with these perception and concerns in mind that the LEDB initiated a massive slum clearance program which began in 1955 and extended three years into the independence period. The scope of the scheme comprised the clearance and redevelopment of seventy acres of built-up land bounded approximately by Broad Street, Balogun Street, and Victoria Street.[146] It was to involve re-housing of about 200,000 people over a period of five to seven years.[147] Streets were to be widened to meet the increased traffic demands and, at the same time, rear access service roads to the commercial premises fronting these main streets were to be provided.[148] This urban planning program degenerated into conflict between the city and the nation on one side and between communities on the other side.

The scheme was, however, difficult to implement and was delayed because of the opposition of the residents and of the Lagos Town Council dominated by AG which presented itself as advocate of the people to be displaced.[149] On October 22, 1955, a letter of protest was written through Chief Secretary of the Federation to the governor general of the federation of Nigeria, signed by over 12,000 residents of central Lagos under the aegis of the Association of Residents in central Lagos.[150] In their letter, it was resolved that the central Lagos slum clearance scheme was not acceptable and should be opposed by all constitutional means.[151] Their resolution was premised on some conditions and reasons: First, they welcome improvements in standard of living, but these standards should be commensurate with the conditions and status of the people at a particular time. Second, that their forefathers had always lived a communal life which was the African living condition as distinct from the isolated non-African system, and so could not afford to live in a three- or four-story building of only eight rooms (according to the building density control) with his whole African family, particularly when the building was to be mortgaged for a loan not below £8000. Therefore, the residents were not convinced that the scheme was intended for the benefit of the people of the area concerned.[152]

Although this protest letter was written and signed by the residents of the area concerned; government felt they were coordinated by the AG members, because central Lagos was dominated politically by the AG. In spite of this protest letter, the scheme came into operations in 1955, in the face of vehement protests from many of the residents.[153]

The government accused the AG of "playing politics with epidemics," while the AG accused the government of having selected the central area of Lagos Island for slum removal, which was its strongest political constituency.[154] An objective evaluation of these accusation and counter accusation reveals that both parties had genuine cases as far as the status of the scheme was concerned. As earlier mentioned in the preceding section, Lagos Island, the most densely populated area of the city, had been hit by severe and recurrent plagues since the nineteenth century, while its two electoral wards were the only ones to have elected AG councilors without interruption from 1950 up to 1955.[155] Although from the chronology and the analysis so far, it is difficult to discard any of these arguments of the parties involved, it is important to note that, in addition to sanitizing central Lagos, the slum clearance scheme paved way for the development of Lagos Central Business District along Marina, Broad Street, and Nnamdi Azikwe Street.[156] This favors the position that the slum clearance scheme was embarked upon by the colonial authorities to make Lagos perform wider political, commercial, and educational functions as the nation's capital and leading urban center. The fundamental problem raised by the Lagos slum clearance scheme is this: how can a neighborhood be physically destroyed, without destroying at the same time the livelihood and way of life of the people who have settled there? Peter Marris argues that if these are disrupted, the clearance of slums is likely to do them more harm than good.[157]

The experiences of the people displaced are both positive and negative. The scheme was embarked upon with the promise by the LEDB to rebuild the demolished houses to be re-occupied by owners, to compensate residents, to grant loans and relocate people to the housing estates in Surulere.[158] Reports from fieldwork and other sources revealed that the implementation of the slum clearance scheme impacted negatively on the dispossessed residents culturally, economically, socially, politically, and psychologically. In fact, only few of those interviewed spoke positively about the slum clearance exercise. Those interviewed comprised the educated elite cum civil servants who were relocated to the housing estate in Surulere, and whose desire to embrace culture of "individualism" instead of the existing extended family and kinship ties system was favored. The account below supports this:

> I really appreciated the slum clearance scheme because, prior to the period, I lived in a family house. We were overcrowded and choked. I married, had children and still living in the family house. There was a strong extended family relationship even to the extent that one's wife family would come, likewise my relatives would come and everybody would jam-pack in a room. This partly explains the prevalence of diseases in Lagos i.e fever, measles (*Igbona*) because we were using hurricane lantern. There was no sewage; bucket latrine (*pokiti*) was in common use, and the night soil men would pass through the passage to evacuate the *pokiti* for one kobo per month. This was the standard of living before the slum clearance scheme. Thus, by the time slum clearance was introduced, larger percentage of us supported it.[159]

This account seems to justify the slum clearance exercise in Lagos. However, Sikiru Akanni belonged to the educated elite or the middle class, because he was a staff of the office of the secretary of state during the implementation of the scheme. Although his reasons on the standard of living has merit, his further comments on the implementation of the scheme contradicts the stories of other residents who narrated the woes and hardships the scheme wrought on them, especially on their livelihood and sociocultural dislocation. Another resident confirmed the cultural implication of the slum clearance exercise:

> Before the slum clearance exercise, the practice had been to bury the afterbirth (placenta) beneath the house where a child is born, and most times the remains of dead persons were also committed to the mother earth within the compound. I could remember that I had traumatic experience when I gave birth to my second child. It was the day that preceded the demolition of our residence at Banjoko Street in Lagos. Then we were confronted with where to bury the afterbirth such that it took us three days before we could do that somewhere very close to the lagoon. Unlike before that we would bury such thing in the compound beneath the ground. Also, there was family dislocation because a lot of families could not afford to rebuild their demolished houses, especially when the compensation given had been shared amongst the relatives. For those that were not ready to move outside Lagos, they resorted to squatting, which, in most cases, the children were scattered and stayed apart from their parents. This to the best of my knowledge affected greatly the communal living system, and marked the beginning of the culture of 'individualism' especially amongst the educated elite.[160]

The most striking aspect of the above experience is the one that has to do with the family dislocation as a result of the slum clearance exercise. Apart from the fact that it affected communal living tradition, dislocation of families resulted in juvenile delinquent behaviors among the youths because Lagos experienced more youths loafing on the streets without any means of livelihood. In fact, it can be said that this exercise promoted criminal activities in Lagos as a result of family dislocation and social change.

There is an important question on the economy of that period: how can a neighborhood be destroyed without physically destroying the livelihood of the people? Central Lagos was densely populated. The population as well as the human traffic facilitated trading activities such that there is hardly a residence without an array of shops for artisans and traders. It was a traumatic experience for most residents as they watched helplessly the destruction of their houses and means of livelihood. The experiences represent those of displaced people of central Lagos whose livelihood was affected, and those that were rehoused outside Lagos, to be precise, in Surulere. Although few aged residents were available for interview, the experience recorded from other sources also illustrates the impact of the slum clearance scheme on the livelihood of those displaced and dispossessed. The experiences are captured below:

> I was a practicing goldsmith at Layeni Street in central Lagos before the slum clearance exercise. Then, my business was recording progress because

Lagosians loved social functions, and wearing of adornments, such as necklace, ring and jewelries generally was part of the conviviality culture of the Lagosians. Suddenly, we were served the notice that the house where my shop was located had been marked for destruction, and that residents were to be rehoused somewhere in the suburbs in a housing estate. Initially, I thought it would not happen but until the LEDB came in 1956 and demolished our residence. Subsequently, I was confronted with two problems, firstly to secure new accommodation because my house had been demolished at Akanni Street, and secondly to look for a new place to practice my trade because my shop had been demolished at Layeni Street. Consequently, life became difficult for me and my family. I had a wife and three children. My wife relocated to Awe town in Oyo province where she hails from with the children. It was a cousin of mine that encouraged me to relocate to Accra in Ghana because goldsmiths were highly sought for at that period. This marked the beginning of my sojourn to Accra in 1956, only to be joined by my family in 1966 shortly before the military coup. This was how I was separated from my family for ten years as a result of the slum clearance scheme.[161]

The experience of Adekunle Faturoti above is just one of the numerous recounts of hardships encountered by the displaced residents of Lagos. Many shops were demolished with houses, and traders became bankrupt. Also, the artisans and civil servants were not left out. A survey carried out by Peter Marris in 1959 in Lagos revealed the livelihood challenges experienced by the residents of Lagos, particularly the reasons why some residents refused to move to the housing estate in Surulere. The fears and anxieties of the people were palpable. A vivid example was that of a bricklayer, who protested that Surulere was too far to Lagos Island, where he had most of his clients. Besides, relocating from Lagos Island to Surulere would affect the business of his wives, who were well-established traders in Lagos.[162]

In addition to the envisaged problems of family dislocation and livelihood destruction, poor urban transport system, and the fear of accessibility to human traffic at the proposed housing estate in Surulere compounded the fears of the residents about the re-housing scheme. The fears expressed by the residents in this regard are succinctly represented thus:

> I'd be sorry to go for two important things, a teacher said. I work in Lagos, and for all my expenditure I depend very much on my wife. Even at the end of the month I depend on her, and thinking now of my salary, it will be very difficult for me, if I go there, to carry all my responsibilities. My wife would have difficulty in trading out there.[163]

This teacher belonged to the category of those residents whose wives engaged in trading either in the household or in the neighborhood in central Lagos as a means of supporting the income of their household. Such people considered the slum clearance scheme and the re-housing project of the government as a threat to their livelihood. Besides, fieldwork and existing body of knowledge reveal that the thick population of Lagos provided a platform for successful trading and patronage for artisans. Therefore, most artisans felt uncomfortable to leave certainty for uncertainty as far as leaving central Lagos for elsewhere was concerned. This is clearly shown in the quotation below:

> It's a matter of busy streets, explained an electrician, whose wife sold poplins and striped cottons from a pavement stall. You look for a market stall in a street where morning and evening people are rushing up and down. At Surulere we might be tucked away in some corner. And my wife has to carry her loads from the market morning and evening: it would be impossible to carry them up and down Surulere.[164]

Apart from the artisans, some civil servants and some of the educated elite were not left out in the fear of uncertainty that gripped the residents of Lagos, particularly the issue of transportation as far as relocating to Surulere was concerned. Their reluctance and apprehension was predicated on the argument that Surulere was too far to Lagos Island, cost of transportation would increase, and poor transport system would make life difficult for them.

Besides all these problems, the facilities in the re-housing estate, that is showers, lavatories, and running water were tempting to the displaced people, but they were reluctant to go because many of them could not afford to pay the bills for the utilities. However, two residents of central Lagos who were affected by the slum clearance exercise and who eventually relocated to the re-housing estates at Surulere phases 1 and 2 eulogized the exercise and even expressed their regrets for not acquiring more than one block of flat as at the time they finally bought the flats from government. Sikiru Akanni, for instance, had been a resident of Randle Avenue in Surulere since 1956. He was a civil servant at the office of the secretary to the colonial government when the slum clearance scheme started. He embraced the scheme because he felt that the conditions of living in Lagos during the period were low and that most residents of central Lagos were vulnerable to diseases.[165] Unlike other residents of central Lagos who were reluctant to move to the new housing estates for fear of uncertainty, Akanni moved into the estate with his family without the fear of the imminent challenges. According to him, one of the challenges of the period was transportation. The government responded to this by providing buses to transport people to and from the island and the mainland. Besides, government established a Post Office at Akerele, and a health center at Randle Avenue to cater for the residents of the estate.[166] Corroborating this view, another long-time resident of Surulere, Fausat Thomas, opined that, initially, most families did not want to come to Surulere which, until then, was referred to as *Obele Odan*, a place notorious for armed robber's activity, but the forceful implementation of the slum clearance exercise in Lagos Island left them with no alternative.

She added that her family was displaced after the destruction of their rented house in central Lagos. Thus, the option left as a young family was to give the new abode offered a trial. She later found the block of flat allocated to her convenient. In fact, she expressed her regret that if only she knew, she would have opted for more blocks of flat when Lagos State Property Development Company (LSDPC) approached them for the final takeover of the building.[167] This is because the name that was once object of ridicule by dwellers of Lagos slums is now one of the most attractive areas to reside in Lagos today.

It is glaring from the experiences of the people affected by the slum clearance exercise in Lagos that it was a paradox. While some of them felt that it impacted negatively on them, some found the scheme necessary as at the time it was carried out. However, it has been argued that beyond livelihood and economic challenges associated with the slum clearance scheme in Lagos, the exercise and other colonial policies also contributed immensely to cultural changes in the city of Lagos. These changes are examined in the subsection that follows.

URBAN CULTURE: FAMILY AND SOCIAL CHANGE IN COLONIAL LAGOS

Every people and every society have a culture. This is the sum total of the integrated learned behavioral patterns characteristic of members of a society, as well as the sum total of a people's customary way of doing things.[168] However, any argument about culture must simply, or make explicit, a powerful political content.[169] For our culture is our way of life—its whole busy action, its values, its arts and symbols, structures, and institutions.[170] More than that, culture is the total, mobile body of feelings and beliefs, intentions, and reasons which inform the ceaseless action.

The response toward the urbanization and modernization drive of the colonialists diluted the existing cultural beliefs, values, structures, and institutions in the city of Lagos. In order for the colonial masters to administer the colony, it was necessary to orientate Nigerians toward Western values.[171] This resulted in a drastic shift from the traditional to the Western values. In fact, the colonial contact initiated a lot of social processes of differentiation and integration.[172] Traditional beliefs and religion, family structure and functions, social stratification and traditional associations were all affected.[173]

The shift toward modernization and industrialization occasioned radical changes in the culture. It brought about a conflict between the indigenous culture and the Western one. The educated elite tilted more to the Western culture, while the illiterate majority, especially the old generations, insisted on tradition.[174] Despite these radical changes, the system still retained some of the basic traditional values, like extended family and kinship ties. The sustenance of kinship ties and extended family in colonial Lagos relied on the concept of social capital and reciprocity. Thus, an attempt is made to clarify the social capital concept as well as the concept of the extended family. This would enable us to understand the workings of the kinship ties, and the survival of the traditional practice of extended family relations in the wake of the Western concept of "individualism" that developed in colonial Lagos as a result of industrialization and urbanization.

Social capital is difficult to define because it is not just a single entity. It is a variety of different entities, sharing two common elements.[175] The search for its meaningful explanation led to over 100 scholarly contributions toward conceptual and empirical development of social capital.[176] James Coleman, James Farr, Robert Putnam, Pierre Bourdieu, and of recent Francis Fukuyama are contemporary scholars identified in the literature in the study of social capital. For the purpose of this study, examples are drawn from one of the earliest pioneers in the subject and the contemporary scholars. Hanifan Lyda Judson was the first to attempt the definition of social capital as:

> Those tangible assets that count for most in the daily lives of people: namely goodwill, fellowship, sympathy, social intercourse among the individuals and families who make up a social unit . . . The individual is helpless socially, if left to himself . . . If he comes into contact with his neighbors, there will be an accumulation of social capital, which may immediately satisfy his social needs and which may bear a social potentiality sufficient to the substantial improvement of living conditions in the whole community. The community as whole will benefit by cooperation of all its parts, while the individual will find in his associations the advantages of help, the sympathy, and the fellowship of his neighbors.[177]

Further, other scholars picked from this explanation, and attempted conceptualization of social capital. Coleman defines social capital by its function and by what it does rather than by what it is. Social capital is not a single entity, but a variety of different entries sharing two common elements. First, they consist of some aspects of social structure, and second, they facilitate certain actions of actors within the structure.[178] Social capital is of extrinsic values that comprise reciprocity, kinship ties, fellowship, goodwill, welfares, sympathy, and extended family relations, all of which can be categorized as platforms through which it is realizable in any social unit. Putting these elements together, social capital, according to James Farr, is complexly conceptualized as the network of associations, activities, or relations that bind people together as a community via certain norms and psychological capacities, notably trust, which are essential for civil society and productive of future collective action or goods, in the manner of other forms of capital.[179] Thus, as far as urban livelihood in colonial Lagos was concerned, kinship ties and extended family relations enhanced reciprocity and welfare as forms of social capital, which played significant roles in the livelihood of the people.

It has been argued that Nigerians are influenced both by their indigenous traditions and by newer values and lifestyles that have been inculcated from the West.[180] Traditional reliance on extended family and kinship networks remains strong throughout Nigeria, but a growing focus on smaller, nuclear families and on individual achievement is recognizable, particularly in urban areas. Extended family relations and kinship ties had been part of the society before the contact with the Europeans. Urbanization and Western culture have affected this practice in the urban areas by promoting individualism and the nuclear family concept. Although examples are given of narratives on the workings of extended family relations in Lagos life from the long residents perspective, attempt was also made to test the hypothesis that extended family relations are absent in West African cities.

There are several criteria that can be used to establish the existence of kinship group and extended family relations.[181] Among these is residence with two or more related nuclear families quarters. A second criterion consists of the joint activities engaged in by the extended family members as an organized unit. These activities can be of various types ranging from economic and legal to welfare and leisure.[182] Another criterion is assistance between individual relatives based on normative expectations whether in the form of gifts or services. Friendship networks joining kinsmen constitute the fourth criterion.[183] The presence of any of these criteria is taken as evidence of the existence of the extended family relations and kinship ties.

In colonial Lagos, all the above highlighted criteria existed. This was because the population of the city comprised largely migrants from the hinterland and villages who had not had time enough to be influenced by urbanization. Besides, among the Yoruba and, to some extent, other groups, family corporations existed, which was meant to orchestrate, arbitrate, and administer the lives of the members of the family collective.[184] The Yoruba *idile* is a named corporate body with membership based on descent; its duties include holding and managing property, seeing to the economic welfare of members in need, caring for the children of incapacitated parents, and arbitrating disputes among members.[185] Although in Lagos, with the exception of the indigenes, the *idile* stood in contrast with the *ebi*. This was because the *ebi* was simply the pull of kindred to which individuals were tied by reciprocal obligatory relations varying in intensity by genealogical distance. Thus, it can be said that the *ebi* was the connecting platforms for extended family relations (*idile*), especially among the migrants in Lagos. Sandra T. Barnes asserts that:

> Neither the passage of time and generations nor lack of residential proximity has managed to diminish the persistence of descent group relationships among migrants. If anything there is a growing tendency toward strengthening these kinds of ties in Lagos. As more and more migrants commit themselves to living permanently in a new location, the number of active *idile* in that place can be expected to increase.[186]

From the above, it can be deduced that of *ebi* and *idile* fostered extended family relations as well as kinship ties in the city. Also with regard to assistance, the residents of Lagos, like their rural counterparts, continued to regard the needs of their kin as their first obligation. They supported aged aunts and cousins as well as parents. It was customary to present their elderly kinsmen with gifts in cash or in kind when visiting them.[187] In addition, they often contributed to the marriage payments of younger brothers, reared nieces, and nephews and helped married sisters.[188] Family, in the Lagos of that period, was more than a refuge for those in need. The content of family ties and exchange cannot all be measured in terms of cash; support has meaning beyond the realm of economics.[189] Marris reported the distress, the longing for news, of migrants to Lagos who were physically separated from kin by the lack of means to visit home or those who found it too expensive to visit home. Here is the way a prosperous Lagos shoemaker described the situations:

> On Sunday the family will come, you know we Yoruba are not like white people, we do not wait to be invited. If I have a brother in Abeokuta, his son may come, let us say, or a cousin. So in the afternoon there is fried yam, beer for an aged person, Coca-Cola for the children. It is because of our belief that in this way they will help us when we are old, and when you die, they will remember the uncle who did this or that for them. That is why we are careful never to offend them, and treat them like that so they will never forget it.[190]

For those with the means, visits among relatives living within easy reach, especially those in the same town, were frequent; visits with relatives in distant towns were often of long durations. Marris claims that there were the formal occasions when the family came together in an expression of unity, with family branches sometimes appearing in *asoebi* (family uniform) allowed this kind of planning and preparation.[191] This fact was corroborated by Esther Akinfenwa. She asserted that, apart from rendering business support to family, funerals, naming ceremonies, house warming and weddings were the concern of all the kin, to which they contributed their quota adequately.[192] She narrated a story to uphold the argument that kinship ties and extended family relations is not only measured in terms of economic support. She described the situation of her uncle who was induced to return from Accra thus:

> In the mid 1940s, there was an uncle of mine—a junior brother to my mother who relocated to Accra in search of greener pastures. By 1957, my mother and his other siblings had become worried about him, especially his marital status. When contacted, my uncle vowed to remain single until he has a roof on his head, and that he would not return to Nigeria until his dream was accomplished. Two years after, precisely on the eve of Nigeria's independence, my mother contacted him again but he remained adamant. It was at this point that my mother invited the remaining two of her sisters to deliberate on the way forward on the only male among them. Eventually, they agreed to find for him a wife, and also build him a house. By 1960, my mother single-handedly built a bungalow type of house for uncle Bashiru, paid the bride price of a lady in preparation for his wedding, only for him to return from Accra and get married at the age of 43 in 1961.[193]

This kind of moral and economic support was not limited to the Yoruba in Lagos. Other groups also enjoyed support in various forms from friends and relations. For instance, Pa Etareko Emmanuel narrated his experience as a long-time resident in Lagos, who ordinarily would have left Lagos as far back as 1955, but for the support of his kinsmen who rallied round him in his period of adversity. He described his ordeal thus:

> I am an Urhobo man from the Delta area. In November 1952, my wife put to bed but rather than deliver safely, she was made to go through operation in the hospital. Eventually she delivered a set of twins to increase the family size to five because we already had a child. At this period, life became difficult because I had expended so much on her while in pregnancy and at the point of delivery. Added to this was the fact that the one - room apartment we occupied at Kadara Street, Ebute-Meta could no longer contain us. In fact, barely four weeks after her delivery I also developed pneumonia. It took the intervention of my home town association -Urhobo Progressive Union- who took me to the hospital, and also assisted us in getting a two room apartment at Adekunle area of Yaba. Again in 1955, armed robbers visited my house at Adekunle Street and made away with my money and the savings of my customers because I am an *esusu* collector by profession. While some of my customers sympathized with me especially when they were confronted with the injuries inflicted on me by the robbers, some threatened to collect their money back because that was their life savings. I wanted to run away, but my home town association came to my aid again, and borrowed me eighty percent of the amount required to settle my customers. In fact, if not for these kinship supports I would have left Lagos since 1955.[194]

The above excerpts reveal the roles of the kinship ties in sustenance of livelihood in colonial Lagos. However, things have changed; kinship bond have given way first to extended family, and later to individualism. During the period, members of extended families, when living apart, were actually within a 10 to 15 minutes' walk from one another and showed a high degree of mutual affection.[195] Friendship networks were maintained by daily meetings which served as opportunities to pass on family news and to discuss family problems.[196] This traditional set up was observed by Peter Marris in his survey of central Lagos in the late 1950s. But when and how did "individualism" dilute the culture of extended family relations and kinship ties in Lagos?

European-Nigerian contact impacted on the traditional value system, beliefs, and religion. The first important effect of urbanization and industrialization is the development of "individualism," which was unknown in traditional African society.[197] In the traditional society, the Nigerian was enmeshed in a web of social relationships, implying obligations and providing security, which left room for the assertion of himself as an individual.[198] According to Westerman "'African society' is characterized by the prevalence of the idea of community."[199] He adds that:

> The individual recedes before the group. The whole existence from birth to death is originally embodied in a series of associations, and life appears to have its full value only on these close ties. Though there is in them a well-ordered gradation between persons who command and obey, yet the prevailing feeling is that of equality. Class distinctions as we know them are absent or but feebly developed. They may be of greater weight in countries where there is a marked distinction between a ruling group and a subject people, but usually with a social unit the consciousness of a strong sense of solidarity is predominant. The group imposes duties on the individual but it also grants privileges; it takes from its members much of their personal responsibility and offers them its protection.[200]

A departure from the above summary of the culture of Africans, especially Nigerians, started with the introduction of monetary economy, which replaced the trade by barter type of economy, which traditional Nigerian was used to. In addition to this, religion, Western occupation and education played significant roles in the cultural dilution in colonial Lagos.

Mission churches and schools, introduced in the 1880s, expanded rapidly after the annexation.[201] Subsequently, by 1912, some 201 Protestant primary schools and 7 Protestant secondary schools scattered throughout the Western province of the protectorate of Southern Nigeria, enrolling 14,484 primary and 769 secondary students.[202] Within the same period, precisely between 1905 and 1912, colonial bureaucracy grew such that it employed 187 Europeans and 405 Africans.[203] This was made possible because the African elite grew steadily between 1880 and 1915 and were readily available for the Europeans who relied heavily on the educated Africans for the development of the colony, partly because Lagos was a very unhealthy place for

Europeans.[204] In fact, between 1880 and 1913, the elite had increased from 54 to 117, respectively, such that members worked as import-export merchants, colonial servants, doctors, lawyers, ministers, headmasters, newspaper editors, and surveyors throughout the period.[205] In addition to these sources of waged employment was the railway corporation which has been credited as the largest single waged employment provider in the colonial history of Nigeria.

During the year ending March 31, 1934, despite drastic measures to meet financial conditions and the lessening of the European staff by twenty-three officials, the number of Africans employed had increased by slightly over 900, mostly in the laboring class.[206] Statistics also revealed that, in the preceding fiscal year, 16,376 Africans and West Indians had been employed by the railway, while the European staff number only 369 officials.[207] Of the total number of native workers including West Indians, 11,075 were laborers, 3,509 artisans and 1,792 salaried staff.[208]

The above statistics lends credence to the fact that appreciable number of residents in colonial Lagos earned wages either as skilled workers or unskilled workers. Their exposure at work and their possession of money greatly affected traditional practices. When a wage earner goes to work, he receives wages as an individual; and he pays tax as an individual. This marks the beginning of his orientation to the culture of "individualism." Some of the workers were quartered very close to their places of work. The housing of the native railway workers showed closer contact with European civilization, as it was the practice of the railway, as of other government departments, to provide housing facilities for its employees.[209] This reinforced the rate at which the native railway workers copied the European lifestyles, which tilted toward individualism in contrast to the traditional practice where the Lagosian thought of himself as a member of a group that was bound together by kinship and communal ties. The social and economic relationship between these wage earners: railway workers, shop assistants, interpreters, clerks, newspaper editors, and so on; and the subalterns: petty traders, artisans, porters, fishermen, musicians, washer men, and female grinder further enhanced the spread of individualism as a way of life. Also, it has been argued that the heavy demands made on those successful in the urban arena by the extended family tends to impede or frustrate individual aspiration and ambition, whether in business or employment, because success only means increased demands from needy relatives.[210] Wayne Nafziger found, in his study on Nigeria that the extended family boosted entrepreneurial activity by financing training and furnishing initial capital outlay but that the expansion of these firms was hindered by increase in the number of dependents asking for support when there was any increase in the size of business.[211] Consequently, the burden placed on urban dwellers as a result of open-handed hospitality and gifts to relatives often made some of them to move away from families and kinsmen.

In addition to the above, conversion to Christianity seemed to have reinforced a social and religious basis for the individualism resulting from monetized economy. The very act of becoming a Christian has generally meant an assertion of someone's individuality in opposition to group pressure. As Westernman has pointed out, "conversion is a personal matter, an affair between man and God."[212] A man may draw his family with him, but, for them as for him, it is a personal step. When a person living in pagan surroundings adopts Christianity, he often loses the protection or even membership of his group and has to stand by himself.[213] This scenario, according to a long-term resident of Lagos, was prevalent in the 1950s.[214] This was the period when the educated elite who had embraced Christianity were highly involved in the conversion of family and friends from either Islam or traditional religion to Christianity. Consequently, there was culture conflict in most families, and the discontent that emanated from such conversion degenerated to individual lifestyle.

The missionaries, in addition to insisting on monogamy type of marriage, urged converts to marry in church ceremonies and taught them Victorian values about proper relationship between and roles of Christian husband and wives.[215] The missionaries also emphasized that Christian marriage should be based on love and companionship, and that husband should support families economically and wives should not work outside the home but devote full time to domestic chores.[216]

Culture conflict arose from the acquisition of Western culture which affects the Nigerian personal orientation and world view. The implication of this is that the traditional practice became affected economically, socially, and religiously. Individualism began to gain ground in Lagos, not only among the wage earners, but also among the subaltern as a result of day-to-day interactions in the markets, on the streets, in the churches, mosques, and at homes. Findings from fieldwork and existing body of knowledge shows that monetized economy, urbanization, and industrialization succeeded to some extent in promoting individualism, but failed to eradicate social capital and kinship ties in the city of Lagos.

CONCLUSION

Waged employment and the need to access money attracted migrants from far and near to the city of Lagos in the nineteenth and twentieth century. The uncontrolled population of the migrants and the unequal municipal administration in Lagos degenerated into "urbanization of poverty." However, the instinct and the need to survive by the residents, especially those in the lower rung of the society created survival strategies through which their threatened livelihood was safeguarded. Besides, the changing nature of the society, particularly the neighborhood cultures, redefined social values, most especially after the implementation of the slum clearance scheme of the late 1950s. However, kinship ties and extended family relations helped the indigenes and the migrants in the city to survive the burden of unemployment and housing during the period under analysis.

NOTES

1. Flanagan and Gugler, *Urbanization and Social Change*, 50.
2. Ibid.
3. Personal Communication with Professor Olakunle Lawal, Lecturer, Department of History, University of Ibadan, 52 years, February 12, 2011.
4. Olukoju, *The Liverpool of West Africa*, 40.
5. Ibid.
6. Pius Sada, "Differential Population Distribution in Metropolitan Lagos," *Journal of Business and Social Studies* 1, no.2 (1969): 121.
7. NAI, CSO 1/19/45 28 of January 16, 1912, Egerton to Harcourt.
8. Sada and Adefolalu, *Urbanization and Problems*, 80–81.
9. Ayodeji Olukoju, *Infrastructure Development and Urban Facilities in Lagos, 1861-200* (Ibadan: IFRA, 2003), 79.
10. Sada and Adefolalu, *Urbanization and Problems*, 81.
11. Olukoju, *Infrastructure Development*, 11.
12. Michael Joseph Echeruo, *Victorian Lagos: Aspects of Nineteenth Century Lagos Life* (London: Macmillan, 1977), 19.
13. Personal Communication with Ibrahim Ayinde, 78 years, May 20, 2009. Also see Abayomi Ferera, an Introduction to "the Lagos We Lost." www.villagesquare.com/forum.
14. Abayomi Ferera, An Introduction to "the Lagos We Lost." www.villagesquare.com/forum, accessed on 20/04/2011.
15. Ibid.
16. Abayomi Ferera, An Introduction to " the Lagos We Lost." www.villagesquare.com/forum.
17. Echeruo, *Victorian Lagos*, 18.
18. Mabogunje, *Urbanization in Nigeria*, 263.
19. For statistical details, see Ibid.
20. Ibid., 262.
21. Ibid., 263.
22. Personal Communication with Lateef Amuda, 78 years, Lagos Island on August 1, 2012.
23. NAI, CSO 1/19/4528, Correspondence from Egerton to Harcourt, January 16, 1912.

24. Ibid.
25. Anthony Hopkins, "The Lagos Strike of 1897: An Exploration in Nigeria Labour History." *Past and Present* 35, (1966): 140.
26. Ibid.
27. See evidence in a court case between Omotosho vs Sedu Olowu, July 13, 1881, Civil 3, Supreme Court Record, Lagos.
28. Hopkins, "The Lagos Strike of 1897," 141.
29. Ibid.
30. Ibid.
31. Wale Oyemakinde, "Wage Earners in Nigeria during the Great Depression," in *Essays in Economic History*, ed. Wale Oyemakinde (Ibadan: Sunlight Syndicate, 2003), 92.
32. Ibid.
33. Ibid.
34. Ibid., 93.
35. Frederick Dawson Hammond, *Report of the Railway System of Nigeria* (1924), 14.
36. Ibid.
37. Williams Kieth Hancock, *Survey of British Commonwealth Affairs*, Vol. II, Part 2 (London: Oxford University Press, 1942), 193.
38. Ukandi Godwin Damachi, *Nigerian Modernization: The Colonial Legacy* (New York, NY: Joseph Okpaku Publishing Company, 1972), 54.
39. Ibid.
40. Olu Ajakaiye and Aderibigbe Olomola, *Poverty in Nigeria: A Multidimensional Perspective* (Ibadan: NISER, 2003), 353.
41. Michael Walton, "Combating Poverty: Experience and Prospects." *Journal of Finance and Development* (September Issue, 1990): 2–6.
42. Tunde Decker, "Social Welfare Strategies in Colonial Lagos." *African Nebula* 1, no.1 (2010): 56.
43. John Iliffe, *The African Poor: A History* (Cambridge: Cambridge University Press, 1987), 49.
44. Ibid.
45. Wande Abimbola, *Ifa Divination Poetry* (New York, NY: Nok Publishers, 1977), 1–4.
46. Ibid.
47. Raymond Okeke, *The Osu Concept in Igboland* (Enugu: Access Publishers, 1986), 9.
48. *The State of African Cities 2008: A Framework for Addressing Urban Challenges in Africa* (Nairobi: United Nations Human Settlement (UN-HABITAT), 2008), 83.
49. Julius Wilson, *The Truly Disadvantaged: The Inner City, the Under Class, and Public Policy* (Chicago, IL: University of Chicago Press, 1987) cited in L.S. Mario and K. Newman, "Urban Poverty after The Truly Disadvantaged: The Rediscovery of the Family, the Neighbourhood, and Culture." *Annual Review of Sociology* 27, (2001): 29.
50. NAI, Comcol 1 file 894, Vol. 1, Unemployment in Lagos, 1929, 34.

51. Ibid.

52. NAI, Comcol 1 file 894, Vol. 1, Response by the Chief Secretary to the Government on the Enquiry by Citizens on the State of Unemployment in Lagos, 35.

53. Mabogunje, *Urbanization in Nigeria*, 254.

54. Herbert Spencer, *A History of the People of Lagos, 1852–1886* (PhD diss., Northwestern University, Evanston, IL, 1964), 127.

55. Ibid.

56. Ibid., 129.

57. Ibid.

58. Personal Communication with Raji Risikat Olanrewaju, 63 years, May 26, 2011.

59. Spencer, *A History*, 130.

60. Ibid.

61. NAI, Comcol 1, File 894, Vol. I, Correspondence between Findlay. G.N. and Chief Secretary to Government, September 21, 1929, 37.

62. Ibid.

63. Ibid., 59.

64. Personal Communication with Pa Oluwole Akinsanya, 83 years, November 17, 2010.

65. NAI, Comcol 1, File no 797/1/Vol. II, "Beggars in Lagos," Colony Welfare Officer to Commissioner of Police and Director of Medical Services, October 16, 1944, 4.

66. Ibid.

67. NAI, Comcol 1, File no 1493, Vol. IV, January 25, 1943, "Letter from J.B. Williams to the Commissioner of Labour," Lagos, 15.

68. Ibid., 16.

69. NAI, Comcol 1, File no 894, Vol. II, "Unemployment in Lagos," Letter from Commissioner of the Colony to the Commissioner of Labour, Lagos, January 25, 1943, 129.

70. Ibid.

71. Ibid.

72. Decker, "Social Welfare," 57.

73. NAI, Comcol 1, File no 894, Vol. II, "Unemployment in Lagos," 129.

74. NAI, Livingstone, Assistant Director of Public Works, to the Chief Secretary on "Suggestion to Alleviate Present Conditions in Lagos and Solve Some of Its Problems," July 6th, 1945, 139.

75. NAI, Comcol 1, File no 797/1, Vol. II, "Beggars in Lagos," a Letter from the Commissioner of Police to the Director of the Medical Services, October 16, 1945, 4.

76. The Editorial, *Lagos Standard*, January 11, 1899.

77. NAI, Comcol 1, File no 797/1, Vol. II, "Beggars in Lagos," 4.

78. NAI, Comcol 1, File no 1493, Vol. 4, "Repatriation of Paupers" Correspondence from Town Clerk to Superintendent of Police, Colony, April 25, 1945.

79. NAI, Comcol 1, File no 1493, Vol. 4, "Repatriation of Paupers" Correspondence from Town Clerk to Superintendent of Police, Colony, November 1st, 1945.

80. Decker, "Social Welfare," 57.

81. Mabogunje, *Urbanization in Nigeria*, 261.
82. *Nigeria: Annual Report on the Department of Labour, 1945* (Lagos: Government Printer, 1946), 12.
83. NAI, Comcol 1, File 2807/S.I, "The Employment of Ex-Servicemen Ordinance No. 48 of 1945."
84. Mabogunje, *Urbanization in Nigeria*, 261.
85. Ibid.
86. Ibid., 262.
87. Ibid.
88. Flanagan and Gugler, *Urbanization and Social Change*, 45.
89. Ibid.
90. Albert Ayorinde Abegunde, "Environmental Management: Coastal Land Reclamation in Lagos," in *Urbanization Process and Problems in Nigeria*, eds. Pius Sada and Julius Oguntoyinbo (Ibadan: Ibadan University Press, 1978), 161.
91. Ibid.
92. Ibid., 162.
93. Ibid.
94. NAI, Comcol 1981, Vol. 1, "Anti-Mosquito Campaign, Lagos Enc. *Report on Anti-Mosquito Campaign*, Lagos by the Medical Officer of Health, Lagos and the Deputy Director of Public Works, December 1929, 2.
95. For description of the settlement pattern and spatial distribution of Lagos Island, see Abegunde, "Environmental Management."
96. Olukoju, "Population Pressure," 37.
97. Pius Sada, "Differential Population Distribution Growth in Metropolitan Lagos." *Journal of Business and Social Studies* 1, no.6 (1969): 117–32.
98. Ibid., 121.
99. *NP*, August 1919, "Overcrowding in Lagos and the Spread of Pulmonary Tuberculosis."
100. Abegunde, "Environmental Management," 165.
101. Peter Marris, *Family and Social Change in an African City: A Study of Rehousing in Lagos* (London: Routeledge and Kegan Paul, 1961), 82.
102. Ibid.
103. Personal Communication with Iyanda Afeez, 82 years, September 25, 2009.
104. Ibid.
105. A remark in the Editorial, *NP*, August 29, 1919.
106. *Lagos Weekly Record* (LWR), September 13, 1919, Editorial: "Overcrowding and Tuberculosis."
107. NAI, Nigeria: Annual Report on the Colony of Lagos, 7.
108. Ibid., 16.
109. NAI, Lagos Town Council, Annual Reports, 1921, 7.
110. Olukoju, "Population Pressure," 40.
111. Ibid.
112. Ibid.
113. *NP*, November 24, 1924, 1.
114. *NP*, December 28, 1928, 4.

115. Olukoju, "Population Pressure," 41.
116. *NP*, November 9, 1928, 3.
117. James Boyce, *The Political Economy of the Environment* (New York, NY: Edward Elgar Publishing, 2002), 7.
118. T.O. Okoye, "Historical Development of Nigerian Housing Policies with Special Reference to Housing the Urban Poor, in *Housing Africa's Urban Poor*, eds. P. Amis and P. Lloyd (Manchester: Manchester University Press, 1990), 73.
119. Daniel Immerwahr, "The Politics of Architecture and Urbanism in Post-Colonial Lagos, 1960–1986." *Journal of African Cultural Studies* 19, no.2 (2007): 7.
120. Mathew Gandy, "Planning, Anti-Planning and the Infrastructural Crisis Facing Metropolitan Lagos." *Urban Studies* 43, no.2 (2006): 375.
121. Akinlawon Mabogunje, "Urban Planning and Post-Colonial State in Africa: A Research Overview." *African Studies Review* 33, no.2 (1990): 137.
122. Olanrewaju Olutayo, *Development of Under-Development: The Rural Economy of Colonial South-Western Nigeria*, A Post-field Work Seminar Presented at the Department of Sociology, University of Ibadan, 1990.
123. Mabogunje, "Urban Planning," 137.
124. Onyeka Nwanuobi, "Incendiarism and Other Fires in Nineteenth Century Lagos." *Africa: Journal of the International African Institute* 60, no.1 (1990): 111.
125. Thomas Gale, "Lagos: The History of British Colonial Neglect of Traditional African Cities." *African Urban Studies* 5, (1979): 11–24.
126. Gandy, "Planning, Anti-Planning," 375.
127. Mabogunje, "Urban Planning," 137.
128. Akinlawon Mabogunje, "The Urban Situation in Nigeria," in *Patterns of Urbanization: Comparative Country Studies*, eds. Goldstein and Sly (Belgium: IUSSP, 1977), 569–641.
129. Frederick Lugard, *Instructions to Political Officers on Subjects Chiefly Political and Administrative, Memorandum No XI-Townships* (London: Waterflow and Sons, 1919), 19.
130. Immerwahr, "The Politics of Architecture," 1. See also: Zeynap Celik, *Urban Forms and Colonial Confrontations: Algiers under French Rule* (Berkley, CA: University of California Press, 1997). Anthony King, *Colonial Urban Development: Culture, Social Power, and Environment* (London: Routledge and Kegan Paul, 1976). A.K. Nevanlinna, *Interpreting Nairobi: The Cultural Study of Built Forms* (Helsinki: Suomen, 1996).
131. Abegunde, "Environmental Management," 163.
132. Ibid.
133. Ibid., 164.
134. Bisola Falola, "On Urban Relations," accessed December 11, 2012, http://www.rachetanurmemorialprize.org/i35-borderland.
135. Abegunde, "Environmental Management," 165.
136. Olakunle Lawal, "The Question of the Status of Lagos: 1953–1967," in *Urban Transition in Africa: Aspects of Urbanization and Change in Lagos*, ed. Olakunle Lawal (Lagos: Longman, 2004), 93.
137. Ibid.

138. Laurent Fourchard, "Lagos, Koolhaas and Partisan Politics in Nigeria." *International Journal of Urban and Regional Research* (2010): 6.
139. Ibid.
140. Ibid.
141. Lawal, "The Question of the Status of Lagos," 93.
142. Flanagan and Gugler, *Urbanization and Social Change*, 46.
143. Ibid.
144. Ibid.
145. A. James, "Rebuilding Nigeria's Capital." *WAR* no.30 (1959): 8–10.
146. Marris, *Family and Social Change*, 84.
147. Ibid.
148. Ibid.
149. Fourchard, "Lagos, Koolhaas," 7.
150. NAI, CSO 1/38322/S845, "Correspondence between the Association of Residents in Central Lagos and the Governor-General of the Federation on the Slum Clearance Scheme in Lagos."
151. Ibid., 2.
152. Ibid., 5.
153. Marris, "Family and Social Change," 86.
154. See, "AG against Slum Clearance Scheme," *Daily Service* (DS), October 4, 1955. Also see, "Playing Politics with Epidemics," *West African Pilot* (WAP), October 7, 1955.
155. Pauline Baker, *Urbanization and Political Change: The Politics of Lagos, 1917–1967* (Berkeley, CA: University of California Press, 1974), 156–57.
156. Immerwahr, "The Politics of Architecture," 8.
157. Marris, *Family and Social Change*, 129.
158. Personal Communication with Akanni Sikiru, 88 years, August 2011.
159. Ibid.
160. Personal Communication with Wuraola Agbalaya, 81 years, August 2011.
161. Personal Communication with Adekunle Faturoti, 83 years, September 2009.
162. For details, see Marris, *Family and Social Change*, 93.
163. Ibid.
164. Ibid., 94.
165. Personal Communication with Akanni Sikiru, 88 years.
166. Ibid.
167. Personal Communication with Fausat Thomas, 62 years, August 2011.
168. Paul Ugboajah, "Culture-Conflict and Delinquency: A Case Study of Lagos." *Eras Edition* 10, (2008): 3.
169. Fred Inglis, "Townscape and Popular Culture," in *Cities, Communities and the Young: Readings in Urban Education*, Vol. 1, eds. John Raynor and John Harden (London: Routledge and Kegan Paul, 1973), 4.
170. Ibid.
171. Damachi, *Nigerian Modernization*, 3.
172. Ibid.
173. Ibid.

174. Ibid., 9.
175. James Coleman, "Social Capital in the Creation of Human Capital." *American Journal of Sociology* (Supplement, 1988): 95–120.
176. Rasheed Ishola Akinyemi, "Social Capital and Development: A Paradigm Shift in Africa's Development," in *Global African Spirituality, Social Capital and Self-Reliance in Africa*, eds. Tunde Babawale and Akin Alao (Lagos: Malthouse Press, 2008), 130.
177. Ibid.
178. Coleman, "Social Capital in the Creation," 99.
179. James Farr, "Social Capital: A Conceptualized History." *Political Theory* 32, no.1 (2004): 9.
180. Falola and Heaton, *A History of Nigeria*, 6.
181. Joan Aldous, "Urbanization, the Extended Family, and Kinship Ties in West Africa." *Social Forces* 41, no.1 (1962): 8.
182. Ibid.
183. Ibid.
184. Flanagan and Gugler, *Urbanization and Social Change*, 131.
185. Sandra Barnes, *Becoming a Lagosian* (PhD diss., University of Winsconsin, 1974), 87.
186. Ibid.
187. Aldous, "Urbanization," 9.
188. Ibid.
189. Flanagan and Gugler, *Urbanization and Social Change*, 129.
190. Marris, *Family and Social Change*, 29.
191. Ibid., 31.
192. Personal Communication with Akinfenwa Esther, 81 years, August 17, 2011.
193. Ibid.
194. Personal Communication with Etareko Emmanuel, 86 years, December 26, 2010.
195. Peter Marris, "Slum Clearance and Family Life in Lagos." *Human Organization* 19, no.33 (Fall, 1960): 124.
196. Ibid.
197. Marx Weber, "Individualism, Home Life and Work Efficiency among a Group of Nigerian Workers." *Occupational Psychology* 41, (1967): 183–92.
198. Damachi, *Nigerian Modernization*, 101.
199. Dietrich Westernman, *The African Today and Tomorrow* (Oxford: Oxford University Press, 1949), 65.
200. Ibid.
201. Jacob Festus Ade Ajayi, *Christian Missions in Nigeria: The Making of New Elite* (London: Longman, 1965), cited in Kristin Mann, "Marriage Choices among the Educated African Elite in Lagos Colony, 1880–1915." *The International Journal of African Historical Studies* 14, no.2 (1981): 203.
202. See, "General Education Statistics," *Blue Book*, Southern Nigeria, 1912.
203. Mann, "Marriage Choices," 203.
204. Ibid.

205. Ibid., 204.
206. Genevieve Oldfield, "The Native Railway Worker in Nigeria." *Africa: Journal of the International African Institute* 9, no.3 (1936): 379.
207. Ibid.
208. Ibid.
209. Ibid.
210. Flanagan and Gugler, *Urbanization and Social Change*, 129.
211. Wayne Nafziger, "The Effect of the Nigerian Extended Family on Entrepreneurial Activity." *Economic Development and Cultural Change* 18, (1969): 25.
212. Dietrich Westernman, *Africa and Christianity* (Oxford: Oxford University Press, 1937), 102.
213. Ibid.
214. Personal Communication with Akanni Sikiru.
215. Mann, "Marriage Choices," 211.
216. Ibid.

Chapter 4

Women and Urban Experience, 1900–1960

There is no way that the social and economic history of Lagos would be written without reference to the activities of women as individuals or as a group. From the pre-colonial period, women played significant roles in the economic and social activities of the city. At the beginning of colonialism, their activities extended beyond the social and economic realms into political activism and partisan politics. This chapter examines the experiences of women in the wake of the modernization and urbanization policies of the British in colonial Lagos, especially from the eve of the World War II to independence in 1960.

WOMEN AND LIVELIHOOD STRATEGIES IN PRE-COLONIAL LAGOS

The concept of livelihood is dynamic, recognizing that the conditions and compositions of people's livelihoods change, sometimes rapidly, and also over time. Livelihood is complex, with households in the developing world undertaking a wide range of activities, as they are not just farmers, or laborers, or factory workers, or fisher folk but engage in self-sustaining activities formally and informally.[1] Thus, it is within this concept that the livelihood strategies of women in pre-colonial Lagos shall be examined, taking into cognizance: the environment, people's culture, contact with neighbors, and contact with Europeans as agents of change that transformed the traditional roles of women in the society.

In spite of the cultural interaction among peoples, it has been argued that every society has a culture that is unique, and such culture contains the norms and values of the people that are different from those of other peoples.[2] In addition, culture is reflected through language, song, works of art, and so on.

The culture of a people affects their actions and reactions to situations.[3] In pre-colonial Lagos, the Yoruba were the predominant peoples, with unique cultural perception. Motherhood is considered to be very important in Yoruba culture because the preservation of humanity depends on the role of mothers in the society.[4] In Yoruba culture, a mother occupies various positions—a mother, a wife, a daughter, a priestess, or even a witch.[5] The way she is perceived depends on the position she occupies, but the highest value is given to a woman as a mother because Yoruba people revere motherhood.[6] In fact, a popular proverb among the Yoruba presents motherhood as precious:

Iyaniwura, Baba nidingi

Mother is gold, Father is mirror.

Even in songs, mother is rated as precious gold:

Iyaniwuraiyebiye, Ti a ko le f'owora

Mother is precious gold that cannot be purchased with money.[7]

Yoruba women occupied a significant place in pre-colonial political organization, religion, family life, and the economy.[8] The nineteenth century accounts and oral records reveal that Nigerian women actively participated in the social, economic, and political development of their societies. Ample testimonies according to Laray Denzer exist concerning their role in local market organization and trade. They occupied a pivotal place in the local and state economy-organizing household industries, operating the local market system, and establishing long-distance trade networks.[9] The pre-colonial Lagos was not an exception. Women in Lagos responded to economic opportunities, part of which was provided by coastal, long-distance and domestic trade. Indeed, being an island, the early Lagosians took to fishing alongside their farming and hunting activities.[10] In fact, long before the beginning of slave trade, Lagos had offered a useful avenue for trade in articles of domestic consumption which Captain J.B. Adams noted toward the end of the eighteenth century at Ebute-Ero Market as being very much in abundant and "well within the reach of the common man."[11] Ebute-Ero Market was particularly popular with people from far and near who came to trade there. So also was the Obun Eko Market, probably established by the Ijebu-speaking people and where periodic market activities were undertaken by all and sundry,[12] the majority of these traders were identified to be women.[13]

A major strategy that Yoruba women used to distinguish themselves and further their own cause was to combine opportunities offered by their unique double status as daughters in their father's lineage and as wives in their husband's lineage.[14] Marriage became a tool for translating social power into economic and political power.[15] This was possible because marriage offered them "new frontiers for the exercise of power and influence in their communities."[16] Coupled with the right they had in their natal homes, these marital opportunities afforded some resourceful women the scope within which to advance themselves significantly.[17]

Before contacts with immigrants and neighbors, production and trade were organized within the families, and a gendered division of labor probably existed between husbands and wives.[18] For instance, in Yoruba land, the husband did the work of hoeing the field, making the heaps and sowing. The wife assisted in reaping and in such work as husking and preparing harvested reaped crops.[19] In addition, the wife was free to follow her own trade independently of the husband, and it was an obligation on the part of the husband to supply her with the means for doing this.[20] However, Mann argues that in pre-colonial Lagos, spouses and children must also have cooperated to meet family needs.[21] That is to say, all adults had a means of livelihood either as an individual or as a group.

Fishing dominated the economy of the island, but the local inhabitants also hunted and farmed a little, despite the fact that the sandy soil was not very good for agriculture.[22] In the case of fishing, its popularity as an economic activity should not be surprising. The people were mostly fishermen; modern metropolis of Lagos was said to have started as "a resting place for fishermen."[23] Most of the fish procured from their fishing expeditions on the Lagos lagoon and the surrounding lakes were mostly for domestic consumption. The remaining quantities were exported.[24] The commonest type of exported fish was the smoked or dried ones, the preparation of which was aided by the availability of salt.[25] A larger percentage of women engaged in the process of smoking fish for export to neighboring towns and villages, and exchange for other items which they needed but did not possess, such as clothing material, palm oil, cassava, and so on. Also in this line of livelihood strategy was salt making. Salt making, from both the lagoon and sea water, was a popular economic activity in Lagos before 1900.[26] It should, however, be pointed out that salt making like fishing was reputed to have been introduced into Lagos by the Ilaje and Ijo peoples who were (and still are) found predominantly in the fishing settlements to the east of Lagos.[27] As a result of this influence, an appreciable percentage of women found engagement in salt making as a way of supporting the livelihood of their household. This salt production and fish smoking stemmed not only from the influence of the Ijo and Ilaje women, but also from the Mahin, who were said to have migrated from their homeland from somewhere in Okitipupa area and extended to the areas close to the Island of Lagos, where such villages as Igbo-Egunrin, Itebu-kunmi, Itebu-Manuwa, Oloto, Igbolomi, Ilu-tuntun, and Mahintedo were established.[28]

Lagos, during the pre-colonial period was more popular for its trading activities—both local and foreign. The foreign trade was facilitated by the city's access to the lagoon, estuaries, and the Ijebu creeks. For instance, "they went in their canoes to Andrah, and Badagry and to the towns situated along the north east extremity of the cradoo lake where they purchased slaves, *jaboo* cloth" and other articles of domestic consumption."[29] Though there were scanty evidence to show that women participated in slave trade and long-distance trade, domestic trade, it had been established was dominated by women.

Indeed, domestic trade was also operated extensively. Daily markets were operated by Lagosians and articles of daily need were exchanged.[30] This shows that trading was the most important activity for women. While a vast majority of women operated at the level of petty trading, a few of them became big-time traders such that in the wake of European contacts, they tapped into the credit system provided by European firms located in the urban centers.[31] A veritable example of such women was Madam Efunroye Tinubu of Lagos, who emerged as one of the leading middlemen in trade between the Yoruba interior, Egbaland, and Lagos in the 1850s.[32] Palm oil merchants reportedly advanced her credit lines of over £5,000.Besides, enterprising female entrepreneurs in Lagos, Abeokuta and Ibadan continued to expand the long-distance trade in textiles (both indigenous and imported) kolanut, palm oil, and imported commodities.[33] Therefore, trading as a platform for women activism in colonial Lagos had been well entrenched in the pre-colonial period.

LIVELIHOOD STRATEGIES: MARKET WOMEN ACTIVITIES AND WOMEN MOVEMENT IN COLONIAL LAGOS

The idea of women's activism, particularly in the context of colonial Nigerian history, often conjures up images of markets and mass movements, of throngs of women vociferously occupying public spaces to assert their rights as gendered and empowered beings.[34] Women livelihood in colonial Nigeria was predominantly in the markets. Besides, markets, particularly in the southern part of the country, were historically understood to be spaces dominated and regulated by women, where they congregated to buy and sell goods, circulate information, and generally interact as a community.[35] This conception of markets partly explains why markets were also frequent sites of struggle with the British colonial state, particularly over issues of taxation, sanitation, street trading, price control and general social, economic, and political matters.

In 1908, the unity of opposition to the government was broken over the water rate issue. The government had decided, for sanitary reasons, to introduce pipe-borne water into Lagos and argued that Lagosians ought to pay a water rate for this amenity.[36] The water rate controversy was an example of grass roots politics. The press, women, traditional, and the elite had different reasons for opposing the scheme.[37] The press for instance, opposed the water rate not because it objected taxation, but on the American colonists' principle of "no taxation without representation."[38] The educated elite argued on the principle of political economy that anything which can be obtained free should not be paid for, and since water could be obtained free in Lagos, then water rate should not be paid for.[39] Others were esoteric in their arguments except for the women.[40] The women, for the first time, announced their determination to oppose all unfavorable colonial policies. On April 2, 1909, 3000 women met in the traditional quarters of Lagos to discuss the protest against the water rate. All markets were closed and serious reprisals were taken against anyone who did not obey the closure.[41] The meeting, which was held from 7:30 h to 13:45 h was to find a viable means of stopping the water rate.[42] Several women speakers suggested a boycott of sales to the European firms and to cooks until the government withdrew the water scheme.[43]

This protest by the women was basically to protect their means of livelihood. As observed, the new water rate would put all the women carriers of water (who were quite a feature in Lagos) out of business.[44] Also, the *Lagos Weekly Record* (LWR) noted that women traders would be particularly hard hit by the water rate, because the female street hawkers (carriers of water) represented the bottom rung of the trade ladder, and the earnings of these sellers hardly exceeded 18d to 2/- weekly.[45] The *LWR* in one of its editorials raised a poser: After providing for body and soul could these people, who form the majority, afford to pay a water rate?[46] In response to this protest, Governor Egerton defended the water rate by maintaining that the poorest classes would not pay it. Only houses within a short distance of the public pump would pay the water rate.[47] This protest was later taken over by the educated elite and the traditional elite until it was finally suppressed in September 1916.

The demography of Lagos from the 1930s up till independence revealed an upward increase in the number of migrant workers. These migrant workers comprised young people, both males and females, and street hawkers were among the most visible young workers.[48] In the late 1940s, anthropologist Suzanne Comhaire noted the existence of eight thousand market women "plus all their assistants and apprentices, both regular and occasional, four or five to one nominal market women."[49] In addition to this, the 1950 census did a breakdown of the population figure, by age and sex, and recorded 1,451 girls aged five to fourteen who worked as petty traders, hawkers, and shop assistants."[50] The children must not spend the money realized from their sales because it belonged to their parents, who used the money realized from child labor to cater for the children's education and welfare as well as parents' immediate needs.[51] The city of Lagos, during and after the Great Depressions of the 1930s, witnessed phenomenal growth in street trading, petty trading, and hawking.

However, this common means of livelihood for females, young and old, in Lagos, faced several objections from colonial authorities and to some extent, the educated elite. For instance, Medical Officer of Health (MOH), Lagos, in one of his memoranda to Secretary, Town Council, Lagos, noted the consequence of petty trading as follows:

> Owing to petty trading, scraps, wrapping leaves and other rubbish are scattered indiscriminately all over the streets of the town creating an excellent attraction to rodents. The "gari" which is to be seen all over the road at Ebute-Ero illustrates my point. The wide distribution of this rubbish resulting from petty trading makes the clearing of it by municipal employees impossible.[52]

Still on the problem of petty trading and street hawking, it was also observed that street traders often resorted to the use of the public drains haphazardly such that the danger of contamination of food either directly or by flies was inevitable, because a large proportion of fish and other food items sold in the town were exposed for sale on the edge of the public drains.[53] There was also the objection of the town engineer, as contained in his correspondence to Secretary, Town Council.

He described the situation thus:

> To my mind the main objection to this petty trading is one which only indirectly affects this office, namely, impediment to traffic, and whilst our transport is inconvenienced by the congestion in certain areas, it is the general public who really suffer from this. In this connection I would specially mention Faji and Araromi markets. In each area there are streets which are practically impassable owing to petty traders, their wares, and their stalls.[54]

Apart from the above social problems identified with street trading and hawking, government also discovered that, of the estimated 4000 people who congregated for trading purposes on the streets of Lagos, 1000 paid £1 per annum as temporary license, for the occupation of Crown Land (squatters), while the permit for trading on streets and areas around market attracted 2/6d per month.[55] The implication of this arrangement is that the remaining 3000 traders that did not pay to the council contributed a great deal to the income leakages experienced by the government. Further, the Town Council also discovered that the petty traders were increasing day by day in the town because the available spaces used in front of houses have been a source of additional income for house owners. In fact, an appreciable number of house owners and touts turned middlemen engaged in this habit for livelihood. Reports from a survey carried out by the Town Council on some major streets in Lagos lend credence to this assertion:

> At 50/52 Palm Church Street, the owner (Joseph Adeodu) collects 30/- per year from one woman (AinaIyalode) who sits in front of the drain and who pays 2/6d a month to the council. If the amount is not paid to the owner he will complain of the woman being in front of his premises. Formerly there was more than one woman paying to him. This information was obtained from a relative of the petty trader. At Ebute-Ero where no payment whatsoever is made to the council, the petty traders are compelled to pay 3d a day to a person called the financial secretary to be permitted to squat on the foreshore. No petty trader who had not paid will be tolerated by the other traders in that locality. This is one of the most overcrowded areas in Lagos on market days which occur every fourth day. In Broad and Victoria Streets the women traders who sit on the pavement outside shops or houses pay a fee of from 2/6d to 5/- a month to the owner or occupier of the premises.[56]

As a follow-up to these discoveries, the administrator of the colony, Lawrence C.T, in his letter to the chief secretary to the government expressed his reservations over the 4000 estimated figure of the petty traders in Lagos. Instead, he posited that there was no street in Lagos or Ebute-Meta where hawking or selling outside houses did not take place. He also observed that small stalls were erected close to the roads inside the fence in Ikoyi as well as the old Colonial Hospital. He, therefore, proposed for either prohibition or prevention of street trading within a certain distance of a recognized market.[57] This proposal was not taken seriously until 1936 when the situation had become embarrassing even to the colonial authorities. The commissioner of police for the colony was asked to enforce bye law No.4 of 1933 prohibiting street trading within the 200 yards perimeter around the following markets: Idumagbo Market, Moloney Bridge Street Market, Anikantanmo Square Market, Lewis Street Market, Ebute-Ero Market, Iddo Market, Oyingbo Market, Ebute Meta *Obada* Market, Yaba Market, and Apapa.[58] However, these questions are pertinent: why did it take so long for the colonial authorities to prohibit street trading in spite of its negative impact on the city? What was the response of the market women to the colonial policies against petty and street trading? Were there market organizations or associations coordinating the activities of market women during the period?

It took the colonial authorities some years to react to trading on the street because of the adoption of Manchester doctrine of minimal financial commitment on colonies. Thus, rather than address the issue of street trading, the government was busy making money from traders in form of charges for stalls and premises in order to generate money for building of infrastructure and general colonial administration. In spite of the earlier warnings by Olajumoke Obasa—leader of the Lagos Women's League—of the moral danger associated with street trading by underageboys and girls,[59] the colonial government did not see it as a problem until 1941 when the colonial welfare office was opened.

Lagos Women's League was the most influential long-standing elite women's organization in the twentieth century Lagos. It was founded in 1901 as the Lagos League under the leadership of young Mrs. Charlotte Olajumoke Obasa, daughter of Emily Blaize and R. B. Blaize, a successful and politically influential merchant in Lagos.[60] It was the formation of the league which provided Mrs. Obasa with the opportunity of putting fully into practice, her talents and enthusiasm for social welfare work.[61] Mrs. Obasa's interests in social welfare work were many and varied, but the most important to this study was her interest in women. She did a great deal in promoting their welfare and championing their standard of living. She not only visited the markets regularly, instructing the women on how to take care of their babies and on general hygiene and sanitation, but also sought ways of improving their livelihood in order for them not to depend entirely on their men folk.[62] For instance, she made *ogi*, pap made out of corn, popular morning meal in Lagos as well as means of livelihood for some women. Prior to this period, the way *ogi* was being prepared for sale was not hygienic and this made it unattractive to the educated members of the society.[63] Mrs. Obasa got some of the women together, taught them how to prepare *ogi* hygienically and how to measure it for sale. These women passed on the knowledge to others. With the hygienic way of preparing it, *ogi* became a popular morning meal, not only for illiterates, but also for literates and well-to-do members of the society and very many women were able to make their living from it.[64]

Opportunities for women in waged or salaried employments were limited to the educated ones. As more girls completed standard 6 or higher schooling, their rate of employment increased.[65] At first, they tended to take up occupations that simply transformed their normal domestic activities into cash-earning opportunities, including washing clothes, cooking, sewing, and looking after children as well as teaching and nursing.[66] The seamstresses discovered that this work paid much better than other jobs (including teaching), combined easily with the responsibilities of family life and required little initial investment. Immediately after World War II, opportunities expanded as Western fashions became increasingly popular and elite women demanded elaborate styles in traditional attire.[67] In fact, fashion training institute such as Singer fashion institute sprang up in central Lagos, and many female residents enrolled as apprentice to learn the act of sewing.[68]

Apart from trading, artisanship, teaching, and nursing, one area where women's activities were particularly important in Southwestern Nigeria was anti-colonial movements. Women possessed a long and rich history of collective organization through which they articulated and protected their interests from pre-colonial times onward.[69] Colonialism altered women's position in their societies.[70] It particularly affected their economic roles and limited their political participation. Southwestern Nigerian women quickly perceived the nature of the threat to their interests and re-grouped their forces in order to preserve their interests.[71]

In the city of Lagos, the first mass-based women's interest group to recognize the power of collective action in protecting and promoting women's rights during the colonial era was the Lagos Market Women's Association (LMWA).[72] The exact date of its foundation is not known, but by the mid-1920s it was an active movement. Madam Alimotu Pelewura was the dynamic leader behind the foundation of the LMWA.[73] Madam Pelewura was an acclaimed market woman of substance in Lagos Colony. She was one of the women born in Lagos who were deeply concerned about the rights of individuals to be fairly treated by state. She was a thorn in the flesh of the colonial authorities, as she fought relentlessly for the improvement of the lot of members of her association and agitated for the rights of women and for independence.[74]

One of the memorable events during Madam Pelewura's time was the famous "*olologbo* case," which took place in 1942.[75] It was a court case in which colonial authorities accused her of violating the price control law. However, Madam Pelewura who felt wrongly accused swore that God would make the judgment of that Magistrate to be the last to take place in that court, as the allegation was deliberately hatched to humiliate her. Ironically, that was the last case the judge heard in that court.[76] Besides, Madam Pelewura resisted government's attempt to move Ereko Market to a new location,[77] and also became actively involved with a much more militant group, then Nigerian National Democratic Party (NNDP).[78]

Alimotu Pelewura was not alone in her struggles for the betterment of women in Colonial Lagos. Among members of Madam Pelewura's market women association were Madam Comfort Ige, Madam Egberongbe, and Madam Bilikisu, Madam Rabi Alaso Oke, and Madam Memunatu, among others.[79] Madam Pelewura's struggles in Lagos represented an expansion of the traditional type of women's organization, and an important step in Nigerian women's attempt to preserve their prerogatives under the changing conditions of the colonial system.[80] In addition, the educated elite also found it necessary to build upon the traditional structures as well as utilize both the traditional and Western protest tactics. Thus, the founding of the Nigerian

Women's Party was their attempt at organizing women along the lines of Western styles association.[81]

Lady Oyinkan Abayomi, while addressing the educated women in Lagos, warned them of their pomposity and inaccessibility by their uneducated counterparts. She opined that unless the so-called highly educated make themselves open and approachable they would have no one to lead.[82] According to a newspaper report, her concern was for the protection of women from the excesses of men. The exploitation of colonial government made her to gather on May 10, 1944, a dozen prominent women in her home at 18, Broad Street, Lagos to discuss the women's political situation.[83] This culminated in the formation of the Nigerian Women's Party (NWP). The NWP stated its aims and objectives as follows:

> The women's party makes its strongest appeal to the women of Nigeria irrespective of class or any other distinction, reminding them of their backward and unenviable position among the women of other rules and calling them to action. It appeals to those who may be outside the ranks of the Women's Party for sympathy and cooperation:

1. To shape the whole future is not our problem, but only to shape faithfully a small part of it according to the rules laid down.
2. To seek by constitutional means the rights of British citizenship in its full measure on the people.
3. To work assiduously for the educational, agricultural, and industrial development of Nigeria with a view to improve the moral, intellectual and economic condition of the country.
4. To work for the amelioration of the condition of the women of Nigeria not merely by sympathy for their aspirations but by recognition of their equal status with men.[84]

In spite of its well-outlined aims and objectives, the NWP seemed not to have enjoyed total support from prominent men and market women in Lagos. For instance, Herbert Macaulay did not give the kind of support he gave to the LMWA to NWP because he felt that the women body threatened his special relationship with market women.[85] The leadership of NWP led by Oyinkan Abayomi, remained undeterred and continued in pursuance of their objectives as spelled out in their constitution. The first remarkable achievement was the appointment of Oyinkan Abayomi as the first female to serve on the Lagos Town Council.[86] Further, NWP advocated the improvement in female education by proposing the establishment of more girls' schools apart from Queens College, as well as broadening the curriculum. Also, NWP demanded scholarships for Muslim girls, more vocational schools, and adult education for illiterate women.[87]

The NWP also fought a long battle in reducing discrimination against women in the civil service employment, especially in the area of discrepancies in salaries and rankings. One of the most important efforts of the NWP was its opposition to the Children and Young Person's Ordinance of 1946, which prohibited children under fourteen from engaging in street trading, required parental permission for girls between fourteen and sixteen to trade, and limited to the hours of daylight the time in which young girls allowed to trade.[88]

The agitation that led to the enactment of the Ordinance was championed by Charlotte Olajumoke Obasa of the defunct Lagos Women's League and was reported in the newspaper of the period. As it would be recalled, Olajumoke Obasa—a voluntary social worker—founded the Lagos Women's League in the 1920s. The league's interests were social reform, social welfare, and moral problems in Lagos.[89] The league came up with "Girl Hawkers Project" in 1926 in order to protect the unnecessary exposure of under aged children to moral danger in Lagos as a result of hawking and street trading. Lagos Women League (LWL) therefore, requested for prohibition of children of both sexes from hawking about the streets until boys have attained the age of twelve and girls sixteen owing to the danger of stealing and the immoral practices to which they are daily exposed to. Also, between 1926 and 1946, several reports were made in the newspapers of girls that were violated, injured, or killed while hawking. One of such reports was the case of an eleven-year-old girl named Olawunmi Olusanya whose dead body was found in the "Dig for Victory Garden" in Lagos barely twelve hours after she was sent out to hawk *foo-foo* in her neighborhood at *Oke popo* area of Lagos.[90]

This inherent danger associated with street trading was the concern of the LWL under the coordination of the elite women in Lagos. The league's position, however, offended the livelihood sensibilities of the market men and women as well as African traditions. According to custom, young girls began their training in trading at an early age, well before the age of fourteen, thus extending the range of the economic activities of their mothers, grandmothers, aunts, and guardians, many of whom were farmers or had businesses elsewhere.[91] Moreover, young hawkers played a major role in supporting the income of their parents, especially those at the lower rung of the society. This practice of child labor stems from Yoruba terminology, *omoenil'omoenii* (my child is my child) this seems to imply that I can treat my child the way I like, "he/she is mine." The children too held the belief that "my mother is my mother, I cannot change her."[92] Therefore, street hawking by the under aged children continued unrestricted in colonial Lagos till the 1940s in spite of the warnings, happenings, and dangers associated with it. Therefore, the Children and Young Person's Ordinance was a contradiction because the custom formed part of the education for the young girls for whom the government failed to provide schools.

The position of the NWP, unlike that of the LWL, was to support the market men and women to fight against the obnoxious ordinance that threatened their livelihood during the period. Thus, NWP, market women movements, and others fought the government to submission on the newly enacted ordinance. After many joint protest meetings and deputations to the authorities, the commissioner admitted that the law needed remedy and agreed to suspend arrests of offenders.[93] Also, the NWP collaborated with other groups, mostly LMWA in the campaign against the "Pullen Price Control Scheme" and other restrictions imposed by the administration during and after the World War II. An expansion of the activities of the NWP and the LMWA during and after the war forms part of the discourse in the next section of this chapter.

WORLD WAR II AND THE FOOD SUPPLY PROBLEM

The outbreak of the World War II had devastating effects on livelihood in colonial Lagos. This was because the city experienced acute shortage of food supply emanating from the dislocation of the world economy, especially the economies of the European belligerents and their colonies.[94] The consequence of this was that the city witnessed increased immigrants of the World War II in addition to those from the province and the hinterlands in search of paid job in the public works and constructions that were ongoing in Lagos. Thus, the labor that was hitherto meant to produce food stuff in the rural areas was in the cities hawking, loafing, conscripted into the colonial army as well as engaging in all forms of informal activities to earn livelihood. The multiplier effect of this was that the demand for food was higher than the supply. Besides, there was significant rise in the prices of imports, especially essential commodities. The price of a bag of cement increased from £2: 11s to £9 6s in the second week of September, 1939.[95] The price of bicycles, sewing machines, and bed-steads increased by £1 on existing levels, those of the 26-gauge corrugated iron sheets moved from £2:11:2 to £4 2s, while prices of the 35 gauge sheets rose from £1155 to £2.[96] Essential commodities, such as salt, sugar, and milk were also in severe short supply from 1942 onwards and this necessitated strict rationing of the available supplies.[97] The import-substitution strategy in which the government attempted to replace imports by domestically produced substitutes, rather than ameliorate the condition, further worsened the situations. In fact, salt scarcity in war-time Lagos was acute to the point that the police once sighted a woman begging for it from house to house along Bucknor Street after she had failed to get any from the market.[98] Although salt was not the only scarce item in Nigeria during the

World War II, it generated the greatest upheavals and dominated most of the comments in both written and oral sources.[99] A report in *West African Pilot* (WAP) described the situation of salt scarcity in Onitsha as follows:

> Nine women received wounds buying salt . . . Onitsha, August 28, (1941). Yesterday morning, thousands of women rushed to the UAC to purchase salt. Reaching there, a struggle began and the following were trampled and wounded . . . After application of brandy Mr. Bushel the Manager, also helped regarding conveyance to hospital where admission took place. Ex-Dispenser Asolo gave first aid and the women are improving. Among the victims was a pregnant woman. The police helped greatly to maintain further peace.[100]

The above, was just one of the numerous unpleasant cases recorded across the country. The colonial government was equally concerned with the scarcity of salt, perhaps more than that of any other product, because of its utmost importance to the people's diets: they could not do without it. Besides, it did not take time before the government of the period took cognizance of the inflationary trend, which translated to high cost of living. In diagnosing the foodstuff problems, the regime ignored the fact that the primary cause was shortage of supply; rather, it assumed that the root cause was a simple desire on the part of the market women to profiteer.[101] Thus, the government faced the task of pegging foodstuff prices in Lagos and its environs by establishing, at the beginning of 1941, the office of the Controller of Native Foodstuffs, which was responsible for fixing maximum selling rates for local foodstuffs.[102]

The food price control scheme itself began in 1941 under the direction of Captain A. P. Pullen, whose name was promptly attached to the operation which soon became the focus of the press and public attack.[103] The initial device was the publication of orders stipulating maximum selling prices for foodstuffs in Lagos. These prices were calculated by obtaining the price of an article at the point of production to which were added all charges up to the railway terminus at Iddo Station.[104] The wholesale price was then determined by adding 10 percent to the landed cost at Iddo, while the retail price was obtained by adding a margin of 20 percent to the landed cost.[105]

The profit margin for perishable items, like vegetables, was fixed at 25 percent to cover losses. The attempt at fixing the prices of commodity by the colonial authorities failed, because the producers, dealers, and traders in the distribution channels argued that those who fixed foodstuff prices were not competent to do so, because the price control officials did not know what it cost to produce a given quantity of a staple and what it cost for it to arrive at the market. Although a report had been carried out earlier in Lagos on the reasons for the variation in the prices of commodities in the Lagos markets, this was not referred to by the colonial authorities before adopting the price control scheme. Indeed, the reports as enumerated by Dare Olusanya—a market survey officer, captured part of what was responsible for the failure of the price fixing approach of the colonial authorities. Part of the report is presented below.

> In Lagos and Districts, Abeokuta and Districts, Ibadan, Ijebu Ode and Districts and Ondo and Districts, there are three principal classes of markets: markets in which people sell every day, five days markets, and nine days, and they all come on in rotation form. There are three classes of dealers working in each of these markets; those who deal in wholesale prices i.e those who go far into the hearts of villages to possess foodstuffs; 1st class retailers, those who wake early in the morning, go fairly far and wait on the roads with the idea to buy foodstuffs from the dealers at reasonable profit on the cost price; and 2nd class retailers, those who wait idly in the markets with the mind to seize the stuffs as soon as their customers come into the markets. This class may be termed rulers of the markets because they sometimes unite together and put forth a strike and thereby compel 1st class retailers to sell at their fixed prices and with their own measures (bowls). This class sells to the 3rd class retailers, who then sell to the majority of the population with miserably flattened bowls and even if sold per heap they will be very small in quantity. It is this class that go about advertising and selling in the nooks and corners of the town in order that they may sell to the unable, lazy, unwary, and unreasonable individuals at reasonable percentage on their cost price that will give them sufficient profits. Majority of this class are so poor that they cannot get a spared 30d monthly to pay to the Lagos Town Council in other that they may sell under the provided shelters in the markets.[106]

Failure to take into cognizance the workings of the distribution channels, as stated in the above report, partly explains why the control prices were never realistic. Further, the prospective buyers apparently felt that officialdom was unrealistic in its price legislation when it was clear that price rise was a function of inadequate supply.[107] The issues involved were not always fully taken into account before setting of prices. Some arbitrariness featured here and there, rendering the target price meaningless.[108] The result was the promotion of black market activities whereby traders ignored official rates and sold at prices convenient for them. A professional butcher who wrote against meat control in the *Daily Service* (DS) of January 30, 1943 claimed that the price of a live cow at the Iddo cattle market had gone up by 100% within two years, making it impossible for him and his colleagues to obey the official ruling on price, in spite of the risk of imprisonment.[109] According to him, a cow which previously £6 in 1941 stood at £12 in January 1943 while that of £7 rose to £14 and that of £8 stood at £15. He concluded that there was no way in which beef could be sold below 9d per pound of weight. It seems clear therefore, that it was more rational for the trader to go idle than to get ruined by selling at an impossible price. He did not, in reality, go idle. He just ignored regulation and sold at a price which guaranteed his own profits.[110] And as long as ready buyers were available, the market performed smoothly, although illegally.[111]

Also, in Lagos, one foodstuff, the shortage of which generated a severe crisis, was *gari*, the staple of an overwhelming majority of Lagosians.[112] The scarcity was so severe that the colonial government had to intervene in its production in Ijebuland.[113] Not only were prices of *gari* fixed at Ijebu Ode and Shagamu, Captain Pullen also established central stores and selling booths in the metropolis. In fact, it was envisaged that there would be about 240 selling booths, allowing a maximum of about 60 booths per store.[114] In spite of these strategies by Captain Pullen and his team, the black market continued to thrive. The reasons for the expansion of the black markets premised on the poor quality of foodstuffs sold at the official markets. They were too crowded that people got injured in the process of queuing to buy foodstuff as well as the alleged harassment of the citizenry by the police at the designated centers. Thus, rather than alleviate the problems for which it was designed, the price control scheme compounded the scarcity by creating tension and panic in the city.

During this period, Madam Alimotu Pelewura was the strong market women leader at the center of the struggle against this retrogressive regulation on the prices of foodstuffs in Lagos. She led market women under the aegis of LMWA to militant protest and formidable resistance to the price control regulations. She engaged not only in mass protests, but also the use of constant petitions, official complaints, and use of legal means, where necessary, to fight the colonial authorities to submission on the price control scheme. For instance, by early 1944, the colonial authorities had realized the ineffectiveness of the price control scheme, decided to engage the market women in a series of meetings in order to reach a compromise, but these attempt failed on about four occasions.[115] Further, Captain Pullen—the Deputy Controller of Native Foodstuffs—sought to influence the market women by arranging for a meeting at the palace of the king where all the chiefs were present.[116] This also proved abortive because at IgaIduganran, in the presence of Oba Falolu and his chiefs, about three thousand market women led by Alimotu Pelewura unanimously refused to agree to Captain Pullen's proposal. In fact, Chief Oluwa, who was the spokesman on that occasion, informed the deputy controller that Madam Alimotu Pelewura was the head of all the Lagos market women and that her decision was binding on all of them. Chief Oniru, Chief Onikoyi, and Chief Onisemo concurred. The deputy controller, however, refused to agree.[117]

Subsequently, Madam Pelewura was accompanied by Madam Barikisu, the Iyalode of Faji Market, to the office of the commissioner of the colony where she implored him to persuade Captain Pullen to leave the trade of the Lagos market women for them or else she would close all the markets in the city.[118] The following day, in the presence of the COMCOL, Pelewura compared the life during World War II with what she remembered of World War I when "no Whiteman sold *gari* in Lagos." In desperation, the harassed official decided to entice her to submission. He proposed to pay Pelewura a monthly allowance of £7 10s and appointment as head of the *gari* sellers of Lagos if she would support his policy.[119] In a scathing rejection of these terms, Pelewura told him that not even if he offered her £100 a month would she help him to "break and starve the country where she was born."[120] Pullen's failure to secure the market's women support made him to succumb to their request to stop interfering with their sources of supply, promising to obtain government supplies directly from the farmers.

Following Captain Pullen's failure to get the cooperation of the market women, government decided to enlighten the general public through the newspaper on the scheme. In June 1945, after nineteen months of unsuccessful operation of the scheme, the controller of local foodstuffs decided to use extensive propaganda through a Lagos newspaper where a daily column could be maintained to educate the people on what the scheme stood for.[121] By June 21, 1945, the first publication of the column known as "Food Facts for Lagos," appeared in *Daily Times*. Forty-three subsequent issues of the food facts column were published, the last of which came out on September 15, 1945.[122] Generally, the column published news items concerning the scheme, informed people on the kinds of foodstuffs that were available at the control markets and, from time to time, indicated changes in the prices of foodstuffs whenever they occurred.[123] In spite of the propaganda, the price control scheme was not successful. Thus, after three months of publishing the facts, it was discontinued.

Apart from the unsuccessful operation of the scheme, it also constituted a huge financial loss to the colonial authorities. For instance, the audited account for the quarter ending 30 September 1945 indicated that, since inception, the scheme had expended 5,778 pounds on the erection of stalls, stores, and offices and 11,990 pounds on the payment of salaries to administrative staff. It had also recorded a cumulative net loss of 4,685 pounds, 8 shillings and 10 pence.[124] Between 1 June and 30 September, 1945, a total of 23,273 pounds 17 shillings and 3 pence was paid out to buying firms as subsidies. Out of the subsidies, palm oil attracted 12,161 pounds, followed by *gari* 4,952 pounds, rice came third with 3,801 pounds and the foodstuff that got the least was millet flour with a subsidy of 56 pounds.[125]

These heavily subsidized foodstuff scheme recorded huge loss due to poor operations and mismanagement. Madam Pelewura's observation on *gari* vividly captured the wastefulness of the scheme as follows:

> Policemen are sent to Ejinrin, 41 miles east of Lagos Town along the Lagos Lagoon, to Ikosi, to Epe, and other villages and towns where every ounce of Gari is commandeered and stopped from being brought for sales to the Lagos Market Women. And any stock of Gari that reaches Lagos and landed at Epetedo Wharf, the police will board the canoes and carry all the Gari on board to the depot of the Deputy Controller of Native Foodstuffs by night and by day where a large stock is piled up until the Gari become rotten and bags upon bags are dumped into the Lagos Lagoon, containing Gari.[126]

As earlier mentioned, Pelewura's observation confirmed the wastefulness of the scheme to the colonial authorities. In fact, it was estimated that, by the time the control market wound up in 1946, the Lagos Foodstuff Scheme had lost 22,313 pounds.[127] Not to be forgotten is the fact that the rising cost of local and imported foodstuffs was compounded by increase in house rents. In the newspaper there were reports that, as a result of the general increase in the prices of foodstuffs and building materials, landlords have responded by increasing the rents of their tenants.[128] Several petitions were also written by the tenants to the commissioner of the colony. In one such letters, signed by seven tenants of the same household, it was alleged that the landlord increased their monthly rentals from 8/6d to 10/6d without light and water. They also attached a quit notice in case they could not pay the new rentals.[129] Failure on the part of government to quickly respond to the envisaged rent profiteering degenerated in Lagos to an extent that an investigation revealed that landlords and their middlemen demanded as much as 25 shillings for rentage per month for rooms which, before the war, were let out for as little as five shillings.[130] Lagosians took advantage of this high demand for accommodation and the inflationary trend of the period, such that an appreciable number of indigenes sublet their family houses at exorbitant rent, only to secure bigger accommodation outside.[131] Government responded by setting up a committee in 1944 to come up with measures for controlling rents in Lagos. The rent control scheme committee proposed that control of rents would be based on room rather than dwelling house. The committee took cognizance of geographical position, type of structure, and dimensions of room in its recommendation.[132] For the purpose of rent control, the township of Lagos was divided into the following areas:

a. Lagos Island,
b. Yaba Estate, Ebute Metta East, Ebute Metta West,
c. All the rest of the township.[133]

The rent statistics in possession of the LTC revealed that, in 1941, the year used as a basis for assessment in sec.6 of regulation No.59 of 1942 as amended by regulation 101 of 1942, the average rates paid in these three areas were approximately in the following proportions, see table 4.1 below:

Table 4.1 Report of the Lagos Rent Board

Location	Rents per Room
Lagos Island	10s
Yaba Estate	8s
Ebute Metta East	8s
Ebute Metta West	8s
Rest of the Township	6s

The variation in the above rents was attributed to the comparative lack of amenities, such as shops, cinemas, social clubs, and so on in the areas remote from the center of Lagos, while transport expenses to the place of work represented an important item in the budget of the average man. Besides, the standard types of structures were classified into four: brick (cement rendered), mud (cement rendered), mud (unrendered) and bamboo/ galvanized/iron or mat.[134] In view of these survey and classifications, the committee proposed the following rates of rent, see table 4.2 below:

Table 4.2 Rents Proposed by Government Committee in 1944

Dimensions	Lagos Island	Yaba, Ebute Metta East and West	Rest of the Township
Rooms of brick (cement rendered)	1s 3d	1s	9d
Rooms of brick (unrendered) or mud(cement rendered)	1s	10d	7.5d
Rooms of mud (unrendered)	9d	7.5d	6d
Rooms of bamboo, galvanized iron or mat walls	6d	6d	5d

In spite of the above proposal, rent profiteering persisted, and there was nothing the government could do to checkmate the profiteering landlords. Rather than cooperate, the latter claimed that they were indeed "suffering to a greater extent than the tenants" by the operation of rent control measures.[135] Subsequently, more demands were made by the landlord associations to which the colonial authorities could not proffer any solution. Thus, the landlords continued in their exploitation of the tenants, and this further increased the high cost of living in Lagos.

Household Challenges and Adaptation in Colonial Lagos

The adaptation and survival strategies of Lagos residents to the high standard of living of the war years are explicable in terms of the responses of the households to the challenges of the period. A description of the classes of people in Lagos would help to understand the different households, their responses and their standards of living. Lagos, as earlier mentioned, was heterogeneous. The Europeans, Syrians, Lebanese, and few Lagosians occupied the upper class. They were mostly found in government employment, textile trade, import and exports trade to mention but few. The rest of the population represented the middle and the lower rung of the society. The small elite were very wealthy, maintaining large trading networks but, for the most part, market women traded with a narrow profit margin, barely making out a living.[136] Also a larger percentage of the immigrants were employed in the informal sectors, while some were unemployed.

The inflationary trend of the war years imposed hardships on the household to the extent that food rationing became a prevalent practice in many household.[137] The same approach was adopted in the education of children in many homes.[138] Buchi Emecheta's novel *"The Joys of Motherhood"* provides a more vivid picture of livelihood in colonial Lagos, especially in the 1940s.[139] The story traces the heroine's struggle to maintain her family in crowded conditions in the face of constant rising prices. Between her husband wage as a laborer and her own irregular income from trading, they barely make ends meet. When he is conscripted into the allied army, she finds it impossible to pay the escalating cost of housing and food.[140] Although a fiction one would call it, available evidence and findings from fieldwork corroborated it. In the market, because the women controlled the distributive trade, especially retail trade, many of them began to engage in unscrupulous means of making profits, particularly in the marketing of food items. For instance, a report on standardization of native retail measures in Lagos described the situation thus:

> As to measures, the diversity of the size, shape, and condition of the bowls used in Lagos Markets is bewildering. In the Ereko market out of thirty-five bowls tested, no two were of the same dimensions. Even allowing a tolerance of 1/8 in both diameter and depth there still remained twenty-three different sizes of bowl, many of them quite distinct from recognized trade sizes. In the Faji market, I found twenty-two different bowl sizes, which even with the 1/8 tolerance still meant 17 diverse sizes. These numbers refer to bowls with some pretensions to being "cash bowls": they do not include the almost endless variety of calabash bowls, crinkled pans, wicker baskets, cigarette tins, sometimes cut down or pressed to a smaller cross-section, cigarette-tin lids, ash-tray, butter tin lids and tins like closed opera hats, which are to be found in these markets.[141]

In addition to these, there was heaping the bowls in the course of measuring food items for customers. The method of heaping the bowls would ordinarily be conical for *gari*, maize, beans, rice and yam flour, the height of the cone being dependent not only on the moistness of the commodity, but most importantly the patience and goodwill of the seller. These were subjected to manipulations by smart sellers to the disadvantage of careless and unsuspecting buyers.[142] Further, women selling imported items such as tin milk, cigarette, and textiles engaged in buying smuggled commodities from ship workers at lower prices in order to maximize profit.[143] Since the business was an illegal one, organized in such a way that the prospective buyers would pay in advance for the commodities before the arrival of the ship, many of them were swindled by dishonest seamen. As a result of the risk of losing financial capital, few people actually explored this means of survival. Also, child hawking, petty trading, and neighborhood trading were prevalent such that hardly could one differentiate between a market and front of houses in Lagos, especially streets in central Lagos.[144]

However, the demands of the family, the pressure to fulfill social obligations, and the desire to be healthy as well as survive fueled borrowings during the period. There were two platforms for borrowings: the organized credit institutions popularly referred to as banks or financial institutions and the informal credit outlets such as esusu collectors' platform or the money lender platform. But because of the collateral involved, many of the people at the lower rung of the society found succor in money lender's platform. This involved the patronage of the traders and the civil servants. Wage earners, for instance, were drawn to lending money for variety of reasons. Moneylenders preferred them both as sureties and lenders because they enjoyed regular salaries, had permanent jobs and addresses, could not risk public embarrassment, and enjoyed the image of responsible people.[145] In addition, civil servants, themselves, when in need of money, used their salaries as collateral. Those who needed money to engage in trade, speculate on business, build a house or meet social expenses took loans from moneylenders.[146] Although the rate of interest was very high, they enjoyed high patronage in Lagos, especially during the war period.

The case was narrated by a long-time resident of Lagos of a woman who resorted to borrowing from a moneylender in order to purchase a singer sewing machine without the knowledge of her husband. The woman, in her bid to support the income of her husband, who then, was a junior clerk with government, opted for training as a seamstress with Singer Training Institute. On completion of her training, she did not have money to purchase the required sewing machine; so the moneylender came to her rescue.[147] Apart from those who borrowed to support their trading activities, small numbers of cases were reported of male civil servants being forced to liquidate loans incurred by their wives. For instance, in Lagos in the 1920s a district clerk was forced to pay the debt of his wife. When the man was slow in paying, the wife was bold enough to petition the administrator of the colony.[148] The petition reads thus:

> Owing to financial stringency caused by lack of support from my husband I was compelled to borrow money from moneylenders in Lagos of an account of £10 net getting my husband to pay this amount with whatever interest shall accrue thereon. The resident ... was then kind enough to forward my complaint ... for investigation which resulted in a promise from Mr. Hamilton that he will pay. The promise I regret to observe has not been wholly [sic] fulfilled as only £4 was paid with further promise to pay the balance at the end of that month which up to date he has not done. As interest is still accruing on the principal and repeated letter from me to him have brought [sic] no reply, I should be greatly obliged if you would be good enough to assist me further in this matter which is causing great unrest in my mind.[149]

The above petition represents one of the examples of household response to challenges of the period by borrowing for survival from different outlets as dictated by circumstances of the period. However, it is important to stress that both the employed and the unemployed devised strategies of survival in war time in Lagos. Government workers were particularly mobilized for war emergency production while artisans in key industries like the railway had to work for about seventy-seven hours a week.[150] In short, overworking was so rampant and prolonged that the resulting exhaustion could not have failed to make people tense and irritable.[151] In addition to the unease of the period was the attempt by government to levy taxes on women. This was envisaged by the women as additional burden that would further deepen their suffering. Therefore, they responded immediately.

The LMWA organized a mass protest immediately to challenge the income tax law. On December 16, 1940, over a hundred women assembled outside the office of the colonial commissioner in Lagos. When the commissioner appeared, Rabiatu Alaso Oke, the Iyalode of Lagos, stepped forward to protest that several women had received "return of income" forms, reminding him of the government's earlier promise not to tax women.[152] The commissioner's unsatisfactory response that only well-to-do women were being taxed infuriated the women, and the following day the women, led by Alimotu Pelewura, closed the markets and marched to protest the tax law to Governor Bourdillion.[153] Initially, the governor was adamant, but after continuous protest, government decided it must revise the law, but it refused to abolish it completely. For their male counterparts, however, demand for wage increment was the strategy of survival as far as the high cost of living was concerned. Government responded with COLA, but this was to the dissatisfaction of the workers because of the alleged racial discrimination in salaries and emoluments of their foreign counterparts. The workers, at their mass rally held at Glover Memorial Hall on May 19, 1945, adopted and forwarded a resolution to government that if their demands for adjustment in the COLA and other demands were not met by Thursday, June 21, 1945, they would go on strike.[154]

The workers argued in their letter that government had, during a period of tremendous rise in cost of living, taken a callous attitude at the sufferings of the masses of Nigerian workers among who were men with large families.[155] They further argued that government had increased the emoluments of their expatriate counterparts and also paid them "local allowances" to take care of the abnormal rise in cost of living in addition to the "separation allowances" previously enjoyed by them, while the same government turned deaf ears to their own request.[156] Workers also criticized the official policy of divide and rule in which "local allowances" of seventy-two pounds (£72) per annum was paid to Africans holding superior posts or what was otherwise known as "Europeans appointments" at a time when ordinary workers had nothing above the ten shillings (10/-) per month which had been granted in the COLA of 1942.[157] Thus, they demanded for a minimum wage for labor to be two shillings and six pence per day, while subordinate grades between labor and standard scale be increased by 50 percent on the existing COLA.[158]

The debate between the workers and the government continued for months. While the workers insisted on the adjustment of the COLA in order to survive, government insisted that such adjustment would translate to more income tax and that the masses would bear the burden. This eventually degenerated to the Nigerian General strike of 1945 led by Michael Imoudu. This strike was supported by the market women, politicians, and nationalists. In fact, it was in the course of the campaign for support that Herbert Macaulay, who was then the President of the National Council of the Nigeria and Cameroon (NCNC), took advantage of the gathering to discuss politics. He concluded his speech with the following statement: "There is not the slightest doubt that the liberation of this country is very near."[159] The opportunity was used to reinforce the need to intensify nationalism and independence movement. It can be said that household challenges and adaptation started with economic strategies on the part of women to support their husband's meager income, which culminated in the agitation for improved standard of living, as well as demand for independence.

CONCLUSION

Women in colonial Lagos were confronted with myriads of challenges ranging from economic hardship to restriction from trading on the streets of Lagos. Besides, the threat of income tax and the rivalry for spaces in the market between the colonial authorities and the women awaken their political consciousness, which translated into agitations and protest on the part of women for improved standard of living, particularly in their bid to jealously guard their livelihood. Thus, it can be said that the experiences of market women, the educated elite and the poor market women in Lagos remained the turning point in the history of women movements in Lagos and in Nigeria, in general.

NOTES

1. Ellis, "Household Strategies," 1–38.
2. Taiwo Makinde, "Motherhood as a Source of Empowerment of Women in Yoruba Culture." *Nordic Journal of African Studies* 13, no.2 (2004): 165.
3. Ibid.
4. For details see Babatunde Lawal, *The Geledespectacle: Arts, Gender, and Social Harmony in African Culture* (Washington, DC: University of Washington Press, 1996), 71–74.
5. Makinde, "Motherhood," 165.
6. Ibid.
7. Ibid.
8. Laray Denzer, "Yoruba Women: A Historiographical Study." *The International Journal of African Historical Studies* 27, no.1 (1994): 2.
9. Ibid., 3.
10. Lawal, "Background to Urbanisation," 13.
11. John Adams, *Remarks on the Country Extending from Lake Palmas to River Congo* (London: G&WB Whittaker, 1823), 96–108.
12. Ibid.
13. Ibid.
14. Tunde Akinwumi, Olufunke Adeboye, and Tosin Otusanya,"Rabi 'Alasooke' of Colonial Lagos: A Female Textile Merchant Encapsulated in a Yoruba Proverb." *Jenda: Journal of Culture and African Women Studies* 8, no.16 (2011).
15. Sandra Barnes, "Ritual, Power and Outside Knowledge." *Journal of Religion in Africa* 20, no.3 (1990): 248–68.
16. Denzer, "Yoruba Women," 1–39.
17. Ibid.
18. Mann, *Slavery and the Birth*, 26.
19. Nathaniel Akinremi Fadipe, *The Sociology of the Yoruba* (Ibadan: Ibadan University Press, 1970), 88.
20. Ibid.
21. Mann, *Slavery and the Birth*, 26.
22. Ibid., 25.
23. See, John Losi, *History of Lagos* (Lagos: CMS, 1921).

24. Lawal, "Background to Urbanization," 14.
25. Ibid.
26. Ibid.
27. Ibid.
28. Olakunle Lawal, "Mahin and Early Lagos." *Journal of West Africa Studies* 38, (1991): 100.
29. NAI, CSO/26/28322/s.887, "Union of Lagos Colony Fishermen to Chief Secretary of the Federation."
30. Ibid., 15.
31. Akinwumi, Adeboye, and Otusanya, "Rabi 'Alasooke'."
32. Saburi Biobaku, *The Egba and their Neighbours, 1872–1882* (Oxford: Oxford University Press, 1966), 57.
33. Denzer, "Yoruba Women," 1–39.
34. Abosede George, "Feminist Activism and Class Politics: The Example of the Lagos Girl Hawker Project." *Women's Studies Quaterly* 35, no.3/4 (2007): 128.
35. See for details, Niara Sudarkasa, *Where Women Work: A Study of Yoruba Women in the Market Place and in the Home* (Ann Arbor, MI: University of Michigan, 1973), Cited in George, "Feminist Activism," 128–43.
36. Patrick Dele Cole, *Modern and Traditional Elite in the Politics of Lagos* (Cambridge: Cambridge University Press, 1975), 98.
37. Ibid.
38. Ibid.
39. Editorial, *LWR*, July 25, 1908, 8.
40. Ibid.
41. Rita Okonkwo, *Protest Movements in Lagos, 1908–1930* (Enugu: ABIC Books, 2011), 9.
42. Ibid.
43. Ibid.
44. Cole, *Modern and Traditional Elites*, 236.
45. For details, see Editorial, *LWR*, August 8, 1909, 2.
46. Ibid.
47. *African Mail*, January 22, 1909, 156.
48. George, "Feminist Activism," 131.
49. Catherine Coquery-Vidrovitch, *African Women: A Modern History*. Translated by Beth Gillian Raps (Boulder, CO: Westview Press, 1997), 95–96.
50. See, *Population Census of Lagos*, Nigerian Department of Statistics, (Nigeria: Government Printer, 1951).
51. Olanrewaju Olutayo, "Systemic Source of 'Working Children' in Africa: The Case of Nigeria." *Childhood* 4, (1994): 210.
52. NAI, Comcol 1, File 1368, Vol. 1, "Memorandum from Medical Officer of Health to the Secretary, Town Council, Lagos." Market and Street Trading in Lagos, March 31, 1932.
53. Ibid.
54. NAI, Comcol 1, File 1368, Vol. 1, Correspondence from Holley. A.G (Town Engineer) to the Secretary, Town Council, Lagos, March 31, 1932.
55. NAI, Comcol 1, File 1368, Market and Street Trading in Lagos, 2.

56. NAI, Comcol 1, File 1368, Reports from a Survey Carried Out by the Town Council on Some Major Streets in Lagos.

57. NAI, Comcol 1, Vol. 1, Correspondence from Administrator of the Colony to Chief Secretary to Government, April 12, 1932.

58. NAI, Comcol 1, File 1368, a Copy of Press Release on Market and Street Trading in Lagos Issued by the President, Lagos Town Council to the Editors: *Daily Times*, *Daily News* and *Daily Telegraph*, 1936.

59. NAI, Comcol 1, File no 498, Lagos Women's League, February 26, 1924.

60. Gabriel Olusanya, "Charlotte Olajumoke Obasa," in *Nigerian Women in Historical Perspective*, ed. Bolanle Awe (Ibadan: Book Craft Ltd., 1992), 123–27.

61. Ibid.

62. NAI, Comcol 1, File 498, Lagos Women's League Letter to the Chief Secretary to Government on the Need to Provide Employment for Women in the Colony, Febuary 26, 1924, 2.

63. Olusanya, "Charlotte Olajumoke Obasa," 133.

64. Ibid.

65. Denzer, "Yoruba Women," 26.

66. Laray Denzer, *The Seamstress in Nigeria: The Evolution of a Popular Woman's Occupation from Colonial Times*. Paper Presented at the Seminar on Women and the Peaceful Transition Programme, Kwara State Polytechnic and Office of Women's Affairs, Ilorin, March 19–21, 1991, 90.

67. Ibid., 91.

68. Personal Communication with Raji Risikatu.

69. For details see, Bolanle Awe, "The Iyalode in the Traditional Yoruba Political System," in *Sexual Stratification: A Cross Cultural View*, ed. Alice Schlegel (New Haven, CT: Yale University Press, 1977).

70. Mona Etienne and Eleanor Leacock, eds., *Women and Colonization: Anthropological Perspectives* (New York, NY: Praeger, 1980), 16.

71. Cheryl Johnson, "Grassroots Organizing: Women in Anti-Colonial Activity in Southwestern Nigeria." *African Studies Review* 25, no.2/3 (1982): 138.

72. Ibid.

73. Ibid.

74. Joke Jacobs, *Market Woman of Substance: A Biography of Alhaja Abibat Mogaji-President General of Association of Nigerian Market Women and Men* (Lagos: Mercantile Press Associates, 1997), 22. Note: An interview was supposed to be held with Alhaja Mogaji, who was trained under late Madam Alimotu Pelewura in Colonial Lagos. However, on getting to her residence, Mama could no longer grant interview as a result of old age (90+), she decided to release a copy of her biography for use in gathering data for this aspect of the book.

75. Jacobs, *Market Woman of Substance*, 22.

76. Ibid.

77. Cheryl Johnson, "Madam Alimotu Pelewura and the Lagos Market Women." *Tarikh* 7, no.1 (1981): 1–10.

78. James Coleman, *Nigeria: Background to Nationalism* (Berkeley, CA: University Press, 1958), 197.

79. Jacobs, *Market Woman of Substance*, 23.

80. Johnson, "Grassroots Organizing," 143.
81. Ibid.
82. Oyinkan Abayomi' Saddress to the Educated Women in Lagos, Herbert Macaulay Papers (HMP), Box 73, File 7, Kenneth Dike Library, University of Ibadan.
83. Editorial, *DS*, May 11, 1944.
84. Private Papers of Mrs. Tinuola Dedeke (Founding Member of NWP), Cited in Johnson, "Grassroots Organizing," 144.
85. *WAP*, June 26, 1944.
86. *DS*, January 8, 1947.
87. NAI, CSO File no 43222, Correspondence from the Secretary NWP to Commissioner of the Colony.
88. Johnson, "Grassroots Organizing," 146.
89. George, "Feminist Activism," 135.
90. *DS* Editorial, "Eleven Year Old Girl Hawker Found Dead in Public Garden," June 21, 1946, 1.
91. F. Adetowun Ogunsheye, "The Women of Nigeria." *Presence Africaine* 32/33 (June–September 1960): 1211–38.
92. Olutayo, "Systemic Source," 209.
93. Editorial, *DS*, April 21, 1948.
94. Olukoju, *The Liverpool of West Africa*, 230.
95. Ibid.
96. NAI, DCI 1/1 4031, Vol. 1, "Control of Merchandise Prices," Minute to P.A.S, September 11, 1939.
97. Ibid.
98. NAI, ComCol 1, File 2283/S.10, Vol. II, "Salt Rationing," Senior Assistant Superintendent of Police, CID to Commissioner of Colony, July 31, 1942.
99. Toyin Falola, "'Salt is Gold': The Management of Salt Scarcity in Nigeria during World War II." *Canadian Journal of African Studies* 26, no.3 (1992): 412.
100. *WAP*, August 30, 1941, cited in, Falola, "'Salt is Gold'," 412.
101. Okuseinde Olumuyiwa, "Managing Urban Food Crisis: The Lagos Foodstuff Marketing Scheme, 1943–1946," in *Urban Transition in Africa: Aspects of Urbanisation and Change in Lagos* (Lagos: Longman, 2004), 65.
102. For details, see *Nigeria, Memorandum on the Organisation and Control of War Time Trade and Production* (Lagos: Government Printer, 1943), 4.
103. Wale Oyemakinde, "The Pullen Marketing Scheme: A Trial in Food Price Control In Nigeria, 1941–1947," in *Essays in Economic History*, ed. Wale Oyemakinde (Ibadan: Sunlight Syndicate Ventures, 2003), 108.
104. Olukoju, *The Liverpool of West Africa*, 233.
105. Ibid.
106. For details, see, NAI, A Report on the Variation of Prices and Retail Trade in Foodstuffs in Lagos, Submitted to the Government Statistician, Chief Secretary Office, June 1929.
107. Oyemakinde, "The Pullen Marketing Scheme," 111.
108. Ibid.
109. *DS*, January 30, 1943.
110. Oyemakinde, "The Pullen Marketing Scheme," 112.

111. Ibid., 113.
112. Olukoju, *The Liverpool of West Africa*, 233.
113. Ibid.
114. Olumuyiwa, "Managing Urban Food Crisis," 67.
115. HMP, Box 13, File 5, Kenneth Dike Library, University of Ibadan.
116. Ibid.
117. Ibid.
118. Ibid.
119. Ibid.
120. Johnson, "Grassroots Organizing," 142.
121. NAI, DCI 1/1, File 4037/S.59, Controller, Local Foodstuffs to Chief Secretary of the Government, June 18, 1945.
122. Olumuyiwa, "Managing Urban Food Crisis," 74.
123. Ibid.
124. NAI, CSO 26, File 41657/S.1, Extracts from the Statement made by the Commissioner of the Colony in Reply to Questions Raised at the Legislative Council, March 18, 1946.
125. NAI, CSO 26, File no 41657/S.1, Correspondence between the Controller, Lagos Market Scheme to Chief Secretary to Government, March 9, 1946.
126. HMP, Box 13, File 5, Kenneth Dike Library, University of Ibadan.
127. NAI, CSO 26, File 41657/S.1, Controller, Lagos Market Scheme to Chief Secretary to the Government, November 13, 1946.
128. Editorial, *Daily Times*, May 13, 1945.
129. NAI, ComCol 1, File no 2438, "Letter of Appeal to the Commissioner of Colony by Tenants Residing at 64 Olonade Street, Yaba, Lagos," Rent and Premises Control, July 28, 1942.
130. NAI, ComCol 1, A Report of the Lagos Rent Board, July 26, 1943.
131. Personal Communication with Professor Kunle Lawal, 52 years, Lecturer, Department of History, University of Ibadan, February 2, 2011.
132. NAI, ComCol 1, "Extract of Reports Submitted by Lagos Rent Control Scheme Committee," Rent and Premises Control.
133. Ibid.
134. Ibid.
135. NAI, ComCol 1, File no 2438, J.G.C. Allen to Commissioner of Labour, November 18, 1944.
136. Johnson, "Grassroots Organizing," 141.
137. Personal Communication with Sikiru Akanni.
138. Ibid.
139. Buchi Emecheta, *The Joys of Motherhood* (New York, NY: Alison and Busby, 1979), Buchiwas born in Lagos to a railway worker father and petty trader mother in 1944.
140. A summary of livelihood challenges in colonial Lagos as depicted in *"The Joys of Motherhood,"* cited in L. Lindsay, "Domesticity and Difference: Male Breadwinners, Working Women, Colonial Citizenship in the 1945 Nigerian General Strike." *The American Historical Review* 1, no.3 (1999): 789.

141. HMP, "Lagos Market: Standardisation of Native Retail Measures in Lagos," Box 13, File 7.
142. Ibid.
143. Personal Communication with Raji Risikat.
144. Personal Communication with Alhaja Raji Risikat.
145. Toyin Falola, "My Friend the Shylock: Money-Lenders and their Clients in Southwestern Nigeria." *The Journal of African History* 34, no.3 (1993): 411.
146. Ibid.
147. Personal Communication with Alhaja Raji Risikat.
148. NAI, ComCol 1/553, Indebtedness of Mrs Hilda Hamilton to Lagos Money Lender. This was cited in Falola, "My Friend the Shylock," 411.
149. Ibid.
150. Wale Oyemakinde, "The Nigerian General Strike of 1945," in *Essays in Economic History*, ed. Wale Oyemakinde (Ibadan: Sunlight Syndicate Ventures, 2003), 155.
151. Ibid.
152. Johnson, "Grassroots Organizing," 140.
153. *Daily Times*, December 18, 1940.
154. *WAP*, May 22, 1945, 3.
155. Oyemakinde, "The Nigerian General Strike," 157.
156. Ibid.
157. For details see, NAI, CE/T9 W, Tudor Davies, Enquiry into the Cost of Living and the Control of Cost of Living in the Colony and Protectorate of Nigeria, London, 1946, 61.
158. Railway Workers Union (RWU), Papers Relating to the General Strike of 1945, cited in Oyemakinde, "The Nigerian General Strike," 157.
159. *WAP*, June 4, 1945, 2.

Chapter 5

Neighborhood Cultures and the Redefinition of Social Values, 1861–1960

The presence of the British colonial administrators, their socioeconomic policies, and their political manipulations impacted greatly on the sub-structure and super-structure of the society. The heterogeneous society of Lagos experienced dilution in cultures which fostered redefinition of social values. In fact, the response of the citizenry to the social, economic, and political challenges of the period translated into several desires, including their aspirations for political independence. This chapter therefore, focuses on popular and neighborhood cultures in Lagos, urban life, and identity in colonial Lagos, crime and criminality, begging culture, destitution, juvenile delinquency, and the growth of informal economic sector in colonial Lagos.

LAGOS AND THE URBAN LIFE: POPULAR AND NEIGHBORHOOD CULTURES

The period of colonialism and its features of urbanization and modernization impacted greatly on the people and their lifestyles. They experienced dilution in cultures and social values. From the mid-nineteenth century when Lagos was ceded to the British, there emerged a new social hierarchy, with the British officials, missionaries, and even traders as the aristocracy, the immigrant black elite as the middle class, and the indigenes of Lagos as the lower class.[1] The two major immigrant groups that exerted considerable influence on the transformation of indigenous Lagos community into an urban metropolis were the Brazillian/Cuban and Sierra Leonian repatriates.[2] There was no doubt that as they began to settle firmly in parts of the town specifically allocated to them, they acquired "foreign" lifestyles in dress, food, religion, education, and language which they brought with them. These became quite noticeable and marked them out as possessing some prestigious social attributes in spite of the historical accident of their previous enslavement.[3]

During the period of their sojourn in Brazil, Cuba, and Sierra Leone, they had acquired considerable skills in several trades and vocations. Many of them had also acquired professional training, a very high standard of education and of cultural sophistication.[4] Echeruo describes these "repatriates" as constituting themselves into "a unique community maintaining ties with the Yoruba homeland, and yet sharing a great deal with the small but prominent and prosperous expatriate community." He continues: "Whether they were repatriates from Brazil and the Americas, immigrants from Sierra Leone and Liberia or simply educated migrants from England, these men were a force in setting Lagos apart as the youngest and fastest growing community on the West coast."[5]

The ego of the Sierra Leonians who wore so much clothing so as to compete with the King of Lagos redefined the attitudes and mode of dressing of the Lagosians in the twentieth century. Before contact with the Europeans, the common Lagosian, male or female, wore very little clothing themselves, but as late as 1933, an observer noted that:

> Lagosians do not care much for clothing as a covering, but they were very fond of it for purposes of display, and on great occasions, exhibit it in great quantities, and in all colors and shades of color. And that on ordinary occasions many people content themselves with less clothing than decency requires. The young of both sexes are very often allowed to go without clothing and when it might be expected that their own sense of propriety would lead them to seek the use of it.[6]

Dress is an image maker and image destroyer. The phenomenon of dress in the social life of Lagos in the nineteenth century, both for its own sake and for the insight it gave into the cultural history of the Yoruba who formed the majority of the population of Lagos cannot be overlooked as far as the changes in social life was concerned. Of all the immigrants in Lagos, the *Saros* were at the forefront of the cultural dilution. The *Saros* wanted the better of the two worlds.[7] They wanted to be English yet never gave up their right to be African, "to go Fantee" as they termed it. But ever mindful of their status as "black English," they tended to be apologetic about their African impulses.[8] The attitude of one contributor to the *Anglo African Times* (AAT) in November 1863 was probably typical of all but the most extreme Saros:

> We in Africa assume a kind of indulgence—we do not hold ourselves amenable to all the formalities and exactions of fashionable life in Europe. We can dine in frock coats or without coats, if by doing so we add to our comfort. We can smoke in the house, even in our dining rooms, and indeed when the cloth is

removed, cigars are as often present as fruits and wine- and not a few of our veritable gentlemen might often, a few always, be seen in collar shirt, waistcoat and sometimes even culottes(except our loose pyjamas are dignified with the name of trousers) so too we are not over-particular as to when we make a call, especially if it be on business, so that we do not arouse a man at midnight; and many of us are all the more pleased if a visitor calls at dinner time, for them we ask him to take a chair and be welcome, and if our neighbors are well behaved and respectable we don't usually make them feel that we esteem ourselves their superiors. Such is life, in the main, amongst us Africans; and it is necessary that it should be so far, far more than it can be at home, we are dependent upon each other.[9]

The above remark reveals the attitudes of the Saros to the Lagosians and other groups in Lagos. These translated into the need to carve for themselves unique identities. Thus, the expression of unique identities in dress and fashion became a popular culture among the Saros, Brazillian returnees, Yoruba Lagosians, and Hausa as well as other groups. Subsequently, the process of cultural dilution and assimilation became entrenched in the city of Lagos.

Islam and Christianity played important roles in the redefinition of social values and the cultural dilution of the society in the nineteenth and twentieth century Lagos. For instance, the Islamic religion was already quite prominent in Lagos during the latter half of the nineteenth century. By the 1870s, a sizable number of indigenous Lagosians had already embraced "Mohamedanism."[10] The assimilatory influences of the Islamic religion of the cultural life of the people of Lagos are evident in the use of Muslim names like *Lateef, Nojeem, Akeem, Monsur, Kassim, Nurudeen, Ibrahim, Bashir*, and so on as first names.[11] These Muslim names are usually used in conjunction with indigenous Yoruba personal or family names as Lateef Kosoko, Sultan Ladega Adele, RabiatuAjala, KudiratOyekan, and so on.[12] In fact, among the nonliterate members of the community, some of these Muslim names had been assimilated into the phonological structure of the Yoruba language, for example, Latifu, Rabiatu, Kudiratu, and so on. Besides, Islamic religion created initially seasonal means of livelihood, which later translated to fully fledged occupation on the entertainment platform. This seasonal means of livelihood was in the form of those Muslims who moved round the town in the early morning during the month of Ramadan to wake up their brethren for prayers by beating of pans, drums, and sticks in return for money from the Islamic faithful.[13] For years, this practice, popularly known as *were*, and the youth involved known as *ajiwere* continued undisturbed, and the number of youths engaged in it increased on a yearly basis. In fact, by the late 1950s, it transformed into what is today known as Fuji music and was no longer a seasonal means of livelihood but a full-fledged occupation.[14]

Christian missionaries in Lagos recognized the importance of music and entertainment in Lagos life, as the Methodist movement opined that the new urban community in Lagos desired entertainment whether holy or profane.[15] As implied in the comment of August 1888, by *Observer*, if Lagos did not have music in their churches, the pews would become vacant, and the music halls and entertainment houses would flourish in consequence.[16] This observation was targeted at discouraging the growth and patronage of entertainment houses and music halls in order for the Christian missionaries to sustain the loyalty and steadfastness of the Christian faithful. During the emancipation celebrations in Lagos in October 1888, the principal sermon was devoted to a condemnation of the concert.[17] The preacher "condemned the tendencies of the rising generation for Balls and concerts with other kindred pleasures to the detriment of those by which man is elevated."[18] Ironically, the report ended with a listing of the rest of the day's program of events, including "A Grand Ball at the Glover Memorial Hall, A Dramatic Entertainment at the Roman Catholic School Room, A musical Party at the Glover Memorial Hall, a Carnival Procession through the town, and a fancy Dress Ball at the Glover Memorial Hall."[19] Apparently, concerts, music, and similar entertainments introduced by the settler population (Brazilian and Sierra Leonian returnees) were satisfying the cultural and the social needs of the people to the disadvantage of missionary activities. This was in addition to the traditional music popularized by Brimah Danmale and Oranyan in the early nineteenth century Lagos. Subsequently, the missionaries had no choice but to adopt entertainment in their styles of evangelism. The *Observer*, in 1888, praised *kerikeri* dance as "the real thing" and when the new C.M.S Yoruba Hymnbook was published in 1888, the *Observer* was quite enthusiastic:

> The Yoruba Nation at least is a nation of poets. Without music, they are inert; without poetry, they are inane . . . Take away singing from the Churches of Lagos today and the pews will be vacant and innumerable music halls and entertainment houses will sprout up.[20]

Corroborating this view, Echeruo opines that traditionally, Lagos was a city of drummers and singers.[21] Similarly, in a report of April 15, 1865, the Anglo-African remarked on this assertion, arguing that:

> Native women were apt at song-making. Every event of interest was, as it were, recorded on the memory of these people in this way; and one could almost produce a history of any locality by compiling the many songs which, from day-to-day, are on the lips of women and children.[22]

The point being made here is that apart from the traditional music and dancing, entertainment had been part of pre-colonial Lagos, this became redefined in the city as a result of the influence of immigrants from the hinterland, the British colonialists, and influence of Islam and Christianity as well as the activity of the Sierra Leoneans and Brazillian repatriates.

LIFESTYLES OF THE EDUCATED ELITE IN LAGOS

The first-generation educated elite were not a product of the Nigerian situation: they were slaves, or children of such slaves who, it was believed by society, were a happy riddance banished forever from Nigeria.[23] Ironically however, in the modern history of Nigeria the banished slaves and their offspring that were hitherto rejected stone was to become the cornerstone of the Nigerian edifice. For when they returned to Nigeria the *Saro*, as the first-generation Western style educated elite came to be widely known, had been metamorphosed in such a way that they began to see themselves as leaders who should be followed by the rest of the Nigerian society.[24] They returned with a different conception of man, his world view, his religion, his life style, his value system, the attributes a leader should have and the course of history society should chart.[25] These educated elite took the entertainment and theater industry in Lagos like a colossus and improved it by setting up dramatic companies as well as organized concerts of various kinds.

Outside the missions, favorable to the growth of the concerts in Lagos was a small, well-educated and "cultured" elite made up mainly of the expatriate colonial civil servants and the missionaries, the Brazilian community which increased in number after the emancipation (1888), Sierra Leonians who came out as professionals with the mission, in the Government Service, or on their own, and a number of "educated" Lagosians.[26] In spite of the mixed culture of the community, concert and entertainment industry assumed an "international character," which in turn gave an impetus to the growth of indigenous participation as a result of the activities of these educated elite. For instance, the Brazilian Dramatic Company, under the patronage of the German Consul, Heinrich Bey, performed a "Grand Theatre" in honor of Queen Victoria's jubilee on May 23, 1882.[27] This concert, according to Echeruo was so humorous, dramatic, and eventful that there were requests for repeat performances.

ENTERTAINMENT, POPULAR CULTURES, AND LIVELIHOOD IN COLONIAL LAGOS

Drumming, singing, concert organizing, stage theater, and cinema business provided employment for the residents of Lagos during the colonial period.[28]

Besides, Lagos had well-established drama festivals and masquerades which provided regular entertainment of near professional quality. Apart from *kerikeri* and *Batakoto* that were indigenous to Lagos, the returnees in Lagos from Sierra Leone and South America featured new forms of entertainment in which many people were engaged.[29]

Ade Ajayi, in his study of Christian missions in Nigeria, has drawn attention to the skills of the slaves from America in theater and singing as emanating from their experiences before emancipation.[30] When these Brazilians came back to Lagos, they brought back their great love for song, and made it more elaborate by the addition of many refinement of European musical practice.[31] Names like J.J. da Costa, J.A. Campos, L.G. Barboza, and P.Z. Silva (for a long-time stage manager of the Brazilian Dramatic Company) were well known in Lagos concert circles.[32] Besides, the Syrian businessmen operated cinema houses, Corona Cinema at Alli Street, Rialto Cinema at Offin Street, and Casino Cinema at Broad Street were the popular spots.[33]

By the middle of the twentieth century, the migrants from the hinterland had introduced different kinds of music to boost the entertainment industry. Theater plays by the late Hubert Ogunde Company were staged at Glover Hall along Victoria Street.[34] Quite dominant were also the social activities that went on most weekends, parties by families naming the newborn, or celebrating marriages, or burying the dead. These were the regular platforms for musicians and musical outfits like Ayinde Bakare, Tunde Nightingale, and Yusuf Olatunji. Thus, an appreciable number of migrants found survival in the entertainment industry in the course of their sojourn in Lagos as singers, dancers, drummers, and theater artistes. Drumming and singing, for example, had been regular (almost daily) features of Lagos life. On several occasions, the chiefs, the police, and the government were in open conflict. The introduction of ordinance prohibiting drumming on the streets of Lagos in 1903 generated grievances and sharp responses from the residents, particularly the chiefs. The chiefs met with the governor and the police over the matter. Out of the report of this meeting (published in Record of January 2, 1904), the responses of Chief Kasumu Giwa and Chief Aromire are worth quoting in *extenso*, because their responses reinforced the challenges such decision posed to the livelihood of those engaged in singing and drumming for survival:

> This is almost strange in the land. If people are drumming in connection with marriage ceremonies, they are prevented from doing so. If those who are drummers by trade go about from house to house to beat for hire, they are also prevented from doing so. A town without a sound of the drum is like a city of the dead. Even those who go about in the early morning during the month of Ramadan to wake up their brethren for prayer by beating of pans were also prevented

from doing this religious act. We have never been dealt with this manner, and we have therefore decided to bring the matter to the notice of the Governor.[35]

Similarly, more concern for drummer's predicament was obvious in Chief Aromire's response:

> It works hardship on the town to stop drumming, and besides this, the drummers would starve. Drumming was their only trade. When they sang the praises of our fathers and their brave deeds we are glad to give them 2d or 3d and so they got something from house to house and make their living.[36]

The above comments by the chiefs were meant to persuade the government on what could be the aftermath of prohibiting drumming on the streets of Lagos. Subsequently, the governor instructed the commissioner to reduce the hours of drumming to 6'oclock in the evening, but still insisted that there should be no night drumming.[37] These regulations culminated in the loss of jobs for drummers in Lagos, especially in the island. Consequently, those who could not find other alternative means of livelihood took to crime in order to survive. A veritable example was Salami Bello Jaguda, who was a famous drummer in Lagos. His drumming career shall be discussed in the next section under crime and criminality in Lagos.

Entertainment brought about the emergence of new neighborhood cultures in colonial Lagos. Behind Marina, Brazilian emigrants settled in the east around campus square, with Sierra Leonians, or "Saro," in the west at Olowogbowo.[38] There was great rivalry between these groups from the beginning, and in terms of their young people, this was symbolically marked every Christmas and Easter when boys from Campus and Olowogbowo carried masquerades—the carreta—and paraded round the town dressed in brightly colored clothes, some riding on horseback.[39] Members of each group carried horsewhips and, wherever the two groups met, they engaged in merciless, ferocious whipping of each other:

> The notorious 'Campus Square boys', the 'Lafiaji Boys', the 'Agarawu Boys' Each of such group of youths had taken their identities from the localities in which they lived and which they concentrated their acts of thuggery during festivals like 'Egungun', 'Eyo', 'Igunnu' and other masquerades' outings. They had readily served as the whip wielding vanguards of such masquerades who taunted opposing masquerades and spectators, so as to ferment and undertake a free-for-all looting of shops and houses.[40]

Youths divided Lagos Island into two districts: those living north and northeast of Tinubu Square were eligible for the "Olowogbowo Alkali Society," with the remainder of the island under the "Lafiaji Alkali Society."[41] It seemed as though the societies interpreted Boxing Day to mean the day when youths were exempted from criminal responsibility for assault:

> Each society recruited fighting squads, and generally on December 26 of each year met each other in inter-district group fighting which, in actuality, were something bordering on internecine warfare . . . The equipment included paper headgear, mask for the face, boxing ring, 'hippo-rod' or the cat (o' nine tails) fitted with a number of nails and sharp-edged blades, daggers and any amount of charms calculated to render the combatant invisible.[42]

It is from this act of stubbornness and bravery that the Agarawu area of Lagos derived a song composed in its praise, which is very popular among musicians and the people of the island:

> *Agarawueriaa*—Agarawu area
> *Bi won tikeremo to yen*—As compact as it is
> *Awonti o wanibe, awoni won oo*—The residents are highly reveres.[43]

Therefore, it can be said that Agarawu area was known for boldness and fearless confrontation against external aggression. It could be concluded that colonialism introduced new sub-cultures in entertainment and lifestyles of Lagosians. It also reinforced the existing youthful exuberance commonly associated with celebration of masquerades such as *Adamuorisha-Eyo* and the notorious *Bamgbose masquerades* in the city of Lagos.

CRIME AND CRIMINALITY IN COLONIAL LAGOS

Criminal activities had been in existence in pre-colonial Lagos as exemplified by the activities of the several migratory fishermen who first used a part of the island as fishing camps.[44] At such a subsistence level, criminality was greatly limited to the theft of fish, canoes, and piratical activities.[45] In addition, the collapse of Oyo Kingdom and the internecine wars of the nineteenth century Yoruba land promoted raiding of weaker neighbors by stronger ones in the quest for survival and dominance. Therefore, merchants and traders as well as other dwellers and visitors to the emerging city became potential victims of robbery attack.[46] For instance, traders were robbed on trading routes while Lagos-bound canoes bearing traders and their goods from the interior were often plundered with the stolen goods often given to soldiers and warring states in the Yoruba interior.[47] Thus, crime in pre-colonial Lagos derived partly from the economic activities of the people and partly from the political situation in the Yorubaland.[48] This was mostly done in order to supply slaves to the flourishing slaves' port of Lagos since the Portuguese had encouraged the participation of the Oba and his people in the obnoxious trade in slaves.[49] However, following the abolition of the slave trade, and the introduction of the legitimate trade, Lagos assumed the position of a great commercial center for traders from the hinterland who demonstrated preference for the attractive prices offered for their goods in Lagos markets.[50]

From the beginning of the twentieth century, Lagos enjoyed boom in commercial activities for almost three decades, although these period, bounded by the economic crisis of 1929 and the end of World War II, marked the development of new forms of urban poverty characterized by rapid growth in unemployment, prostitution, and delinquency, which eventually led to a rise in criminal activities.[51] The economy mostly dictated the nature of crime and was greatly aided by environmental factor.[52] In the colonial period, these became redefined to include burglary, armed robbery, murder, smuggling, juvenile delinquency, gambling, pickpocket activities, and currency counterfeiting.

A clarification of the concept of crime would enhance our understanding of its changing trends as far as livelihood is concerned in colonial Lagos. Although a complex and culturally relative term to define, it can mean different, even opposed things, depending on one's point of view.[53] Crime is conceptualized as something that threatens the community, or something generally believed to do so or something committed with evil intent or something forbidden in the interest of the most powerful sections of the society.[54] This study views crime as an action prohibited by law or a failure to act as requested by law.

Analyzing the changing form of crime is not an easy task because the primary sources, available newspapers, administrative reports, police and justice records, and oral sources present crime from a specific angle.[55] For instance, newspapers reported mainly exceptional events, such as robberies, burglaries, and kidnappings. They emphasized serious offenses whereas minor offenses against property, such as stealing are more common offenses in Nigeria during the colonial period.[56] Therefore, there was a wide gap in the statistics on crime because reliable crime rate data for the period are difficult to obtain.

This section of the chapter is not interested in the review of all the crimes perpetrated in Lagos during the period, but only crimes that have had some links with the rise of urban poverty and livelihood challenges. In southern Nigerian cities, particularly Lagos, the period saw a growing number of petty offenders who were convicted several times. It also saw the development of a class of more serious offenders who expanded their criminal activities.[57] Collective actions were now organized around gangs that employed violence; their offenses became more sophisticated: children were exploited by adults to steal for them and prostitution became prevalent in Lagos.[58] Although it is still not clear whether trade fluctuations and economic depression had any direct impact on crime, but it had on the image of Lagos as a land of inexhaustible opportunities.[59]

As the experience of Salami Bello Jaguda illustrates, Lagos was a place where the possession of a skill or talent—drumming for him—could guarantee a means of livelihood.[60] He had enjoyed this trade for almost two decades when, in 1903, the noise control Ordinance introduced in Lagos hampered the use of his talent.[61] This was meant to restrict drumming all night on the street of Lagos to the inconvenience of other citizens. Consequently, the ordinance against noise making reduced the potential of drummers to make enough for a living, such that some of them, including Salami, resorted into crime as an alternative means of livelihood.[62] Jaguda came to Lagos sometimes in the late 1880s from Okitipupa with the intention of selling his talent—drumming—which was in high demand in Lagos because Lagos people enjoyed dancing and praise singing.[63] However, as the law on noise making was enacted and enforced in Lagos around this time, it made the vocation unprofitable.[64] He resorted to organizing and training young boys as pickpockets.[65] Subsequently, he was sentenced to nine months' hard labor for stealing a huge sum of money from a rich merchant in Lagos in 1924.[66]

The appearance of Jaguda and Boma boys in many Nigerian cities constituted one of the main changes that occurred between the 1930s and the 1940s.[67] Jaguda began to mean pickpocket activities and stealing in Yoruba.[68] The activities of the former is examined in this section, because pickpocket activities as practiced by *Jaguda* Boys were a means of livelihood, but the latter is examined in the subsequent section as a form of juvenile delinquency. Jaguda Boys in their operative system roamed the main business and traffic arteries of Lagos Island looking for pockets to pick from or using public menaces to get their way.[69] They deliberately bumped into people in crowded places and then picked money from their pockets. Some even went as far as to hold people while others went through the victim's pockets.[70] Sometimes two or more of them would engage in a seeming scuffle; an innocent man with money in his pocket unaware of the tricks and approaching as a go-between would find to his horror that he had been relieved of it all.[71]

The menace of Jaguda Boys was so pervasive in Lagos that they operated day and night. Jaguda Boys operated from the porch of Tom Jones Memorial Hall on Victoria Street or the mosque opposite, from empty meat stalls at Ereko Market along Idumagbo Avenue every evening, at Ebute-Ero's daily foodstuffs markets, at Idumagbo Marina on market days, and at Ido Railway Station.[72] Thus, their activities in the major streets of Lagos gained the attention of almost all the newspapers of the period. It was reported that Jaguda Boys along Agarawu and Ereko Streets demanded "gifts on the basis of 'give me or I' will take it."[73] Near the Island's banks, they watched those withdrawing money, saw where the money had been stowed, and then followed behind to pick from their pockets.[74]

Another report, it was claimed that outside the tax office on Reclamation Road and at Jankara Market in the evening, "these heartless brute congregate, ready to attack innocent people who might come their way."[75] Even needing the cover of darkness proved no barrier: for instance, "Sango" and his gang stole Beatrice Iyalode's £13 of gold trinkets in broad day light at Idumagbo Avenue in early September 1940 in front of dozens of witnesses.[76] Another stunning example was when One Jaguda Boy even plied his trade in the Supreme Court building itself until he was caught in the process of stealing six pence. With two previous convictions, he returned to court, in the dock this time, to receive three months' hard labor.[77]

As a result of these widespread operations of Jaguda Boys in Lagos, government became challenged to devise strategies of curtailing them. In response to such crimes, the police tried hard to remedy the situation. For example, half the ten reported cases of stealing from Ereko Market in 1941 resulted in arrests.[78] The police rounded up Jaguda Boys, but many hauled before the courts on various offenses had no parents or guardians. This lack of roots negated the belief of the colonialists and Native Authority that the simple solution to juvenile delinquency in the capital involved the repatriation of offenders back to their home area.[79] Although different strategies were used by the colonial authorities to checkmate the situations, the pickpocket phenomenon still survived beyond the colonial period.

Another shortcut to making money was to engage in its private manufacturing. In 1937, the British colonial government became alarmed over high rate of currency counterfeiting and the ease with which such illegal money circulated all over Nigeria.[80] Although several means were used to acquire wealth and money in pre-colonial societies, rituals and charms to invent money, stealing, the use of power by chiefs to exact tributes, fines, war booty and so on, counterfeiting was not a possible option.[81] Monetization of the economy and the introduction of wage labor enabled those with jobs to have access to the new money and to cultivate a taste of Western products.[82] Their new lifestyles and tastes also added to their high visibility. While many people understood that they acquired money through their engagement in salary jobs and trading, there were those who believed that they too could have access through other means.[83]

Subsequently, several techniques of making money were sought, and counterfeiting became one of them, after all, the new money was "just paper or small metals"[84] that looked as if they could be duplicated. Indeed, they were duplicated, initially as toys, with available objects.[85] Jokes too began to spread that blacksmiths and goldsmiths could make the money, and it was no coincidence that many of the initial suspects in forgery were smiths.[86] In fact, forged coins and to a larger extent paper money were attributed to the Ijebus. This was because appreciable numbers of the Ijebus were practicing goldsmiths. Thus counterfeit coins were popularly referred to as *owo Ijebu* (Ijebu-made money).[87]

Apart from tracing the source of counterfeiting business to the Ijebus, there was also a source, derived from oral documentation. Most informants were quick to allege that counterfeiting was brought to Nigeria by the Lebanese and Indians.[88] The British administrators, however, exonerated this group of aliens from the crime, attributing everything to "Africans of criminal disposition."[89] In contrast to this position of the British colonial authorities was the claim by some informants that the Lebanese were the brains behind the currency counterfeiting in Lagos. Their argument was that, apart from the fact that Nigerians at that period had limited knowledge and technological shortcomings in making money, paper money, especially, were imported into the country by the Lebanese businessmen.[90] Agbongbon, for instance, cited a scenario in 1940 when some Lebanese businessmen were caught in Lagos with ten pieces of mattress laced with fake British pounds imported into the country.[91]

An attempt was made to search for newspaper report of such events during the period without success, but this was corroborated by Sikiru Akanni, who narrated how his friend who was a cashier in the bank confided in him that he was introduced into currency counterfeiting by some Lebanese businessmen, who brought the money to the bank for them, to help circulate to the members of the public. While these allegations could not be said to be untrue, currency counterfeiting in the colonial period transcended the involvement of Nigerians alone as the British administrators would want us to believe.

Currency counterfeiting, it has been argued, flourished through certain aspects of indigenous attitudes about money. At the root of counterfeiting was this belief that work, especially hard work, could be circumvented in the search for money.[92] "If hard work brings money," goes a popular proverb, "all the Hausa in Sabo would have become rich." Sabo (or Sabongari) is the strangers' quarters in southwestern towns and cities where the Hausa from Northern Nigeria resided.[93] An addition to this thinking was the notion that the way out of poverty is *"isekekere owo nla"*—"little work, big money" This was to serve as a kind of encouragement to counterfeiters who, rather than work hard and await the blessing of God, preferred smart work. In fact, a suspected counterfeiter told the police in 1935 that *iseni monse, mi ki se ole, iselile ni isewa* (I work for a living, I am not a thief. This is hard work).[94]

The implication of this position is that, counterfeiters never saw themselves as thieves, nor did the public see them as such. Although many of them were aware of the position of government on counterfeiting, they did not believe that their work should be criminalized. Instead, their activities and "work" were described as "*fi ogbonorijeun*" (using one's brain or cleverness to survive) and far better than approaching money lenders for loans on high interest or even pawning oneself.[95] In spite of the fact that the business was risky, and offenders were jailed after arrest, many people engaged in the business for survival not only in Lagos, but across the country in the colonial period.

The economic status of Lagos in the colonial period could be linked to crimes in the city. This partly was why the city enjoyed concentration of police to ensure security. However, in the municipal area where policing should have been more effective given the number of men deployed, stealing of a minor degree was often recorded.[96] The strength and distribution of the police in the Western province reveals that, out of the five hundred fifty-six men deployed in the Western province in 1908, Lagos alone, that is, the municipal area including Ebute-Meta had three hundred twenty-four men representing about –58 percent of the total strength of the police in the province.[97] This mal-distribution and over-concentration of police in the municipal area degenerated into a situation whereby the district where policing was poor, experienced prevalent burglary and robbery with violence, while the municipal area experienced theft and minor stealing. The disparity in the criminality of the two areas, that is the city and the suburbs of the colony area, had also been pointed out by Barnes, with reference to their political set up.[98]

In the 1930s, the stealing of safes in which people kept mostly cash was high as reported by the newspapers of the period. The victims were mostly Lagosians who lived on the island who did not have their safes securely fixed with concrete.[99] It was reported that the thieves distanced themselves from those with fixed and concrete safes, while they went after those who loosely placed their safes either on the floor or on a chair.[100] The modus operandi of this category of thieves was solid, and their networking unimaginable. For instance, a safe was stolen from an office in Marina and transported by canoe to the Badagry creeks where it was later recovered unlocked.[101] To the thieves, they never saw anything bad in helping careless people to keep their hard-earned money, provided the owners were not injured or killed by them.

However, from 1928 to 1946, various crimes considered to be serious were reported in the Lagos District. Consequently, there was a shift of the center of authority of the district from the Island to Agege and later Ikeja, but this did not immediately translate to the restoration of order in a district that had long been sidelined for about sixty-six years during which time the area had undergone a lot of changes.[102] First, new villages had been established in the area by the constant stream of migrants of various backgrounds into the area.[103] Barnes has described some of these villages as being loosely organized and less bound together by the rights and obligations of kinship found in the son-of-the-soil villages.[104] Second and closely related to the first, is the fact that, as the population of the area became heterogeneous, village authority in the area became somewhat inadequate to cope with the expansion in space. Thus, lawlessness, which manifested mostly in robberies, was just a fait accompli.

The wave of crime in Lagos in the 1930s and 1940s has been traced to be the consequence of unemployment occasioned by the world trade Depression which began in 1929.[105] Villages or farmsteads round about Ikeja were rendezvous to which a certain class of criminals chased out of the colony after repeated convictions, decamped. Once in the district, they disguised as potential farmers or newly arrived unemployed people seeking for land upon which to settle in apparently peaceful occupation only for them to perpetrate heinous crimes later.[106] The district of Ikeja and the suburbs experienced enormous proportions of burglaries and armed robberies with violence during the period of study. For instance, on the night of November 17/18, 1930, at about 2 am, the house of one Oseni Opeifa at Hausa village was broken into by a gang of burglars, with all his goods stolen and the man seriously wounded with machetes.[107] Also, on the night of 19/20, at about 2 am the house of one Mrs. Bamgbola of Abule Williams along Idimu road, was broken into by a gang of burglars, the goods in the house were stolen and the woman was seriously wounded with machetes.[108] In the same vein, on the night of 20/21, at about 2 am, the house of Olaewe, of Olaewe village, near Oshodi, was broken into. His goods were rifled and Olaewe was murdered with machetes. There was in the house the daughter of the deceased, and her infant child as well as the deceased's wife.[109] Although the wife of the deceased could not identify any of the miscreants, she suspected that they were either Ijaw or Sobo people as they spoke in a tongue similar to theirs. This observation, to some extent, lend credence to the assertion that, perhaps, unemployment and the uncontrolled influx of migrants to Lagos, in search of better means of livelihood provided platforms for burglaries and robberies as livelihood strategies for the lazy and the wicked ones.

In the early 1930s and up to the 1940s, Ikeja district acquired a negative image in the press and with the police. According to Tamuno, the most troublesome areas during the 1930s were Warri and Owerri provinces in eastern Nigeria and the Ikeja district near Lagos.[110] Armed gangs, carefully disguised and belonging to the secret organization known as *Egbe Enumenu*, raided homes and committed murder or rape.[111] Apart from membership of secret societies, most of the burglars were in possession of criminal charms (*juju*) reputed to possess the power to protect them.[112] Two such charms were generally used: the most common one to prevent people from waking up during the night; the other to prevent burglars from being arrested.[113] The use of charms by burglars was so prevalent that, in the 1930s in Ikeja district, no fewer than forty offenders were brought to court because of illegal possession of criminal charms, a fact that reveals the power attributed to these criminal charms among colonial officers and judges.[114]

The colonial government was undoubtedly baffled by the nature and prevalence of robbery in the environs of Lagos and sought to understand the problem. A pointer to this was found in the report of Wilkes, which gave a clue as to why robbery was prevalent in the district of the colony.[115] The report suggested a nexus between crime, economy, and unemployment among farm laborers in Lagos. Wilkes argued that the crime rate in other parts of Yorubaland was lower than in Lagos during this period because of the favorable and less expensive labor condition in the former.[116] According to Wilkes, it was unthinkable that organized crime of the nature that occurred in the districts of Lagos could occur in any part of the Yoruba country.[117] He premised his argument on the fact that, in the Yoruba province, a farmer cultivated his land with the assistance of his whole family and possibly *Iwofas*. If he employed outside help, he engaged local men whom he paid by piece work, that is, at so much for 1,000 heaps cleared, and who lived in their own homes.[118]

However, the labor situation was different in the colony district where a farmer had to employ regular laborers whom he paid at a monthly rate in addition to accommodating them.[119] A contract was usually entered into by the two parties. The general pattern of the contract was that the labor would agree to work for a year but would receive only 5/-per month with the whole balance payable at the expiration of the contract.[120] Thus, a laborer on 15/-per month was owed £6 at the end of a year, a sum sufficient to carry him home and, perhaps, marry a wife.[121] The success of this contractual labor system pulled a lot of strangers into the district, the majority of who were Egun, Bariba from Dahomey, and Kabba province.[122] However, in the period of slump, as was the case between 1929 and 1933 when there was depression in world trade, most employers became incapacitated in meeting and fulfilling their obligations to their laborers with far-reaching consequences.[123] Although many sought judicial assistance, many continued to work on the same terms in the hope of eventual payment. Others accepted payment in kind. The greatest impact of this situation on the city was that an unpaid laborer whose contract had expired and who, more often than not, was without a means of subsistence or money to transport him back home, ended up in crime, as he was compelled to steal to survive.[124] Therefore, from the forgoing chronology and analysis of crime and livelihood in colonial Lagos, one can deduce that an appreciable number of people found succor in engaging in criminal activities in order to survive, because urban poverty was prevalent in a city considered by many as land of opportunities.

BEGGING CULTURE, DESTITUTION, AND JUVENILE DELINQUENCY IN COLONIAL LAGOS

Between 1930 and 1950, Lagos witnessed phenomenal growth in population. This resulted from the economic crisis, which provoked an unparalleled development of unemployment in contrast to previous decades of relative scarcity of labor.[125] According to the commissioner of police in charge of a report on unemployment in Lagos, in 1927, "there are probably 1000 or more unemployed persons in Lagos, even if it was difficult to know the exact figure on account of the movement into and out of the town."[126] Before this time, precisely in 1915, a Lagos newspaper had to decry the ease with which people migrated into the city and forewarned of its consequences. It noted that many of these people were "indigent persons . . . without feasible means of support and without friends"; the newspaper declared that "if some means are not devised to stem the flow of these undesirables, a serious problem will confront the administration, which will entail a good deal of handling, careful handling."[127]

Several years later, the same newspaper observed that Lagos had "outgrown herself"[128]; in 1927, it described the city as the "dumping ground for all sorts and conditions of the poor and the maimed (sic) from everywhere, even from the neighboring Colony of Dahomey."[129] The uncontrolled movement of the migration is attributable to the loose transport system of the period, especially the railway system. As mentioned in chapter 2, the experience of Alhaji Sherifdeen Abubakar Namama, who traveled to Lagos from the far North in 1947 on board a passenger train from Nguru (Northern Nigeria) in company of his kinsmen numbering fifteen, aged between ten and twenty to Lagos, without any job and definitely with no plan on what to do, was just one of the numerous ways through which the city became flooded with the beggars and destitute.[130] He emphasized that, for ten years, he slept at the railway terminus in the absence of any worthwhile accommodation. In addition, hundreds of boys between ten and fourteen, commonly known as *alaaru* (porter) worked as carriers at the train station and in large markets of the township. They came in bands from Oyo and Ilorin and lived together, twenty, or thirty in a room.[131] "They lived in the slum districts of Lagos Township, kept on their person the same dirty clothes for several days, sleeping in them and without a bath for days in succession . . . Their death rate is said to be very high."[132] They generally sent money to their indigent families in the country. This uncontrolled movement of immigrants, and their search for livelihood culminated in the increase of destitute and beggars in the city of Lagos.

Besides juvenile destitution, begging was also used by the poor as a strategy for survival in colonial Lagos. What appeared confusing was whether begging had been part of the culture of the indigenes or a redefined cultural practice. According to Iliffe, the Yoruba were few compared to the number of Hausa beggars who flooded Yorubaland during the twentieth century.[133] As earlier mentioned the beggars invaded the streets of Lagos and became problems to the colonial authorities. Subsequently, steps were taken, and the police found 153 beggars in 1944, but the real number was probably much greater.[134] According to the census carried out on beggars, they were said to be mostly Muslim and Hausa (90 percent), they were often married (65 percent), and they were very often blind (77 percent).[135] Their "profession" was so entrenched in the city that by 1921, the beggars in Lagos elected the leader with the title "Head of the Blind."[136] The fact that most of the beggars were disabled supports the view that they probably came to Lagos as professional beggars from the North in order to earn a living. The opinion of the long-time residents of Lagos interviewed is that begging was not part of the Lagos culture; rather, it can be said to be one of the redefined neighborhood cultures introduced by migrants. In fact, Fausat Thomas and Raji Olanrewaju asserted that an average Lagosian is so proud that he or she could embark on the street begging when in need; instead, he or she would prefer to depend on family and friends for survival.[137] In spite of this argument, this redefined culture became so entrenched in Lagos that even in the post-independence period, it was modified by the street urchins, popularly known as the "area boys" most of whom were young men of Yoruba background, perhaps those that grew up in Lagos from the 1950s.

JUVENILE DELINQUENTS AND LIVELIHOOD IN LAGOS

Apart from the beggars and the destitute, juvenile delinquents were obsessions of the late colonial period. Vagrant youths were nothing new.[138] In the nineteenth century they had joined East African war bands or the "swarms of ragamuffins" around the Freetown docks.[139] Lagos and Freetown had youth gangs in the 1920s, Dares Salaam in the 1930s.[140] Although mention had been made of the activities of Jaguda Boys and their pickpocket activities in the preceding section under crime and criminality, the Boma Boys, Cowboys, Alkali Boys, the teenage female sex hawkers, and the under aged street hawkers constituted formidable set of juvenile offenders that cannot be overlooked.

According to a 1948 report on juvenile delinquency in the British Empire, continually increasing numbers of juvenile delinquents were evident in Nigeria, Kenya, and Northern Rhodesia. The report saw it as a specifically urban phenomenon.[141] The 1930s and the 1940s saw an increase in the number of juvenile offenders and the appearance of organized juvenile groups.[142] There were fifty to hundred cases of juvenile offenders brought before courts in Southern Nigeria a year between 1923 and 1929 and around 1,000 cases a year for all Nigeria between 1945 and 1947.[143] Donald Faulkner in his report on vagrant boys of Lagos in 1941 found hundreds of them sleeping in gutters, parks, railway yards, markets, mosques, and graveyards:

> Here at night come stealthy figures. Small and agile, they scale the walls quickly and dropping lightly on the other side, disappeared into the gloom. Some carry fowls under their arms, some yams, while others come swaggering, smoking cigarettes, with money chinking in their pockets. They are desperadoes of 12–14 years of age who make this graveyard their home, stealing food from the market places, cooking and eating it communally in the evening, later sleeping under the stars. Their days are spent in gambling and loafing, pimping for prostitutes, and picking pockets. Criminal because that is the way to live, carelessly, irresponsibly, among good companions.[144]

One boy in three had a home in Lagos. Those under twelve "have been left stranded in Lagos, are orphaned, and truants from school or runaways from home."[145] They lived by begging and petty theft. Older youths fell into three groups: newly arrived, inexperienced boys who found themselves destitute and lived rough, boys entirely adapted to a vagrant life of petty theft, and older, generally unemployed "Boma Boys" who acted as guides or touts for brothels.[146]

Ugboajah argues that, between 1920 and 1950, three important features shaped juvenile delinquency: the increase in the number of young offenders, the affirmation of the existence of male offender youth groups, and the emergence of an organized network of juvenile prostitution.[147] He classified the young offenders as those involved in petty theft of less than five pounds, which comprised half of the cases brought before the Juvenile Court of Lagos in 1945–1947 and in the 1950s.[148] The second feature of the period, according to Ugboajah, was the emergence of youth criminal groups.[149] Prominent among these groups were Jaguda Boys, who were synonymous with pickpocket activity and stealing. Since their activity had been discussed in the preceding section on crime and criminality in Lagos, focus shall be on Boma Boys, whose activities as unlicensed tourist guides, and agents of prostitution lend credence to the position of this study that, there was a nexus between livelihood and redefinition of social values in the city of Lagos. Alkali boys and the Cowboys also belonged to these youth criminal groups. Unlike Jaguda Boys and Boma Boys, they were known for molestation and hooliganism. The inspector general of police gave a vivid description of them:

> Cowboys clad themselves in cowboy's dresses, armed themselves with horsewhips, cudgels and sticks, and some dangerous weapons during Xmas and New Year festivities, and parade the township with their banners and flags singing native songs and when anyone comes on their way he will be whipped, beaten and cudgeled.[150]

The last of the features identified by Ugboajah is the emergence of an organized network of juvenile prostitution. He avers that child prostitution, the commercial provision of heterosexual labor by female juveniles occupied the most strategic position among the numerous social questions of this period.[151] Child prostitution was prevalent, especially among the immigrants from the hinterland. This study also argues that this practice redefined the cultural lifestyle of the young girls in the neighborhood from the hardworking teenagers providing economic support to their families as street hawkers and traders to teenage sex hawkers, and instrument of exploitation in the hands of the greedy adults.

The term "Boma" was brought down to the West Coast of Africa from America, where "bum" means a vagrant good-for-nothing.[152] It is also claimed that Boma Boys were repatriated Nigerian stowaways from Freetown in Sierra Leone, where "bom" meant to beg.[153] The important point, however, is that the term "Boma" was foreign and can be said to be a creation of the colonial capitalist formation in the Lagos urban domain. Thus, a Boma Boy is defined as one who acts as a guide or a tout for houses of ill-fame.[154] Initiation into the Boma Boys way of life took different stages of development. At the first stage, he was a simple unsophisticated out-of-work boy introduced to the trade by a friend, a casual guide without an arrangement with a particular house. He had not the experience to make the work very remunerative, so he still slept outside and led rather a meager existence.[155] When he became more experienced and by his glib tongue and polite manner could get more customers, he lived in a house, dressed well and fed well. He might earn upwards of £2 per month. He probably had a definite arrangement with special harlots or particular houses.[156] Further, he was gradually deteriorating morally and eventually became a sophisticated cynical youth, up to all the tricks of the trade, lazy and immoral, perhaps acting as a master to a group of younger Boma Boys. Lastly, he became mature to the stage of working on a percentage basis as an important partner of an organized trade.[157]

Many Boma Boys were not initially inclined to commit crimes; guiding sailors and seamen was a convenient means of livelihood, particularly those who had reached a high standard of elementary education. They were ashamed of the work but regarded it as the only means of supporting themselves.[158] With no ships in harbor, Boma Boys took to gambling on the sandy patch on Marina in front of the Kingsway Store. When ships docked, Boma Boys sprang into action: "cheeky ragamuffins who force their loathsome services on seamen and voyaging tourists at the Marina."[159] Indeed, Boma Boys filled a necessary economic function: proprietors of hotels and bars wanted hard drinking, free-spending customers, and sailors needed guides. Boma Boys guided many unwary sailors and seamen to brothels, "sordid and disreputable places, and even when the victims are drunk they 'bomb' them by relieving them of what money they have in their pockets."[160]

The menace of Boma Boys had negative effects on social values. These are explicable in two ways. Firstly, Boma Boys succeeded in changing the orientation of the youths, by treating local boys to glamorous stories that fired their imagination; ambition to see "life" abroad was usually all that was required for entrapment. Because of the Boma Boys relationships with the seamen, the stories had always been that, if the boys could find some money, they would be introduced to someone on board a ship who would take them to Europe or America as a stowaway.[161] Consequently, youngsters who were duped in the process by Boma Boys, mostly of their school fees, discovered they had been deceived, became afraid to go home and face the punishment and began to loiter about, gradually degenerating into Boma Boys themselves.[162]

Secondly, Boma Boys occupation as unlicensed tourist guides promoted juvenile prostitution in Lagos. For instance, European seamen were persistently accused by the public for helping child prostitution to thrive. Constable Ajani, a policeman who was sent on a fact-finding mission to Apapa, reported that European seamen had strong "love" for girls in their teens.[163] Child prostitution during this period flourished on the activities of the Boma Boys, especially their intricate network with taxi drivers, sailors, and seamen as well as the owners of brothels, nightclubs, and long chains of greedy adults, who found livelihood means in bringing young girls from the hinterland for the purpose of prostitution, and, in some cases, hawking. Child prostitution was a well-entrenched social, sexual, and economic relation.[164] The significant indices include the presence of brothels, and other places where child prostitutes solicited, the method employed in procuring them, and the entire conditions that facilitated demand and supply.[165] Child prostitution was an aspect of urban subculture that was widely known as an "inevitable" social and sexual network in the culturally heterogeneous domain of colonial Lagos.[166]

Most of the available evidences relating to the place of birth of child prostitutes indicate that they came from places outside Lagos and were brought to the city as child prostitutes or became child prostitutes after they had worked as girl hawkers, traversing the major streets of Lagos, selling wares, or placed under poor parental control.[167] The experience narrated in a petition written by Rose Ojenughe, a child prostitute, in establishing criminal charges against her procurer, Alice Etovsodia, of child prostitutes in Lagos illuminates the fact that various unscrupulous means of making livelihood out of child prostitution were devised by the parties involved:

> In the year 1945, she asked me to follow her to Ikeja where I shall be better trained. We arrivedIkeja early in 1945 when I was given to a certain army who took my virgin and he paid £3 to this woman, from there I was forced by her to

become a harlot. Sir, all the money that I have been gathering from this harlot trade from 1945 is with this woman . . . I do not claim for all the pounds that I have foolishly worked for her. I want £10 only from her and the £3 my virgin fee all £13...please sir, ask me and I will tell you how I, a little girl like this will be forced to keep three over-sea soldiers at a time.[168]

This petition was later accepted as evidence in a Lagos court on the 21st of December that same year, 1945. Alice was sentenced to two years in prison for violating sections 222B and 223 subsections 1, 2, 3, and 4, of the Criminal Code Ordinance (1944 Amendment) of Nigeria. These sections of the Criminal Code Ordinance prohibit the procurement, defilement, illegal guardianship, and allowing an "underage" girl to live and work as a prostitute in a brothel.[169]

The above example represents one of the numerous strategies adopted by those who made procuring child for prostitution their livelihood. Excerpts from archival materials identified the network of those involved in child prostitution to include aunts; cousins; uncles; relatives of an orphan; Boma Boys; and other agents. The modes of operations are described as follows:

In the case of child marriage, a girl of 15 from Owerri said that a woman came to her village and paid dowry for her to marry her son. She was brought to Lagos and told by the woman that the son was still too young for intercourse, so these other men were provided.[170]

The above reveal that the usual practice was for women to go up-country and bring girls as wives ostensibly to train them, actually for prostitution. Another strategy employed by parties involved in child prostitution is succinctly described below:

At twelve midnight, the Europeans were standing around Tinubu Police Station. There were several stationary taxis around, and the drivers began offering to take them to girls. The Europeans stated that no man would have any difficulty in being provided with a girl of any age, virgin if desired. The young girls would undress to show the men their breasts to prove their age. Some of the girls appeared passive; others enjoyed themselves and were evidently being used to being given money and cigarettes. The usual price appeared to be about 10/-, and more for a virgin. These places are patronized by European seamen[171]

The above explains the role of taxi drivers who acted as touts; scouting for drunken seamen that they conveyed to clubs, hotels, and other places notorious for prostitution. Available evidences also buttressed the fact that child hawkers were vulnerable to prostitution. Elderly men, especially, enticed young hawkers into their homes, gave them money to cover their goods, and then engaged them in intercourse. Also, girls' hawkers were often sent out late at night to solicit and lead men to adult prostitutes.[172]

Child prostitution redefined the lifestyles of girls in Lagos, particularly the child hawkers as a result of the prevailing moral dangers in the community. This became a matter of serious concern to the residents of Lagos and the British administrators. As a follow-up to the police investigation report, it was suggested that: (A) there was need for ordinance to prevent the dangers of child hawking, (B) which would enable action to be taken against the procurers and seducers, give the means and opportunities for rehabilitating the children through boarding; (C) making registration of girls entering or leaving Lagos compulsory would help this department to check the girls who are married as children; and (D) police could be asked to take more frequent actions against brothel-keepers and be asked to bring in more girls suspected as being in danger.[173]

These suggestions, particularly the prohibition of street hawking in Lagos, generated reactions from the women's party led by Oyinkan Abayomi, Tinuola Dedeke, and Iyalode Rabiatu Alaso Oke. In a letter to the Editor of *Nigerian Daily Times* (NDT), the women movement condemned and described the thought to prohibit street hawking as prejudice, ignorance, and hypocrisy.[174]

In spite of the position of the women, it is important to point out the fact that hawking by children evolved under the peculiar circumstance of life and trade in a metropolitan area. Therefore, the vulnerability of the girls to immorality and prostitution is explicable not in the context of custom as the women would want us to believe. Rather, it was an informal means of livelihood for all the parties involved, which impacted negatively on the existing culture and redefined the social values.

THE GROWTH OF THE INFORMAL ECONOMIC SECTOR IN COLONIAL LAGOS

It is imperative to attempt a conceptual clarification of informal sector in order to give focus to the analysis that follow. The concept "informal sector or economy" was born in Africa in the context of studies on the urban labor market. The economic anthropologist, Keith Hart, who coined the term, used it to express the "gap between my experience there and anything my English education had taught me before."[175] He was referring to the popular entrepreneurship, dynamism, and diversity of activities of the self-employed in Accra and other African cities, which were at odds with Western discourse on economic development, dynamism, and diversity.[176] Keith Hart divided the income opportunities faced by the urban labor force in Africa into two: wage employment and self-employment. Over time, this view of the informal sector as a repository of entrepreneurship and dynamism was lost, and the term "informal sector" became coterminous with poverty and the survival mechanism in response to the inability of the urban formal sector to absorb the excess labor in the cities.[177]

Further, Mabogunje conceptualizes informality to be the term applied to "most attempts by Africans to transform and adjust their pre-capitalist mode of production to the dictates of the free market economy."[178] Expanding this scope, depending on who is reckoning, the informal sector includes those involved in hawking, street vending, prostitution, and drug peddling; mechanics, carpenters, shoeshine boys, and sellers of matches; and those involved in metal working, arts and crafts, and credit provision "people taking back in their own hands some of the economic powers that centralized agents sought to deny them."[179] For the purpose of this study, informality is interpreted to be all unregulated economic activities; that is, economic actions that do not adhere to established institutional rules in colonial Lagos.

The economy of Lagos before contact with the British had been a direct response of the people to their environment and the opportunities it had to offer. The early Lagosians took to fishing alongside their farming and hunting activities.[180] Although Lagosians participated in the slave trade business, by the end of the nineteenth century, especially after the annexation of Lagos, a picture of the economic organization and commercial activities of Lagos had become clear and easy to discern.

Broadly, these activities included fishing, farming, hunting, Smith work, salt making, wine tapping, and a wide intricate network of trading systems that involved not only daily and periodic market activities but also short- and long-distance trading practices.[181] Blacksmith work was a popular occupation in the nineteenth century Lagos. Within the traditional set-up, artisans had separate areas where they practiced their trade. For instance, the blacksmiths were quartered at Isale Agbede, popularly referred to as Arooloya, a place designated for blacksmith business.[182] Isale Agbede, today, had given way to Saint John's Church, Arooloya in Lagos.

The informal sector in the late nineteenth century was much more buoyant than the formal sector. The subalterns of the period were in control of the domestic goods traders in Ebute-Ero, ObunEko; artisans, such as blacksmiths at Arooloya; the musicians; the boat builders; salt makers; and, most importantly, the palm wine tappers, who traversed the Ibeju Lekki area from Lagos Island to tap palm wine.[183]

However, by the opening decade of the twentieth century, Lagos had become "by far the largest commercial coast town in British West Africa."[184] This boom in trade and the urbanization process, attracted people from the hinterland and the neighboring colonies to Lagos. Consequently, the urban economy, especially the formal sector, could not create jobs fast enough to support the growing urban labor force. Thus, the migrants and the natives who could not secure livelihood means in the formal sector had to find succor in the informal sector. Indeed, the informal sector ably supported the growing population in Lagos even up till the present time.

For the purpose of analysis, this book analyzes the growth of the informal economic sectors using the indigene migrant response approach to the available opportunities. The indigenes as used here comprised the Awori of Isale Eko, the Sierra Leonean returnees/descendants, and the Brazillian returnees. The migrants comprised other categories of people from the hinterland and the neighboring colonies, but not extended to the Asians, Italians, Germans, and British officials.

For the indigenes, fishing, hunting and farming, boat building, palm-wine tapping, blacksmith business, and most importantly, trading was synonymous with them. Trading for instance pre dates colonial period. However, the extent, pattern, and articles of trade changed in 1852 following the bombardment of the town by the British, which brought about an effective end to slave trading in this part of West Africa. The news and the economic opportunities associated with the bombardment immediately attracted a number of European merchants to Lagos.[185] According to Geary, there were five of them by the end of 1852: Sanderman Scala (an Italian), Grotte (a German), Diedrichsen (agents of Messrs. W. Oswald of Hamburg), and Johanssen.[186] Two more arrived in 1853, namely Barner and McCosky and within a decade, there were several others, notably Southern Wilke, Chilling Worth, Regis Aine (agents of a French firm), and Madam Pittiluga, a spinster of Austrian descent.[187]

This first batch of European traders settled on the southern shores of Lagos Island, which was then the largest area of vacant land nearest to the existing town. Others came later and expanded the trading network. Some Africans and Asians were involved in importing but they accounted for a very small proportion of the total.[188] All the three groups—European, Asian, and African—were engaged in the retail trade. Most of the European firms were vertically integrated so that, besides importing and wholesaling, they also operated retail establishments. Among the Asians, the Lebanese showed a decisive preference for textile trade, while the Indians handled a greater variety of general goods, including textiles.[189] Neither the European nor the Asian reached directly more than a small fraction of the final consumers, usually those in the salaried class. Most of their African customers were sellers who sold to still other resellers until the final link between distributions was reached in the markets, the itinerant traders, the hawkers, or street vendors.[190]

The subalterns availed themselves of the opportunities growth in trade offered. Thus, they worked as shop assistants, porters at railway termini, bus-stops, cartwheel pushers, retailers in the markets, sellers in front of houses, hawking on the streets to mention but few.[191] All through the twentieth century, markets were contested places of power among market women, traders, and the state.[192] This informal trading network, provided spectral of livelihood means for the teeming population of Lagos. This partly explains the difficulty experienced by the municipal authority in forbidding street trading and stalls in and around the main commercial centers as well as the large "indigenous city."[193] The pervasiveness of this informality in the trading activities of the citizenry received the attention of the colonial authority when, in 1932, the administrator of the colony complained that 10,000 non-registered traders were operating in a town which had only 100,000 inhabitants.[194] This trend continued and by the late 1950s and the early 1960s, the main avenue in the commercial center (Lagos Island) was occupied by an army of merchants and street traders, by goods and by parked cars.[195]

Trading also had with it other ancillary livelihood means. Human porterage was another example of informal occupation. The porters were mostly seen at the railway termini, motor parks, and markets carrying goods for traders from one place to another. This aspect of trade was dominated by the *Zabaruma* (migrants from the Northern Nigeria).[196] Also, the use of cartwheel (*omolanke*) was introduced by the second decade of the twentieth century. Thus, energetic men who could not secure jobs at the construction sites, Railway Company, or colonial office, embraced the cartwheel pushing business. Unlike the porters, who were mostly from the North, the cartwheel pushing business was dominated by the Yoruba migrants in Lagos.[197]

It is important to state that, among the returnees, trading, especially mercantile ones and European-oriented artisanship and craft, became noticeable features. The Sierra Leonean returnees, known locally as Krio (Creole) or Saro, were mostly traders and did much to improve import and export trade among the population of Lagos.[198] The freed slaves from Cuba and Brazil on the other hand developed into a vast population of bricklayers, tailors, carpenters, and other artisans.[199] Thus, a larger percentage of the population engaged as apprentices or laborers in order to survive. For a newly arrived youth with half education, the best hope of survival was often apprenticeship. In the early 1960s, Nigeria alone had about two million apprentices, four times its labor force in large organizations.[200] The period of apprenticeship was usually between three and five years in Lagos, depending on the nature of the work. Many worked unpaid in return for accommodation, a daily meal, occasional presents, and whatever skill they could pick up.[201] Many paid fees, which were usually modest in West Africa—the longer the apprenticeship, normally, the lower the fee—but higher in East Africa, especially in modern trades, and so high in Brazzaville that apprenticeship was closed to the poor.[202]

The environment of Lagos created jobs for the migrants. For instance, the migrants from the hinterland, specifically Oyo, Igbomina, Ogbomosho, and Abeokuta, were mostly found in laundry business. They took the advantage of the Lagos River to develop the business of washing clothes for money. They were referred to as *alagbafo*. Similar to that are the *Oloolu*—those engaged in the business of removing dirt from clothes not by washing, but by beating the fabrics. The traditional *asoofi, sanyan*, and *alaari* are examples of clothes in this category.[203] Their female counterparts, specifically the migrants from Oyo, Sepeteri, Okeho and Saki, engaged in grinding business (*alagbalo*) at Ebute-Ero, using grinding stones for pepper at a fee before the introduction of grinding machine.[204]

Inadequate infrastructure and absence of good sewerage system also provided opportunities for the night soil men (*agbepo*) in Lagos, who specialized in the evacuation of bucket latrine from houses to the river. The night soil men would go round the town at 9 p.m., under the cover of darkness to empty slop pails in the yard of each householder, and continued till 4 a.m. to 4.30 a.m. to finish the rounds of the houses in town for which they were engaged.[205] The main reason for their mode of operation has been traced to the fact that, in the day light, despite their wearing of masks to conceal their identities from the public, they were usually embarrassed. In fact, there was a popular song composed for the night soil men in Lagos. It goes thus:

Bi eba nlo si Ikoyi Ebuomidanioo, Egbeo'ra moto bi omoagbepo

On your journey to Ikoyi, It is necessary to carry water along
Egbe never bought a vehicle[206] like the son of a Night soil man

The shame of associating with this job accounted for why it was dominated by the *Egbe*—a group of people from the hinterland, specifically from present day Kogi State. Available evidences show that, by 1943, night soil cleaning provided jobs for nothing less than two thousand men in colonial Lagos.[207]

Similarly, another group of people who carved a niche for themselves in their trade were the Tappa—who became synonymous with an informal exchange trade (*Paaro*) in which articles mostly household utensils were exchanged for used clothes. The existence of the Tappa in Lagos predates colonial Lagos. Their leader Oshodi Landuji—the Tappa of Lagos—was said to have reigned as a prominent war general, who played valiant role during the political crisis that rocked the Lagos royal family over successions in the 1830s and 1840s.[208] They are mostly found in Lafiaji area of Lagos. By the middle of the twentieth century, they dominated the trade in informal exchange of European goods for used clothes, and operated at Jankara Market in Lagos. As a result of the boom in the business, their kinsmen from Lafiaji, a town in present day Niger State, migrated into Lagos in large numbers in order to seek for this profitable means of livelihood.[209]

In the city of Lagos, drumming and music provided jobs for many people. Apart from *kerikeri* and *Batakoto* that were indigenous to Lagos, the returnees in Lagos from Sierra Leone and South America featured new forms of entertainment in which many people were engaged.[210] Also, by the middle of twentieth century, the migrants from the hinterland had introduced different kinds of music to boost the entertainment industry. Thus, an appreciable number of migrants found survival in entertainment. Closely related to entertainment is the use of ornaments for ceremonies by Lagosians. The goldsmith, mostly of Ijebu extraction, dominated this business in colonial Lagos. It was a kind of informal sector occupation that commanded respect during the period under review.

The process of destruction and re-creation was the general experience of the urban informal sector.[211] Modernization destroyed many petty occupations but created others. Leatherworks and blacksmith work decayed, tailoring was overcrowded and ill paid, but there was opportunity in photography, electrical work, vehicle repair, and metal manufacture.[212] Also, the baking industry flourished only through "the vigor of the hawkers" response. The multiplicity of the petty traders was itself a symptom of poverty, for poor consumers could only buy in minute quantities and poor sellers would compete relentlessly for minute rewards.[213] These minute rewards were in the form of commissions on every unit of bread sold. Hawking was dominated by females, both young and old. This practice was not only synonymous with Lagos, as traders were most numerous in West Africa because of its tradition of female marketing. In 1960, Ghana had 323,900 traders, or slightly fewer than 5 percent of the population; of these, 83 percent were women. In central Lagos in 1958–1959, 87 percent of the women traded.[214]

Urbanization created opportunities for food vendors in Lagos. Lagos cooked-food business thrived in the nooks and crannies of the city. Areas such as Itafaji, Cow Lane, Pashi, Shakiti, Agarawu, Okepopo, Isale Ofin, and Odan (Race Course), all had numerous food vendors responding to the food demand of the populace.[215] The pervasiveness of these food vendors was because of the ease of entry and exit into the business. In the late 1950s, a popular food vendor was Iya Odan whose food children around Odan, now Race Course, usually awaited with glee any day they went to Odan to play. As soon as she arrived with her girl assistant, both of them carrying their wares, the shout went round, "*Iya Odanti de o*! (Iya Odan has arrived)." She, in response, called back "*omo Odan*" (children of Odan) in the twinkling, they would be surrounded by customers.[216] Also, migrants from the neighboring countries such as the Aganyin from Benin and Togo became popular in Lagos with their specially cooked beans otherwise known as "*ewa Aganyin*."[217] This was complemented with several *bukateria* owned by the people from the hinterland, *Ara oke*, where traditional delicacies, such as *amala* and *iyan*, are sold to the populace. Similarly, most of the migrants from Igboland, Calabar, and the Delta area, apart from trading, were employed by the Europeans as gardeners, cooks, laundrymen, laborers, and domestic servants.[218] In this line of occupations were also the Ajase, Kurumo, and the Aganyin from the neighboring colonies of Benin, Liberia, and Togo, respectively.[219] The Ajase and the Aganyin in the colonial period, especially in the 1950s, dominated the domestic servant market, priding and encouraging child labor as a means of livelihood for three classes of people, namely the middlemen, the parents of the child and the child himself/herself.[220]

The residents of Lagos also engaged in occupations that were considered untidy by the society and the colonial authorities: prostitution, currency counterfeiting, touting, unlicensed tourist guide, money lending, gambling, begging, and pick pocketing. All these have been discussed in the preceding sections of this study.

CONCLUSION

I argue in this book that the city of Lagos experienced a dilution in cultures and lifestyles as a result of colonialism, which created means of livelihood for residents of Lagos as well as redefined their social values. Also, this study observes that from the second decades of the twentieth century, the informal sector economic activities in Lagos was very large; it eased the urban unemployment burden and contributed meaningfully to economic production up to independence. In fact, without the buoyant informal economic sector, livelihood in colonial Lagos would, to some extent, have been difficult for those outside waged employment.

NOTES

1. Titilola Euba, "Dress and Status in 19th Century Lagos," in *History of the Peoples of Lagos State*, eds. Anthony Adefuye, Babatunde Agiri, and Jide Osuntokun (Ikeja: Literamed, 1987), 142.

2. Funso Akere, "Linguistic Assimilation in Socio-Historical Dimensions in Urban and Sub-Urban Lagos," in *History of the Peoples of Lagos State*, eds. Anthony Adefuye, Babatunde Agiri, and Jide Osuntokun (Ikeja: Literamed, 1987), 160.

3. Ibid.

4. Ibid.

5. Michael Echeruo, *Victorian Lagos: Aspects of Nineteenth Century Lagos Life* (London: Macmillan, 1977), 16.

6. Buckley Wood, *Historical Notices of Lagos, West Africa and on the Inhabitants of Lagos, their Character, Pursuits and Languages* (Lagos: CMS Bookshop, 1933), 53–55.

7. Euba, "Dress and Status," 150.

8. Ibid.
9. *Anglo African Times* (AAT), November 14, 1883.
10. Akere, "Linguistic Assimilation," 173.
11. Ibid.
12. Ibid.
13. Personal Communication with Mabinuori Kudirat, 68 years, Trader, on August 1st, 2012.
14. Ibid.
15. Echeruo, *Victorian Lagos*, 72.
16. *Observer*, "Comment on Emancipation Celebration in Lagos," August 13, 1888.
17. Ibid.
18. *Observer*, Editorial Comments, August 20, 1888.
19. Echeruo, *Victorian Lagos*, 73.
20. *Observer*, August 11 and 18, 1888.
21. Echeruo, *Victorian Lagos*, 67.
22. *Anglo Africa*, Music in Lagos, April 15, 1865.
23. Emmanuel Ayokanmi Ayandele, *The Educated Elite in the Nigerian Society* (Ibadan: Ibadan University Press, 1974), 9.
24. Ibid.
25. Ibid.
26. Echeruo, *Victorian Lagos*, 73.
27. Ibid., 73–75.
28. Personal Communication with Muritala Isiwatu, 70 years, Trader, Lagos on August 2nd, 2012.
29. *Keri Keri* and *Batakoto* were so popular that women often followed its musicians for days without going back to their houses. See M.J.C. Echeruo, *Victorian Lagos* (London: Macmillan, 1978).
30. Ajayi, *Christian Mission in Nigeria*. Cited in Echeruo, *Victorian Lagos*, 74.
31. Echeruo, *Victorian Lagos*, 74.
32. Ibid.
33. Wale Akin, *The Lagos We Lost* (Forthcoming Book on Lagos) www.villagesquare/forum, Retrieved on January 27, 2009.
34. Ibid.
35. This was Chief Kasumu Giwa's response at the meeting held on "The Drumming Question" in Lagos published in the *Record* of January 2, 1904.
36. This was Chief Aromire's response at the meeting held on "The Drumming Question" in Lagos published in the *Record* of January 2, 1904.
37. Ibid.
38. Lindsay Lindsay, "To Return to the Bossom of Their Fatherland': Brazilian Immigrants in Nineteenth Century Lagos." *Slavery and Abolition* 15, no.1 (1994): 22–50.
39. Anthony Laotan, "The Brazilian Influence on Lagos." *Nigeria Magazine* 69, (1961): 165.
40. Simon Heap, "Their Days are Spent in Gambling and Loafing, Pimping for Prostitutes, and Picking Pockets: Male Juvenile Delinquents on Lagos Island,

1920s–1960s." *Journal of Family History* 35, no.1 (2010): 55. The indent also includes information from oral interview with Mrs Oluwole Comfort, 72 years, Pensioner at 2 Allistreet, Lagos Island on August 2nd, 2012.

41. Heap, "Their Days are Spent," 55.

42. Ibid.

43. Personal Communication with Oluwole Comfort, 72 years, Lagos August 2nd, 2012.

44. Babatunde Agiri and Sandra Barnes, "Lagos Before 1603," in *History of the Peoples of Lagos State*, eds. Anthony Adefuye, Babatunde Agiri, and Jide Osuntokun (Ikeja: Literamed, 1987), 25–26.

45. Toyin Falola, "Brigandage and Piracy in Nineteenth Century Yorubaland." *Journal of the Historical Society of Nigeria* 12, no.1 & 2 (1995): 83–105.

46. Ibid.

47. Ibid., 92–95.

48. Paul Osifodunrin, *Violent Crimes in Lagos, 1861–2000: Nature, Responses and Impact* (PhD diss., University of Lagos, 2008), 41.

49. Ibid.

50. Ibid.

51. Toyin Falola and Steve Salm, eds., *African Urban Spaces in Historical Perspectives* (Rochester, NY: University of Rochester, 2005), 287.

52. Ibid.

53. Williams Clifford, *An Introduction to African Criminology* (Nairobi: Oxford University Press, 1964), 1.

54. William Kornblum, Julian Joseph, and Carolyn Smith, *Social Problems*, 8th Edition (NJ: Prentice Hall/Eaglewood Cliffs, 1985), 199.

55. Laurent Fourchard, "Urban Poverty, Urban Crime, and Crime Control: The Lagos and Ibadan Cases, 1929–1945," in *African Urban Spaces in Historical Perspectives*, eds. Toyin Falola and Steve Salm (Rochester, NY: University of Rochester, 2005), 296.

56. Ibid.

57. Ibid., 297.

58. Ibid.

59. Osifodunrin, *Violent Crimes*, 59.

60. Ibid.

61. Echeruo, *Victorian Lagos*, 68.

62. Personal Communication with Akanni Razak, 77 years, at Lagos Island, August 2nd, 2012.

63. Oral Interview, Dr. Yomi Akinyeye, Professor of History, Department of History and Strategic Studies, University of Lagos, Cited in Osifodunrin, *Violent Crimes*, 59.

64. For details on prohibition of drumming, see Echeruo, *Victorian Lagos*, 67–79.

65. *NP*, Editorial on Pickpocket in Lagos, August 8, 1924.

66. *NP*, "Pickpocket in Lagos," December 4, 1924.

67. Fourchard, "Urban Poverty," 297.

68. "Boma Boys," *WAP*, November 16, 1940.
69. Heap, "Their Days are Spent," 56.
70. Ibid.
71. "*OmoJagudal'Eko* (Pickpockets in Lagos)," *Yoruba News* (YN), September 20–27, 1938.
72. Heap, "Their Days are Spent," 56.
73. "Jaguda Boys," *African Advertisers*, June 22, 1942.
74. "Hooliganism and Worse," *Nigerian Daily Times* (NDT), November 6, 1940.
75. "Robbers Increase in Number, by Big Man," *DS*, May 30, 1950.
76. "Pickpockets' Exploit at Idumagbo," *NDT*, September 7, 1940; "The Underworld of Lagos," *NDT*, September 9, 1940.
77. "Pocket Picking in Supreme Court," *NDT*, September 13, 1940.
78. "Lawlessness at Ereko Market," *DS*, August 26, 1941.
79. Ordinance No. 43 of 1933 to Prescribe the Powers and Duties of Native Authorities, Clause 12(1).
80. Toyin Falola and Akanmu Adebayo, *Culture, Politics and Money Among the Yoruba* (USA: Transaction Publishers, 2000), 219.
81. See for details, Robin Law, "Slaves, Trade and Taxes: The Material Basis of Political Power in Pre-Colonial West Africa," in *Research in Economic Anthropology*, ed. George Dalton (New York: JAI Press, 1978), 1.
82. Toyin Falola, "Manufacturing Trouble: Currency Forgery in Colonial Southwestern Nigeria." *African Economic History* 5, no.25 (1997): 123.
83. Ibid.
84. Ibid.
85. Ibid.
86. Ibid.
87. Personal Communication Sikiru Akanni, 88 years.
88. Oral Interviews, Ebenezer Ojo: Adenuga Oyekan (80+) Lagos, 1985 and 1991, Cited in Falola, "Manufacturing Trouble."
89. Toyin Falola, "Lebanese Traders in Southwestern Nigeria, 1900–1960." *African Affairs* 89, (1990): 523–53.
90. Personal Communication with Agbongbon Adewale, Alhaji Sikiru Akani, 78 years and 88 years respectively. Interviews held at Alasalatu Area of Mushin and Randle Avenue, Surulere Lagos.
91. Oral Interview, Pa Agbongbon Adewale, 78 years, held at Alasalatu Area of Mushin.
92. Falola, "Manufacturing Trouble," 128.
93. Ibid.
94. Ibid.
95. Ibid., 129.
96. *NDT*, Lagos, April 18, 1930, 4.
97. Osifodunrin, *Violent Crimes*, 76.
98. Sandra Barnes, *Patrons and Power: Creating a Political Community in Metropolitan Lagos* (Manchester: Manchester University Press, 1986), 19–46.
99. *NDT*, Lagos, Wednesday April 22, 1930.

100. Ibid.
101. Ibid.
102. Osifodunrin, *Violent Crimes*, 80.
103. Ibid.
104. Sandra, *Power and Patrons*, 19–46.
105. NAI, File no G80, "Crime in Ikeja District, 22.
106. Ibid.
107. NAI, Comcol 1, File 1257, "A Memorandum from the Assistant District Officer to District Officer on Crimes in Lagos and the Districts."
108. Ibid.
109. Ibid.
110. Tekena Tamuno, *The Police in Modern Nigeria, 1861–1965: Origins, Development and Role* (Ibadan: Ibadan University Press, 1970), 190.
111. Fourchard, "Urban Poverty," 305.
112. Ibid.
113. Ibid.
114. Ibid.
115. Wilkes Report on Crime in Colonial Lagos cited in Osifodunrin, *Violent Crimes*, 80.
116. Ibid.
117. NAI, File G8, "Crime in Ikeja District," 8.
118. Ibid.
119. Osifodunrin, *Violent Crimes*, 86.
120. NAI, File G8, "Crime in Ikeja District," 8.
121. Ibid.
122. Ibid., 8–9.
123. Osifodunrin, *Violent Crimes*, 86.
124. Ayodeji Olukoju, "The Travails of Migrant and Wage Labour in the Lagos Metropolitan Area in the Inter-War Years." *Labour History Review* 61, no.1 (1996): 62–63.
125. Ibid., 59.
126. NAI, ComCol 1, File 69, Report by the Commissioner of Police of Lagos, September 2, 1927.
127. *NP*, July 1, 1915, "Random Notes and News."
128. *NP*, December 2, 1921.
129. *NP*, June 24, 1927, "Random Notes and News."
130. Personal Communication with Sheriffdeen Abubakar Namama, Age 74 years, Lagos, on September 26, 2009.
131. NAI, Comcol 1, File 2600, D.E. Faulkner, Report on Juvenile Welfare in the Colonies, July 15, 1943.
132. NAI, Comcol 1, File 2600, *Alaaru* Question in Lagos, August 26, 1943.
133. Iliffe, *The African Poor*, 192.
134. NAI, Oyo Prof, File 1176, Resident Oyo Province to District Officer, Ibadan, January 7, 1935; Comcol 1, 791/1, Vol. 2, The Secretary Town Council to the Superintendent of Police, March 5, 1945.

135. NAI, Comcol 1, 791/1, Vol. 2, Census of Beggars in Lagos, 1944.
136. Iliffe, *The African Poor*, 192.
137. Personal Communication with Fausat Thomas, Raji Olanrewaju ….
138. Iliffe, *The African Poor*, 187.
139. Ibid.
140. Ibid.
141. Fourchard, "Urban Poverty," 297.
142. Ibid.
143. Police Annual Report, 1945, 1946, and 1947.
144. NAI, Faulkner, D.1941, *Social Welfare Report on Lagos*, 1.
145. Ibid.
146. Ibid.
147. Paul Ugboajah, *Juvenile Delinquency and Its Control in Colonial Lagos, 1861–1960* (PhD diss., University of Ibadan, 2010), 130.
148. Ibid.
149. Ibid.
150. NAI, Comcol 1/2403, Inspector-General of Police versus O. David, K. Oneman, A. Jonathan, A. Labayiwa, Lagos Magistrate Court, June 1, 1953.
151. Ugboajah, *Juvenile Delinquency*, 132.
152. "Boma Boys," *WAP*, November 16, 1940.
153. Ibid.
154. NAI, Comcol 1, File 2471, Boma Boys in Lagos, 3.
155. Ibid.
156. Ibid.
157. Ibid.
158. Ibid.
159. Heap, "Their Days are Spent," 59.
160. "The 'Boma Boy' Problem," *African Mirror* (AM), August 14, 1940, cited in Heap, "Their Days are Spent," 59.
161. Heap, "Their Days are Spent."
162. Ibid.
163. NAI, Comcol 1, File no 2844, Officer Alani's Report. Cited in, Saheed Aderinto, "The Girls in Moral Danger: Child Prostitution and Sexuality in Colonial Lagos, Nigeria, 1930s to 1950." *Journal of Humanities and Social Sciences* 1, no.2 (2007): 3.
164. Aderinto, "The Girls in Moral Danger," 3.
165. Ibid.
166. Ibid.
167. Ibid., 9.
168. NAI, Comcol 1, 2844, Child Prostitution in Lagos 1942–1944.
169. Ibid.
170. Ibid.
171. Ibid.
172. NAI, Comcol 1, 2844, Police Investigation Report on 'Child Prostitution in Lagos, 1944," Appendix E.
173. Ibid.

174. *NDT*, "Moral Dangers in the Community," November 24, 1944.

175. Portes Alejandro, "The Informal Economy and Its Paradoxes," in *The Handbook of Economic Sociology*, eds. Neil Smelser and Richard Swedberg (Princeton, NJ: Princeton University Press, 1994), 427.

176. Toyin Falola, *Africa: Contemporary Africa*, Vol. 5 (NC: Carolina Academic Press, 2003), 646.

177. Ibid.

178. Akinlawon Mabogunje, "Introduction," in *Urbanization in Africa: A Handbook*, ed. James Tarver (Westport, CT: Greenwood Press, 1994), xxvii.

179. Hart Keith, "The Idea of Economy: Six Modern Dissenters," in *Beyond the Market-Place: Re-Economy and Society*, eds. Roger Friendland and A.F. Robertson (New York, NY: Aldine de Gruyter, 1990), 158.

180. Lawal, "Background to Urbanization," 13.

181. Ibid.

182. Personal Communication with Professor Olakunle Lawal, 52 years Lecturer, Department of History, University of Ibadan.

183. Personal Communication with Professor Kunle Lawal, 52 years Lecturer, Department of History, University of Ibadan.

184. NAI, CSO 1/19/45 28 of January 16, 1912, Correspondence from Egerton to Harcourt.

185. Akinlawon Mabogunje, "The Evolution and Analysis of the Retail Trade Structure of Lagos, Nigeria." *Economic Geography* 40, no.4 (1964): 305.

186. William Neville Montgomerie Geary, *Nigeria under British Rule* (London: F. Cass, 1927): 24.

187. Percy Amaury Talbot, *The People of Southern Nigeria*, Vol. 1 (London: Oxford University Press, 1926), 104.

188. Mabogunje, "The Evolution and Analysis," 305.

189. Ibid., 307.

190. Ibid.

191. Personal Communication with Thomas Fausat ….

192. Fourchard, "Lagos, Koolhaas," 10.

193. Ibid.

194. Ibid.

195. Ibid.

196. Personal Communication with Abubakar Namama and Professor Olakunle Lawal.

197. Ibid.

198. See Jean Herskovits Kopytoff, *Preface to Modern Nigeria: The Sierra Leonians in Yoruba, 1830–1890* (WI: University of Wisconsin, 1965).

199. Laotan Ade "Brazillian Influence in Lagos," *NM*, Vol. 69, 1961.

200. Iliffe, *The African Poor*, 174.

201. Donald Faulkner, *Social Welfare and Juvenile Delinquency in Lagos* (London: Howard League for Penal Reform, 1950), 6–7.

202. Iliffe, *The African Poor*, 175.
203. Personal Communication with Raji Olanrewaju, Felele Ibadan.
204. Ibid.
205. HMP, Box 14, File no 4, "Correspondence between Association of Night Soil Men and Captain D.H. Holly-Town Engineer, Lagos Town Council," Kenneth Dike Library, University of Ibadan, Ibadan.
206. Personal Communication with Professor Olakunle Lawal ….
207. HMP, Box 14, File no 4 …, 2.
208. Olakunle Lawal and Mufutau Olusegun Jimoh, "Oshodi Landuji (Tapa): From Slavery to Stardom, African Notes." *Journal of the Institute of African Studies* 36, no.1 & 2 (2012): 51.
209. Personal Communication with Sikiru Akanni.
210. See Echeruo, *Victorian Lagos*.
211. Iliffe, *The African Poor*, 174.
212. Ibid., 175.
213. Peter Kilby, *African Enterprise: The Nigerian Bread Industry* (CA: Stanford University Press, 1965), 71.
214. Claude Mellasoux, ed., *The Development of Indigenous Trade and Markets in West Africa* (London: Oxford University Press, 1971), 380.
215. Personal Communication with Agiri Rafatu, 72 years at Lagos Island on August 1, 2012.
216. See Wale Akin, *A Preface to the Lagos We Lost* (upcoming book on Lagos), www.villagesquare/forum.
217. Personal Communication with Agiri Rafatu, 72 years at Lagos Island on August 1, 2012.
218. Personal Communication with Alayaki Raifu, 78 years, at Mushin, Lagos, December 26, 2010.
219. Ibid.
220. Ibid.

Conclusion

This book examined the critical relation of urbanization and livelihood strategies with the background of social capital as being important for human survival in colonial Lagos. British urban policy and modernization drive of the nineteenth and twentieth century, no doubt, was partly responsible for the transformation of Lagos from an essentially rural, swampy terrain used by some itinerant fishermen and migrant sojourners to a "modern" metropolis. This modernization process, enunciated through monetized economy, improved transport and communication systems, and banking facilities, created a rather hybrid settlement of many immigrants from different parts of modern Nigeria.

Though Lagos grew as a strong trading center, providing opportunities for all and sundry, the trade of the port failed to generate structural change in the economy of the port city and the hinterland.[1] Thus, the rapid growth of the population had very significant effect on the development of the neighborhood and also over-stretched urban facilities. Consequently, from 1861 to 1960, colonial authorities fashioned out infrastructure to accommodate the population which rose from 25,083 persons in 1866 to 73,766 in 1911.[2] The phenomenal increase in population was such that, by 1960, Lagos and its suburbs had a total population of over one million persons, the first city in West Africa to attain that mark.[3] The demographic characteristic of Lagos between the periods of study (1861–1960) remains a paradox. Initially, its primary role as a center of trade and transformation underlies its attraction for ever-increasing migrants from rural areas and the hinterland. For these people, the relative poverty resulting from the subsistence agriculture stood in sharp contrast to the wealth and glamour of the city. By moving to the city, most of them hoped to improve their skills, earn more money, and raise their social standing.[4] However, the reverse was the case because the colonial white-collar jobs could only cater for a few. Besides, increase in population in the absence of strong urban planning and economies put a lot of pressure on housing and food supplies in the city. Hence, unemployment, poverty, and the emergence of slums and shanties became the characteristics of the city from the first decade of the twentieth century to the late 1950s.

This study also examined the role of wage employment, the concept of social capital in relation to extended family roles in the economic and social strategies of livelihood in colonial Lagos. Colonial economy occasioned monetization of labor. Labor attracted wages. In fact, the expansion in the PWD provided a platform through which more Nigerians were progressively drawn into wage employment. The colonial authorities wasted no time in establishing an administration that had to be manned at the lower level by indigenous workers. Products of missionary education were at hand for this purpose and when later the imperial rulers participated in the provision of educational facilities, the products of such institutions joined.[5] Thus, it became fashionable to try and secure wage employment and to train to become employable. The implication of this for the city is that as heterogeneous as the city was, so was the labor market which comprised unskilled, semi-skilled, and skilled labor spread across the formal and informal sectors.

Mercantile houses recruited men and women to operate shops, factories, and warehouses in the country. But by far the single largest employer of labor was the Nigerian railway. Most Africans were employed as laborers. This was the deliberate policy of the colonial government to employ indigenous workers to fill the positions for which they had competence. This was to ensure that the services would be cheaply run since expatriate staff earned a lot higher than their local counterparts. It was also to secure operational stability since foreign staff, whether from Europe or the West Indies, tended to be "birds of passage."[6]

This study argues that modernization and monetization of Lagos economy with the features of inequality in municipal administration and poor urban planning degenerated into "urbanization of poverty." Therefore, nineteenth and twentieth century Lagos was a pioneer in the changing nature of poverty in Africa with the birth of new categories such as delinquents, unemployed, and prostitutes.[7] These supplemented the older states of being incapacitated and hungry or living in a position of servitude. Although a slum clearance scheme adopted in Lagos Island during the period of study showed that many Lagosians were already living in very poor housing conditions,[8] the 1930s crisis and the depressed war economy extended these new forms of poverty.

The Great Depression of the 1930s impacted negatively on the economy and the labor market. In fact, all categories of employers were affected by the economic crisis. As elsewhere in West Africa, African network traders were affected by the competition of European and Levantine companies.

This was enhanced by the construction of roads, which enabled European and Levantine merchants to buy produce in areas which had hitherto been accessible only to African middlemen. Consequently, about 30,000 people that were deriving their livelihood by patronizing these district markets reduced considerably to below 2000 or one fifteenth of its original.[9] The point here is that, the decrease of trade caused many merchants to become unemployed or led them to turn to street trading and hawking for survival.

In addition to the above impact was the mass retrenchment of railway workers in 1932. A total of 20,104 railway workers lost their jobs.[10] Also, the stopping of public work provoked great loss for the artisan class and for the floating population who formerly sought employment during the dry season.[11] Among the semi-skilled artisans, there was a large number of carpenters, tailors, blacksmiths, and bricklayers for whom there was little demand by October 1929.[12] In fact, this loss of jobs coupled with the will to escape taxation on market goods culminated in the expansion of street trading and hawking in Lagos. By 1932, these activities became central issue for the Lagos Town Council. "There is no street in Lagos or Ebute Metta where hawking or selling outside the houses does not take place," complained the administrator of the colony.[13]

It is, however, important to state that beyond the skilled, semi-skilled and unskilled labor categorization of the unemployed in Lagos, the beggars, paupers, and ex-servicemen also constituted the bulk of the unemployed residents of Lagos. Colonial authorities responded by adopting strategies of combating unemployment and improving standard of living in Lagos. This ranged from compulsory repatriation of the undesirables back to their native lands, use of labor bureau, employment of ex-servicemen, slum clearance scheme, and introduction of taxes as well as prohibition of street trading. Though the socioeconomic strategy of alleviating the condition of the poor in the city of Lagos helped as far as the survival of the war returnees, both able and disable were concerned, the slum clearance scheme had negative impacts on the livelihood of the people. This became noticeable particularly on those who relied on the human traffic in Lagos such as traders and artisans. Most importantly, it degenerated to cultural redefinition and social dislocation. Hence Lagos witnessed growth in juvenile delinquency, increased crime rate, and expansion of the informal sectors.

The citizenry responded to the tax regime of the colonial authorities with strong protest movements as exemplified by the activities of the LMWA under the leadership of Alimotu Pelewura. This was also complemented with other women's movement in Lagos such as NWP and LWL. For instance, in the protest against the water rate scheme, several women speakers suggested a boycott of sales to the European firms, and also suggested to their cooks to stop working until the government withdrew the water scheme. This protest by the women was basically to protect their means of livelihood. As observed, the new water rate would put all the women carriers of water (who were quite a feature in Lagos) out of business.[14] Also, the LMWA, along with the LWL, fought, among others, the Ordinance prohibiting street trading and hawking by young people in Lagos. Further, these women movements, particularly the LWMA, in order to protect the livelihood means of men and women, fought to stand still, Captain Pullen's price control scheme on foodstuffs in Lagos. This was proposed by the colonial authorities to alleviate the problems of food supply shortage in Lagos, but considered to be disadvantageous to the market women of Lagos.

Social capital in the forms of reciprocity, kinship ties, fellowship, goodwill, welfares, sympathy, and extended family relations played significant roles in the sustenance of livelihood in colonial Lagos. This was premised on the communal living system that was characteristic of the town before the annexation of 1861. Although the new urban culture, especially Christianity, as well as other economic relationship between the wage earners: railway workers, shop assistants, interpreters, clerks, editors, and so on and subalterns: petty traders, artisans, porters, fishermen, musicians, and washermen further enhanced the spread of "individualism" as a way of life; yet, social capital in the forms of kinship ties, mutual credit support, trust, reciprocity and extended family relations survived and are still relevant as far as livelihood is concerned in the city of Lagos.

Kinship ties, for instance, found expression in the coming together of people of the same descents for the purpose of uplifting their standard economically and socially. This culminated in the rise of home town associations and group identities. These group identities became the platform for ethnic consciousness. In fact, the ethnic associations remained strong in (the African) cities, providing an alternative welfare system.[15] Among other functions, they awarded scholarships, assisted orphans and widows, contribute toward burial expenses, aided unemployed, provided cultural and recreational activities, socialize new arrivals from village into urban life and provided access to highly placed persons.[16] Thus, I argue that kinship ties bonded all groups economically, socially and, to some extent, politically, in order to ensure the survival within, between, and against the dominant colonial structures and official bureaucracies.

Lastly, this book posits that in the nineteenth and twentieth century Lagos, "urban poverty" which resulted from rapid urbanization and high population growth rate was minimized by the buoyant informal sector and social capital. The informal sector includes those involved in street trading, hawking, prostitution, artisans, palm wine tapping, clothes dry cleaning, night soil cleaning, unlicensed tourist guides (*Boma Boys*), porterage (*Alaaru*), trading, touting, prostitution, transportation, boat building, hunting, fishing, money lending, currency counterfeiting to mention few. In fact, this study has been able to establish that economic adjustment, slum creation, and ethnic and social bonding were the strategies that the migrants and indigenes in colonial Lagos adopted for livelihood. These strategies, respectively, provided employment in the informal sector and thus reduced poverty, eased the burden of housing among the lower class, and provided social and economic support.

I have examined in this study the various challenges associated with livelihood in colonial Lagos. I want to show that though the city of Lagos after independence has witnessed dynamic change and continuity in the experience of livelihood, there is an ample of similarities in the strategies adopted by the colonial authorities to address the livelihood challenges and the ones adopted by the post-colonial successive administrators of the city of Lagos.

The city of Lagos in the post-independence period has transformed significantly to a mega city. This enviable status has associated with it: increase in population, over-stretched infrastructural facilities, housing and environmental challenges, child labor and street trading, inadequate transportation, crime and security challenges, and youth unemployment. In spite of all these however, the contemporary mega status of Lagos and its attendant economic opportunities has made it a hot spot for livelihood seekers in Nigeria such that its heterogeneous nature encompasses the presence of Nigerians from all parts of the country and foreigners of different nationalities with heavy investment portfolios. This enviable status attests to the position of the late professor Kunle Lawal, who buttressed the fact that Lagos had always been an *Eldorado*, even before the contact with the Europeans.

Successive governors and administrators of Lagos city have implemented different policies to address the challenges associated with livelihood and survival in Lagos. A brief example would suffice: Lateef Kayode Jakande: transport revolution, housing estates, and building of schools for the youths in the 1980s cannot be forgotten in the annals of history of Lagos as well conceived and implemented policies put in place to cater for the growing population of Lagos. Similarly, Asiwaju Bola Ahmed Tinubu: massive infrastructural development, revenue generation, and employment creation laid the foundation for the advancement of the state in the twenty-first century. Likewise, Babatunde Raji Fashola's consolidation on transportation, urban renewal, housing, and environment cannot be forgotten by Lagos residents and Nigerians. In fact, Lagosians and residents of Lagos have also responded to the new social and economic structures undermining their dream of maximizing the gains of living in the city, which cannot be isolated from the challenges thrown up by urbanization and population explosion. One of such measures is public-private partnership scheme, which has been in use to address transportation, sanitation, and trading spaces in the commercial city of Lagos.

In spite of these however, contemporary Lagos still shares similar strategies as used in the colonial period to address livelihood challenges. For instance, Babatunde Raji Fashola in his determination to achieve certain standard and practices by the inhabitants of Lagos decided to repatriate non-Lagosians with no feasible means of livelihood, relations, and contact in the city. Thus, this generated controversies as it affected some non-Yorubas who considered it to be discriminatory against their people. It would be recalled that British colonial authorities repatriated non-indigenes in the colony of Lagos in the 1940s.

Post-independence Lagos witnessed slum clearance just like it did in the colonial period. Settlement like Maroko had to give way for planned environment in the urban renewal policy of Lagos in the 1980s. The dispossession that was synonymous with this exercise brought untold hardship on the residents just as experienced in the slum clearance of central Lagos in the 1950s. But despite the development of new planned urban settlements in Lagos, slums and shanties still exist in Makoko, Oko baba, and Apapa Ajegunle.

High rate of unemployment is a serious problem in the contemporary city of Lagos. The youths, however, have taken negative advantage of technology and internet to engage in cybercrime for livelihood in addition to the existing crime of pick pocketing, touting, and armed robbery. In fact, child labor, kidnapping, and human trafficking are also serious issues in contemporary Nigeria, and the city of Lagos is no exception in this regard. This book traces child labor and prostitution in Lagos to the colonial period when the immigrants from hinterland and neighboring West African countries adopted it as means of livelihood.

The city of Lagos no doubt, deserves serious academic engagement in the twenty-first century. This is in order to understand the post-colonial challenges of nation building as well as for the purpose of policy formulation and implementation for the present and the future. It is in view of this that this study would serve as foundation for another ongoing study to be titled: *Livelihood in the post-independence Lagos, 1960–1999*.

NOTES

1. Olukoju, *The Liverpool of West Africa*, 247.
2. Ayodeji Olukoju, *Infrastructure Development and Urban Facilities in Lagos, 1861–2000* (Ibadan: IFRA, 2003), 11.
3. Pius Sada and Ayokanmi Adefolalu, *Urbanization and Problems of Urban Development of an African City* (Lagos: Longman, 1975), 79.
4. This represent the opinions of Alhaji Sikiru Akanni, Alhajo Abubakar Namama and others who resided in Lagos during the period of study.

5. Oyemakinde, "Wage Earners in Nigeria," 93.
6. Hancock, *Survey of British*, 193.
7. Iliffe, *The African Poor*, 185.
8. Olukoju, "Population Pressure," 91–106.
9. NAI, Comcol 1, Memorandum on Trade Depression, Unemployment and Income Tax Collection Prepared by the National Democratic Party, 1929.
10. Wale Oyemakinde, *A History of Indigenous Labour on the Nigerian Railway, 1895–1945* (PhD diss., University of Ibadan, 1970), 147.
11. Laurent Fourchard, "Urban Poverty, Urban Crime, and Crime Control: The Lagos and Ibadan Cases, 1929–45," in *African Urban Spaces in Historical Perspective*, eds. Toyin Falola and Steve Salm (Rochester, NY: University of Rochester Press, 2005), 294.
12. Ibid.
13. NAI, Comcol 1, 1368, Letter of April 2, 1932 from the Administrator of the Colony to Chief Secretary to the Government, Lagos.
14. Cole, *Modern and Traditional Elites*, 236.
15. Claude Ake, "The Nigerian State: Antimonies of a Periphery Formation," in *Political Economy of Nigeria*, ed. Claude Ake (London: Longman Group Ltd., 1985), 26.
16. Ibid.

Bibliography

Abayomi, Ferera. An Introduction to "The Lagos we lost." Accessed April 20, 2011, https://www.villagesquare.com/forum.s

Abegunde, Albert. "Environmental Management: Coastal land Reclamation in Lagos." In *Urbanization Process and Problems in Nigeria*, edited by Pius Sada and Julius Oguntoyinbo, 161–68. Ibadan: Ibadan University Press, 1978.

Adalemo, Ayinde. "The Physical Growth of Metropolitan Lagos and Associated Planning Problems." In *The Spatial Expansion and Concomitant Problems in the Lagos Metropolitan Area*, edited by D.A. Oyeleye, 5–16. Lagos: Department of Geography, University of Lagos, 1981.

Adedamola, Ademola. *Factors Affecting Livelihood Activities in Ile-Ogbo Community of Aiyedire Local Government Area, Osun State, Nigeria*. Msc diss., University of Ibadan, 2010.

Adefuye, Anthony, Agiri Babatunde, and Osuntokun Jide. Eds. *History of the Peoples of Lagos State*. Lagos: Literamed Publications, 1987.

Aderibigbe, Adeyemi Bamidele. "Early History of Lagos to About 1850." In *Lagos: The Development of an African City*, edited by Adeyemi Bamidele Aderibigbe, 1–26. Lagos: Longman, 1975.

Aderibigbe, Adeyemi Bamidele. Ed. *Lagos: The Development of an African City*. Nigeria: Longman, 1975.

Aderinto, Saheed. "The Girls in Moral Danger Child Prostitution and Sexuality in Colonial Lagos, Nigeria, 1930s to 1950." *Journal of Humanities and Social Sciences* 1, no.2 (2007): 3–15.

Adewoye, Omoniyi. "Legal Practice in Ibadan, 1904–1960." *Journal of Legal Pluralism* no.24 (1986): 57–76.

Agiri, Babatunde and Sandra Barnes. "Lagos before 1603." In *History of the Peoples of Lagos State*, edited by Anthony Adefuye, Babatunde Agiri, and Jide Osuntokun, 18–32. Ikeja: Literamed, 1987.

Ajakaiye, Olu and Aderibigbe Olomola. Eds. *Poverty in Nigeria: A Multidimensional Perspective*. Ibadan: NISER, 2003.

Ajayi, Jacob Festus Ade. *Christian Missions in Nigeria*. London: Longman, 1965.
Ake, Claude. "The Nigerian State: Antimonies of a Periphery Formation." In *Political Economy of Nigeria*, edited by Claude Ake, 33–61. London: Longman Group Ltd., 1985.
Akin, Wale. *The Lagos We Lost*. Accessed January 27, 2009, https://www.villagesquare.com/forum.
Akinyemi, Rasheed Ishola. "Social Capital and Development: Paradigm Shift in Africa's Development." In *Global African Spirituality, Social Capital and Self-Reliance in Africa*, edited by Tunde Babawale and Akin Alao, 127–44. Lagos: Malthouse Press, 2008.
Aldous, Joan. "Urbanization, the Extended Family, and Kinship Ties in West Africa." *Social Forces* 4, (1962): 6–12.
Alejandro, Portes. "The Informal Economy and its Paradoxes." In *Handbook of Economic Sociology*, edited by Neil Smelser and Richard Swedberg, 426–37. Princeton, NJ: Princeton University Press, 1994.
Ali, Danladi. "Environmental Influence and Crime in Lagos Metropolis, 1880–1999." In *Technology, Knowledge and Environment in Africa: Perspectives from Nigeria*, edited by Akinwunmi et al., 337–49. Keffi: Keffi International conference, 2009.
Ake, Claude. *The Political Economy of Nigeria*. London: Longman Group Ltd., 1985.
Apter, David. *The Politics of Modernization*. Chicago, IL: Chicago University Press, 1995.
Ayandele, Emmanuel Ayokanmi. *The Educated Elite in the Nigerian Society*. Ibadan: Ibadan University Press, 1974.
Baker, Pauline. *Urbanization and Political Change: The Politics of Lagos, 1917–1967*. Berkeley, CA: University of California Press, 1974.
Barnes, Sandra. "Ritual Power and Outside Knowledge." *Journal of Religion in Africa* 20, no.3 (1990): 19–46.
Bergel, Egor Ernest. *Urban Sociology*. New York, NY: McGraw-Hill, 1955.
Biobaku, Saburi. *The Egba and their Neighbours, 1872–1882*. Oxford: Oxford University Press, 1966.
Boyce, James. *The Political Economy of the Environment*. New York, NY: Edward Elgar Publishing, 2002.
Buchanan, Keith and John Charles Pugh. *Land and People in Nigeria*. London: University of London Press, 1955.
Campbell, Aidan. *Western Primitivism: African Ethnicity: A Study in Cultural Relations*. London: Cassell, 1997.
Celik, Zeynep. *Urban Forms and Colonial Confrontations: Algiers under French Rule*. Berkley, CA: University of California Press, 1997.
Chamber, Robert and Gordon Conway. *Sustainable Rural Livelihoods: Practical Concepts for the 21st Century*. Brighton: Institute of Development Studies, 1992.
Clifford, Williams. *An Introduction to African Criminology*. Oxford: Oxford University Press, 1964.
Cole, Patrick Dele. "Lagos Society in the Nineteenth Century." In *Lagos: The Development of an African City*, edited by Adeyemi Bamidele Aderibigbe, 27–58. Lagos: Longman, 1975.

Cole, Patrick Dele. *Modern and Traditional Elites in the Politics of Lagos*. Cambridge: Cambridge University Press, 1975.

Coleman, James. *Nigeria: Background to Nationalism*. Berkeley and Loss Angeles, CA: University of California, 1971.

Coleman, James. "Social Capital in the Creation of Human Capital." *American Journal of Sociology* (Supplement) 94, (1988): 95–120.

Daily Service (DS), 1946–1957.

Damachi, Ukandi Godwin. *Nigerian Modernization: The Colonial Legacy*. New York, NY: Joseph Okpaku Publishing Company, 1972.

Davies, Herzekiah Oladipo. *The Birth of Service Press Ltd*. Lagos: Service Press, 1961.

Decker, Tunde. "Social Welfare Strategies in Colonial Lagos." *African Nebula* 1, no.1 (2010): 56–63.

Denzer, Laray. *The Seamstress in Nigeria: The Evolution of a Popular Women's Occupation from Colonial Times*, paper presented at the seminar on "Women and the Peaceful Transition Programme." Kwara State Polytechnic and Office of Women's Affairs, Ilorin, 1991.

Denzer, Laray. "Yoruba Women: A Historiographical Study." *International Journal of African Historical Studies* 27, no.1 (1994): 1–39.

Dioka, Leo. *Lagos and Its Environs*. Lagos: First Academic Publishers, 2001.

Echeruo, Michael. *Victorian Lagos: Aspects of Nineteenth Century Lagos Life*. London: Macmillan, 1977.

Ekundare, Femi. *An Economic History of West Africa, 1860–1960*. London: Methuen & Co, 1972.

Ellis, Frank. "Household Strategies and Rural Livelihood Diversification." *Journal of Development Studies* 35, no.1 (1998): 1–38.

Emecheta, Buchi. *The Joys of Motherhood*. New York, NY: Alison and Busby, 1979.

Etiene, Mona and Eleanor Leacock. Eds. *Women and Colonization: Anthropological Perspectives*. New York, NY: Praeger, 1980.

Euba, Titilola. "Dress and Status in the 19th Century Lagos." In *History of the Peoples of Lagos State*, edited by Anthony Adefuye, Babatunde Agiri, and Jide Osuntokun, 139–59. Ikeja: Literamed, 1987.

Fadipe, Nathaniel Akinremi. *The Sociology of the Yoruba*. Ibadan: Ibadan University Press, 1970.

Falola, Bisola. *On Urban Relations*. Accessed December 11, 2012, http://www.rachetanumemorialprize.org/i35-borderland.

Falola, Toyin. "Brigandage and Piracy in Nineteenth Century Yorubaland." *Journal of the Historical Society of Nigeria* 12, no.1 & 2 (1995): 83–105.

Falola, Toyin. "Lebanese Traders in Southwestern Nigeria, 1900–1960." *African Affairs* 89, (1990): 523–53.

Falola, Toyin. "Manufacturing Trouble: Currency Forgery in Colonial Southwestern Nigeria." *African Economic History* 5, (1997): 121–47.

Falola, Toyin. "My Friend the Shylock, Money Lenders and their Clients in South Western Nigeria." *Journal of African History* 34, no.3 (1993): 403–23.

Falola, Toyin, "Salt is Gold: The Management of Salt Scarcity in Nigeria During the World War II." *Canadian Journal of African Studies* 26, (1992): 402–25.
Falola, Toyin and Akanmu Adebayo. Eds. *Culture, Politics and Money among the Yoruba*. USA: Transaction Publishers, 2000.
Falola, Toyin and Mathew Heaton. Eds. *A History of Nigeria*. Cambridge: Cambridge University Press, 2010.
Falola, Toyin and Salm Steve. Eds. *African Urban Spaces in Historical Perspectives*. Rochester, NY: University of Rochester, 2005.
Fourchard, Launrent. "Lagos, Koolhaas and Partisan Politics in Nigeria." *International Journal of Urban and Regional Research* 35, (2010): 1–17.
Funso, Akere. "Linguistic Assimilation in Socio-Historical Dimensions in Urban and Sub-Urban Lagos." In *History of the Peoples of Lagos State*, edited by Anthony Adefuye, Babatunde Agiri, and Jide Osuntokun, 160–88. Ikeja: Literamed, 1987.
Gale, Thomas. "Lagos: The History of British Colonial Neglect of Traditional African Cities." *African Urban Studies* 5, (1979): 11–24.
Gandy, Mathew. "Anti-Planning and the Infrastructure Crisis Facing Metropolitan Lagos." *Urban Studies* 43, (2006): 371–96.
Gbadamosi, Tajudeen. "Aspects of Socio-Religious History of Lagos." In *Lagos: The Development of an African City*, edited by Adeyemi Bamidele Aderibigbe, 173–97. Lagos: Longman, 1975.
Gbadamosi, Tajudeen. *The Growth of Islam among the Yoruba: 1847–1908*. London: Longman, 1979.
Geary, William and Nevile Montgomerie. *Nigerian under British Rule*. London: Fcass, 1927.
George, Abosede. "Feminist Activism and Class Politics: The Example of the Lagos Girl Hawker Project." *Women's Studies Quarterly* 35, no.314 (2007): 128–43.
Gugler, Josef and Williams Flanagan. Eds. *Urbanization and Social Change in West Africa*. Cambridge: Cambridge University Press, 1978.
Gutkind, Peter. "Migration, Urbanization, Modernity and Unemployment in Africa: The Roots of Instability." *Canadian Journal of African Studies* 3, no.2 (1969): 343–65.
Hailey, Lord. *An African Survey*. London: Macmillan, 1957.
Hancock, William Keith. *Survey of British Commonwealth Affairs*, Vol. II, Part 2. London: Oxford University Press, 1942.
Hart, Keith. "The Idea of Economy: Six Modern Dissenters." In *Beyond the Market-Place: Re-economy and Societies*, edited by Roger Friendland and A.F. Robertson, 155–73. New York, NY: Aldine de Curyter, 1990.
Heap, Simon. "Their Days are Spent in Gambling and Loafing, Pimping for Prostitutes and Picking Pockets: Male Juvenile Delinquents' on Lagos Island, 1920s–1960s." *Journal of Family History* 35, no.1 (2010): 48–70.
Herbert Macaulay Papers: Boxes 13, 14 and 73, Kenneth Dike Library, University of Ibadan.
Hodgkin, Thomas. *Nationalism in Colonial Africa*. New York: New York University Press, 1962.
Hopkins, Anthony. "The Lagos Strike of 1897: Exploration in Nigerian Labour History." *Past and Present* no.35 (1966): 133–55.

Hugh, Smythe. "Urbanization in Nigeria." *Anthropological Quarterly* 33, no.3 (1960): 143–48.
Immerwahr, Daniel. "The Politics of Architecture and Urbanism in Post-Colonial Lagos, 1960–1986." *Journal of African Cultural Studies* 19, no.2 (2007): 1–25.
Iliffe, John. *The African Poor: A History*. Cambridge: Cambridge University Press, 1987.
Inglis, Fred. "Townscape and Popular Culture." In *Cities, Communities and the Young: Readings in Urban Education*, edited by John Raynor and Jane Harden, 4–13, Vol. 1. London: Routledge and Kegan Paul, 1993.
Jacobs, Joke. *Market Woman of Substance: A Biography of Alhaja Abibat Mogaji – President General of Association of Nigerian Market Women and Men*. Lagos: Mercantile Press, 1997.
James, Akpan. "Rebuilding Nigeria's Capital." *West African Review* no.30 (1959): 8–10.
James, Farr. "Social Capital: A Conceptual History." *Political Theory* 32, no.1 (2004): 6–33.
Johnson, Cheryl. "Grassroots Organizing: Women in Anti-Colonial Activity in Southwestern Nigeria." *African Studies Review* 25, no.2/3 (1982): 137–57.
King, Anthony. *Cities as Texts: Paradigms as Representation*. London: Macmillan Press, 1986.
King, Anthony. *Colonial Urban Development: Culture, Social Power, and Environment*. London: Routledge and Kegan Paul, 1976.
Kopytoff, Jean Herskovits. *Preface to Modern Nigeria: The "Sierra Leonians" in Yoruba, 1830–1890*. Madison, WI: University of Winsconsin Press, 1965.
Lagos Weekly Record (LWR), 1909–1919.
Lawal, Adebayo Ayinla. "Industrialisation as Tokenism." In *Britain and Nigeria: Exploitation or Development?* edited by Toyin Falola, 114–24. London: Zed Books, 1987.
Lawal, Babatunde. *The Gelede Spectacle: Arts, Gender, and Social Harmony in African Culture*. Washington, DC: University of Washington Press, 1996.
Lawal, Olakunle. "Background to Urbanization: Lagos Society before 1900." In *Urban Transition in Africa: Aspects of Urbanization and Change in Lagos*, edited by Olakunle Lawal, 1–24. Lagos: Longman, 2004.
Lawal, Olakunle. *Britain and the Transfer of Power in Nigeria, 1945–1960*. Lagos: Lagos State University, 2001.
Lawal, Olakunle. "Mahin and Early Lagos." *ODU Journal of West Africa Studies* 38, (1991): 99–111.
Lawal, Olakunle. "The Question of the Status of Lagos: 1953–1967." In *Urban Transition in Africa: Aspects of Urbanisation and Change in Lagos*, edited by Olakunle Lawal, 88–103. Lagos: Longman, 2004.
Lawal, Olakunle. Ed. *Urban Transition in Africa: Aspects of Urbanization and Change in Lagos*. Lagos: Longman, 2004.
Lewis, Mumford. *The City in History*. New York: Mariner Books, 1961.
Lindsay, Liza. "Domesticity and Difference: Male Breadwinners, Working Women and Colonial Citizenship in the 1945 Nigerian General Strike." *The American Historical Review* 104, no.3 (1999): 783–812.

Lindsay, Liza. "To Return to the Blossom of their Fatherland: Brazilian Immigrants in Nineteenth Century Lagos." *Slavery and Abolition* 15, no.1 (1994): 22–50.
Lloyd, Peter. "The Yoruba: An Urban people?" In *Urban Anthropology*, edited by Anthony Southall, 107–23. Oxford: Oxford University Press, 1973.
Losi, John. *History of Lagos*. Lagos: CMS, 1921.
Mabogunje, Akinlawon. Eds. *Cities and African Development*. London: Oxford University Press, 1976.
Mabogunje, Akinlawon. "Evolution and Analysis of the Retail Structure of Lagos, Nigeria." *Economic Geography* 40, no.4 (1964): 304–23.
Mabogunje, Akinlawon. "Urban Planning and Post-Colonial State in Africa: A Research Overview." *African Studies Review* 33, no.2 (1990): 121–203.
Mabogunje, Akinlawon. "The Urban Situation in Nigeria." In *Patterns of Urbanization: Comparative Country Studies*, edited by Golstein Sidney and Sly David, 569–641. Belgium: IUSSP, 1977.
Mabogunje, Akinlawon. *Urbanization in Nigeria*. London: University of London Press, 1968.
Makinde, Taiwo. "Motherhood as a Source of Empowerment of Women in Yoruba Culture." *Nordic: Journal of African Studies* 13, no.2 (2004): 164–74.
Mann, Kristin. "Choices among the Educated African Elite in Lagos Colony, 1880–1915." *The International Journal of African Historical Studies* 14, no.2 (1981): 201–28.
Mann, Kristin. *Slavery and the Birth of an African City: Lagos, 1760–1900*. IN: Indiana University Press, 2007.
Mario, Luis and Newmen Katherine. "Urban Poverty after the Truly Disadvantaged: The Rediscovery of the Family, the Neighbourhood, and Culture." *Annual Review of Sociology* 27, (2001): 23–45.
Marris, Peter. *Family and Social Change in an African City: A Study of Rehousing in Lagos*. London: Routledge and Kegan Paul, 1961.
Mitchell, Clyde. *Cities, Society and Social Perception: A Central African Perspective*. Oxford: Clarendon, 1987.
Nafizger, Wayne. "The Effect of the Nigerian Extended Family on Entrepreneurial Activity." *Economic Development and Cultural Change* 18, (1969): 15–30.
Nevanlinna, Anja. *Interpreting Nairobi: The Cultural Study of Built Forms*. Helsinki: Suomen, 1996.
National Archives Ibadan (NAI), CE/T9 W, Tudor Davies Enquiry into the Cost of Living and Control of Cost of Living in the Colony and Protectorate of Nigeria, 1946.
National Archives Ibadan (NAI), Comcol 1 498, Lagos Women's League, 1924.
National Archives Ibadan (NAI), Comcol 1 69, Reports by the Commissioner of Police of Lagos, 1927.
National Archives Ibadan (NAI), Comcol 1 G.80, "Crime in Ikeja District," 1930.
National Archives Ibadan (NAI), Comcol 1 553, Indebtedness of Mrs Hilda Hamilton to Lagos Money Lender.
National Archives Ibadan (NAI), Comcol 1 791/1, Census of Beggars in Lagos, 1944.
National Archives Ibadan (NAI), Comcol 1 797/1, Vol. II, "Beggars in Lagos," Colony Welfare Officer to Commissioner of Police and Director of Medical Services, 1944.

National Archives Ibadan (NAI), Comcol 1, 2807/S.I, "The Employment of Ex-Servicemen Ordinance No. 48 of 1945."
National Archives Ibadan (NAI), Comcol 1 894, Vol. I & II, Unemployment in Lagos, 1929 and 1943.
National Archives Ibadan (NAI), Comcol 1 1170, Correspondence from Senior Electrical Engineer to District Officer, 1948.
National Archives Ibadan (NAI), Comcol 1 1257, "Crime in Lagos and the Districts," 1930.
National Archives Ibadan (NAI), Comcol 1 1368, Vol. I, "Memorandum from Medical Officer of Health to the Secretary Town Council," on Market and Street Trading in Lagos.
National Archives Ibadan (NAI), Comcol 1 1493, Vol. IV, "Repatriation of Paupers," Correspondence from Town Clerk to Suprintendent of Police, Colony, 1945.
National Archives Ibadan (NAI), Comcol 1 1505, "The Waterworks Ordinance," 1933.
National Archives Ibadan (NAI), Comcol 1 1981, "Anti-mosquito Campaign, Lagos," 1929.
National Archives Ibadan (NAI), Comcol 1 2283/S.10, Vol. II, "Salt Rationing," Senior Assistant Superitendent of Police CID to Commissioner of Colony, 1942.
National Archives Ibadan (NAI), Comcol 1 2403, Inspector General of Police versus O. David, K. Onerman, A. Jonathan, A. Labayiwa, Lagos Magistrate Court, 1953.
National Archives Ibadan (NAI), Comcol 1 2438, "Rent and Premises Control, 1942 and 1944.
National Archives Ibadan (NAI), Comcol 1 2471, "Boma Boys in Lagos," 1940.
National Archives Ibadan (NAI), Comcol 1 2600, "Alaaru Question in Lagos," 1943.
National Archives Ibadan (NAI), Comcol 1 2600, D.E. Faulkner Report on Juvenile Welfare in the Colonies, 1943.
National Archives Ibadan (NAI), Comcol 1, Report of the Lagos Rent Board, 1943.
National Archives Ibadan (NAI) and Michael Crowder. *West Africa under Colonial Rule*. London: Hutchinson, 1968.
National Archives Ibadan (NAI), CSO 1/1/8, Rowe to Kimberley, "Introduction of Public Wells in Lagos," April 1882.
National Archives Ibadan (NAI), CSO 1/1/13, Denton to Knutsford, "Correspondence on Poor Lighting in Lagos," June 1891.
National Archives Ibadan (NAI), CSO 1/1/16261, Correspondence from Denton to Chamberlain, December, 1896.
National Archives Ibadan (NAI), CSO 1/1/22, Governor, Lagos to Chamberlain, "Enquiry for Mistakes Made by DPW," July 1897.
National Archives Ibadan (NAI), CSO 1/1/28, Governor to Chamberlain, December 1899.
National Archives Ibadan (NAI), CSO 1/19/4528, Memo from Egerton to Harcourt, January 1912.
National Archives Ibadan (NAI), CSO 1/2/2, Lugard to Harcourt, "Acting GRM's Memo," May 1913.
National Archives Ibadan (NAI), CSO 1/38322/S845, "Correspondence between the Association of Residents in Central Lagos and the Governor-General of the Federation on the Slum Clearance," 1955.

National Archives Ibadan (NAI), CSO 19/2/2634, Proposal to Extend Branch of Railway from Ifo to Ilaro, 1914.
National Archives Ibadan (NAI), CSO 26/28322/S.887, "Union of Lagos Colony Fishermen to Chief Secretary of the Federation."
National Archives Ibadan (NAI), CSO 26/41657/S.1, Extracts from the Statement made by the Commissioner of the Colony in Reply to Questions Raised at the Legislative Council, March 1946.
National Archives Ibadan (NAI), CSO 26/43222, "Correspondence from the Secretary NWP to Commissioner of the Colony."
National Archives Ibadan (NAI), DCI 1/1/4037/S.59, "Controller Local Foodstuffs to Chief Secretary to the Government," 1945.
National Archives Ibadan (NAI), DCI 1/1403, Vol. I, "Control of Merchandise Prices," Minutes to PAS, 1939.
National Archives Ibadan (NAI), Nigeria: Annual Report, 1938.
National Archives Ibadan (NAI), Nigeria: Annual Reports of the Labour Department, 1945.
National Archives Ibadan (NAI), Nigeria: Annual Reports of the Nigerian Police Force, 1945–1948.
National Archives Ibadan (NAI), Oyo Prof/1176, Resident Oyo Province to District Officer, Ibadan, 1935.
Nigerian Daily Times (NDT), 1930–1945.
Nigerian Magazine (NM), Vol. 69, 1961.
Nigerian Pioneer (NP), 1915–1928.
Nwanuobi, Onyeka. "Incendiarism and Other Fires in Nineteenth Century Lagos." *Africa: Journal of the International African Institute* 60, no.1 (1990): 111–20.
Ogundana, Babafemi. "Seaport Development in Colonial Nigeria." In *Topics on Nigerian Economic and Social History*, edited by Adeagbo Akinjogbin and Segun Osoba, 159–81. Ile-Ife: University of Ife Press, 1980.
Ogunsheye, Adetowun. "The Women of Nigeria." *Presence Africaine* 32, no.33 (June–September 1960): 1211–38.
Ojiako, James. *Nigeria: Yesterday, Today and?* Onitsha: African Educational Publishers, 1981.
Okeke, Raymond. *The Osu Concept in Igboland*. Enugu: Access Publishers, 1986.
Okonkwo, Rina. *Protest Movement in Lagos, 1908–1930*. Enugu: ABIC Books, 2011.
Olanrewaju, Stephen. "The Infrastructure of Exploitation: Transport, Monetary Changes and Banking." In *Britain and Nigeria: Exploitation or Development?* edited by Toyin Falola, 66–78. London: Zed Books, 1987.
Olawale, Kehinde. "Slum Life in Nigeria: Lagos Experience." In *Nigeria: People and Culture*, edited by Layi Olurode, 140–66. Lagos: Rebonic Publication, 2005.
Oldfield, Genevieve. "Native Railway Worker in Nigeria." *Africa: Journal of the International African Institute* 19, no.3 (1936): 379–402.
Olukoju, Ayodeji. *Infrastructure Development and Urban Facilities in Lagos, 1861–2000*. Ibadan: IFRA Occasional Publications, 2003.
Olukoju, Ayodeji. *The "Liverpool" of West Africa: The Dynamics and Impact of Maritime Trade in Lagos, 1900–1950*. Trenton, NJ: African World Press, 2003.

Olukoju, Ayodeji. "Nigerian Cities in Historical Perspectives." In *Nigerian Cities*, edited by Toyin Falola and Steve Salm, 11–46. Trenton, NJ: African World Press, 2005.

Olukoju, Ayodeji. "Population Pressure, Housing and Sanitation in West Africa's Premeir Port City: Lagos, 1900–1939." *Journal of Austrialian Association of Maritime History* 5, no.2 (1993): 91–106.

Olukoju, Ayodeji. "The Travails of Migrants and Wage Labour in the Lagos Metropolitan Area in the Inter-War Years." *Labour History Review* 61, no.1 (1996): 40–65.

Olumuyiwa, Okuseinde. "Managing Urban Food Crisis: The Lagos Foodstuff Marketing Scheme, 1943–1946." In *Urban Transition in Africa: Aspects of Urbanisation and Change in Lagos*, edited by Lawal Olakunle, 65–78. Lagos: Longman, 2004.

Olutayo, Olanrewaju. *Development of Under-Development: The Rural Economy of Colonial South-Western Nigeria*. A Post Field Seminar Paper Presented at the Department of Sociology, University of Ibadan, 1990.

Olutayo, Olanrewaju. "Systemic 'Source of Working Children' in Africa: The Case of Nigeria." *Childhood* 4, (1994): 207–11.

Osifodunrin, Paul. *Violent Crimes in Lagos, 1861–2000: Nature, Responses and Impact*. PhD diss., University of Lagos, 2008.

Oyemakinde, Wale. Ed. *Essays in Economic History*. Ibadan: Sunlight Syndicate, 2003.

Oyemakinde, Wale. *A History of Indigenous Labour on the Nigerian Railway, 1895–1945*. PhD diss., University of Ibadan, 1970.

Oyemakinde, Wale. "Wage Earners in Nigeria during the Great Depression." In *Essays in Economic History*, edited by Wale Oyemakinde, 92–104. Ibadan: Sunlight Syndicate, 2003.

Peil, Margery. *Lagos: The City is the People*. London: Bellhaven Press, 1991.

Population Census of Lagos. A Publication of the Nigerian Department of Statistics, Nigeria: Government Printer, 1951.

Rodney, Walter. *How Europe Underdeveloped Africa*. Nigeria: Panaf Press, 1972.

Sada, Pius. "Differential Population Distribution Growth in Metropolitan Lagos." *Journal of Business and Social Studies* 1, no.6 (1969): 121.

Sada, Pius and Ayo Adefolalu. "Urbanization and Problems of Urban Development." In *Lagos: The Development of an African City*, edited by Adeyemi Bamidele Aderibigbe, 79–107. Lagos: Longman, 1975.

Simone, Abdoulmalique. "On the Worlding of African Cities." *African Studies Review* 44, no.2 (2008): 15–41.

Sjoberg, Gideon. "The Pre-Industrial City." *American Journal of Sociology* 60, (1955): 438–45.

Smith, Robert. *The Lagos Consulate, 1851–1861*. London: Macmillan Press Ltd., 1978.

Spencer, Herbert. *A History of the People of Lagos, 1852–1886*. PhD diss., Northwestern University, Evanston, IL, USA, 1964.

State of the Lagos Megacity and Other Nigerian Cities Report. A Publication of the Lagos State Ministry of Economic Planning and Budget, 2004.

Stevenson, Deborah. *Cities and Urban Culture*. Philadelphia, PA: Open University Press, 2003.

Talbot, Percy Maury. *The People of Southern Nigeria*, Vol. 1. London: Taylor and Francis Ltd, 1926.

Tamuno, Tekena. *The Police in Modern Nigeria, 1861–1965: Origin, Development and Role*. Ibadan: Ibadan University Press, 1970.

The State of African Cities: A Framework for Addressing Urban Challenges in Africa. Nairobi: United Nations Human Settlement (UN-HABITAT), 2008.

Tijani, Hakeem and Saidi Ologunro. "Stages in Economic History of Lagos." In *Fundamentals of General Studies*, edited by A.O.K. Noah, 146–51. Lagos: Rex Charles, 1997.

Ugboajah, Paul. *Juvenile Delinquency and Its Control in Colonial Lagos, 1861–1960*. PhD diss., University of Ibadan, 2010.

Vidrovitch, Catherine Conquery. "The Process of Urbanization in Africa: From the Origins to the Beginning of Independence." *African Studies Review* 34, no.1 (1991): 1–98.

Wallman, Sandra. *Eight London Households*. London: Tavistock, 1984.

Walton, Michael. "Combating Poverty: Experience and Prospect." *Journal of Finance and Development* 27, no.3, (1990): 2–6.

Wande, Abimbola. *Ifa Divination and Poetry*. New York, NY: Nok Publishers, 1977.

Weber, Marx. *The City*. New York, NY: Macmillan Publishing, 1958.

Weber, Marx. "Individualism, Home Life and Work Efficiency among a Group of Nigerian Workers." *Occupational Psychology* 41, (1967): 183–192.

West African Pilot (WAP), 1941–1957.

West African Review (WAR), 1959.

Westerman, Dietrich. *The African Today and Tomorrow*. New York, NY: Oxford University Press, 1949.

Wilson, William Julius. *The Truly Disadvantaged: The Inner City, the Underclass, and Public Policy*. Chicago, IL: University of Chicago Press, 1987.

Wirth, Louis. "Urbanism as a Way of Life." *American Journal of Sociology* 44, no.1, (1938): 1–24.

Wood, Buckley. *Historical Notices of Lagos, West Africa and the Inhabitants of Lagos, their Character, Pursuits and Languages*. Lagos: Lagos Printer, 1933.

Yaeger, Patrick. "Dreaming of Infrastructure." *Publication of Modern Language Association of America* 122, (2007): 1–18.

Yoruba News (YN), 1938.

Index

Abakaliki, 28
Abegunde, Albert, 42
Abeokuta, xii, xv, 4, 13, 20, 74, 123
Action Group (AG), 48, 49
Adamuorisha-Eyo, 106
Ade, Ajayi, 10
Adele, Ajosun, 4
Aderibigbe, Adeyemi, 2
Adiyan River, 16
Africa, xv, 1
African countries, xi
African regions, xi
Afro-Brazilians, 35
Aganyin, 125, 126
Agarawu, 28, 105, 106, 108
Agbonmagbe Bank, 14
Agege, 5, 17, 111
Ajeromi, 28
Akinsemoyin, 2, 3
Akitoye, 9, 10
Alferd, Jones, 14
America, xv
Anglo–African Times, 100, 102
Anikantanmo, 43, 44
Anja, Nevalinnia, 47
annexation, xiii, 3, 5, 27, 59, 121, 138
Anthony, King, 47
anti-colonial movements, 79

Apapa, 28, 77, 118, 140
apprenticeship, 30
architecture, 16
armed robbers, 54, 58
Ashton and Kinder, 19
Asians, 29, 122
Atlantic slave trade, 2
Awka, 28
Awori, 1, 11, 28
Ayoola, Tijani, 21

Badagry, 4, 74, 111
Balogun, 4
Bamgbose, 28
Bank, 14
banking, 12
Banking Ordinance, 14
Bank of British West Africa (BBWA), 14
Barclays Bank, 14
Baro-Kano line, 31
Batakoto, 124
beggars, 36, 115
begging culture, 6, 113
Benin, xi, xv, 12
Bight of Benin, 1, 3
Bini hegemony, 1, 12
Black Africa, 1

153

black market, 84
Blacksmith, 20, 30, 121, 137
Blackstock and Co, 19
Boma boys, 108, 116, 117–18
Braimah, Igbo, 20
Brazil, xvi, 123
Brazilian, 10, 42
Brazilian repatriates, 11, 28, 35, 99
bricklayers, 30, 33, 52, 137
Brimah, Apatira, 30
British, 6, 9, 13, 19, 121
British annexation, 20, 30, 121, 137
British bombardment, 10
British currency, 13, 14
British imperialist, 9
British trade, 9
British West Africa, 28, 121
Broad street, 29, 50, 80
Buchi, Emecheta, 89

canoemen, 30
capital, 1
Captain Pullen, 85–86, 138
carpenters, 20, 30, 33
Carter Bridge, 13
census, 41
census officer, 41
Central Bank, 14
Central Lagos, 51, 52, 78, 140
Chief Secretary, 35, 36
Chief Secretary's Office (CSO), 5
child labour, 41, 139, 140
Christianity, 4, 60, 101
city, 2, 5, 15, 17, 36
city of Lagos, xvii
cocoa, 13
colonial authorities, 4, 37, 38, 77, 84, 85, 110, 135, 137
colonial government, 15, 83
colonial governor, 15
colonial infrastructure, 9
colonialism, xv, 33, 45, 79, 126
colonial Lagos, xvii, 6, 9, 27, 41–42, 56, 59, 81, 92, 113, 118, 139

colonial monetary system, 14
colonial rule, 5, 10
colonizer, 12
colony of Lagos, 34, 50, 106
colony welfare officer, 36
Commercial Bank, 14
Commissioner of Colony, 5
Commissioner of Police, 36
community, 18
Cost of Living Allowance (COLA), 36, 91, 92
cotton, 13
creeks, 1
crime, 6, 105, 106, 112, 113
Criminal Code Ordinance of Nigeria (CCON), 119
criminality, 6, 106
Cuba, 123
currency, 12, 20, 107
currency counterfeiting, 107, 109, 110, 139

Dahomey, 17, 28–29
Daily Service (DS), 84
Daily Times, 86
David, Apter, 9
Delta, 28
demography, xiii, 17
destitution, 6, 113
development, 10
Director of Medical Services, 36
disease epidemics, 44
dispossession, 5
Donald, Faulkner, 115
drumming, 103–4

Eastern Region, 32
Ebute-Ero, 2, 72, 77, 121, 124, 139
Ebute-Meta, 5, 28, 47, 77, 111, 137
Echeruo, Michael, 12, 102, 103
economy, 1, 4, 5
Edo speakers, 1
educated elite, 50, 53, 55, 75–76, 103
education, 11

Egypt, xi
Ehingbeti, 19
Eko, 1
Eldorado, 21, 27, 139
electricity, 15
Electricity Corporation of Nigeria (ECN), 15
electricity ordinance, 15
Elegbata, 43
elite, 15
employment, 5, 78
England, 15
entertainment, 102, 105
Enugu, xiii
equator, 3
Ereko, 29, 109
Europe, xv
Europeans, xv, 1, 2, 5, 10, 12, 16, 19, 20, 29, 34, 42, 46, 59, 89, 118, 136–37
European traders, 122
Ewa Aganyin, 125
export, 3, 10, 20
export of slaves, 3
ex-servicemen, 35, 40, 137
extended family, 5, 21, 27, 55–57, 59, 138

Faji, 12, 29
Falola, Toyin, xiv
farming, 1, 5
Federal Capita Territory (FCT), 48
first bank, 14
fishermen co-operative, 2, 10
foreign, 14
foreign slave trade, 2
French, 18, 19
Fulani, 28

Gaiser, 19
gambling, 116, 126
Garri, 76, 85–87, 90
Gbadamosi, Tajudeen, 4
geographical zones, xi

George, Denton, 15
German firm, 19
Germans, 18
Gideon, Sjoberg, xiv
Glasgow, 13
Gold Coast, 20, 29
Gordon, Conway, xvi
Government House, 10, 15
Governor-General, 16
great depression, 35, 76, 136

Hausa, 28–29, 38, 101
hawking, 76, 118, 121, 137–38
health, 11
health ordinance, 45
Heaton, Mathew, xiv
Herbert Macaulay, 80, 92
hinterland, 12, 17–18, 28, 117, 123, 140
historical, 5
historical analysis, 5
historiography, 4
hospital, 15
housing, 11, 41, 45

Ibadan, xiii, xv, 4, 13, 74
Iddo, 1, 11, 17
Idejo, 2
identity, 6
Idumagbo, 42, 44, 109
Ifo–Ilaro, 13
Ijebu, 4, 74, 110, 125
Ijora, 15
Iju, 16
Iju stream, 16
Ikeja, 28, 111
Ikoyi, 1, 12, 16, 29, 42, 44, 47
Ile-Ife, xii
Ile Olofin, 10
Ilorin, xii
immigrants, xvi, 42, 99, 100, 117, 135
import substitution, 82
indigenes, 5, 10, 34, 54, 74, 87, 104, 139
indigenous, 14, 20, 124

industrial estate, 21
industrialization, 56, 59, 61
influx, 17, 21, 36, 40, 42
informal sector, 4, 21, 41, 121, 126, 138, 139
infrastructure, 11–12, 77, 124, 135
institutions, 9
Isale Eko, 28
Isale Ofin, 28
Islam, 101, 103
Isoko, 28
Ita Faji, 28, 125
Ivory Coast, 28

Jaguda boys, 116
Jankara market, 109, 124
Jebba, 13
John, Glover, 15, 46
John Holt and Company, 19
Juvenile delinquency, 6, 107, 113, 116
Juvenile empowerment, 40

Kaduna, xiii
Kano, 13
Kasumu, Giwa, 104
Kerikeri, 102, 104, 124
King Leopold, 12
kinship ties, 5, 55–56, 58, 138
Kosoko, 10
Kristin, Mann, 2

labour market, 27
lagoon, 1, 10–11, 42
Lagos, x, xii–xiv, xvi–xvii, 1–7, 9–24, 27–38, 40–67, 71–95, 97, 99–131, 133, 135–140
Lagos Executive Development Board(LEDB), 47, 50, 52
Lagosians, 2, 18, 52, 74, 75, 87, 89, 100.103, 111, 121, 139
Lagos Island, 5, 10, 49, 52, 53, 87, 105, 121, 136
Lagos labour bureau, 37
Lagos Market Women Association (LMWA), 79, 82, 137

Lagos Railway, 31
Lagos Standard, 37
Lagos Stores Ltd, 19
Lagos Town Council, 38, 49, 80
Lagos Township Young Persons Ordinance, 40
Lagos weekly Record (LWR), 75
Lagos Women's League, 78, 81, 82, 137
land reclamation, 45–47
land settlement, 37
Laray Denzer, 34, 72
Lebanese, 18–19, 29, 89, 110, 122
Levantines, 18, 19–20, 136–37
Lever brothers, 19
Lewis, Munford, xii
liberated slaves, 12
Liberia, 28–29
livelihood, xi–xvi, 4–6, 14, 20–21, 27–28, 33, 35–36, 41, 50–52, 58, 71, 76, 78, 89, 101, 103–4, 107–8, 112, 118, 122, 124, 126, 135–36, 138–40
Liverpool, 11, 13
livestock, 32
London, 10, 13, 15
Louis Wirth, xiv, xvi

Mabogunje, Akinlawon, xv, 29, 121
Macgregor Canal, 12, 42, 47
MacIver and Company Ltd, 19
Madam Efunroye Tinubu, 74
Marina, 10, 19, 28, 42, 50, 105, 111, 117
marriage, 73
masons, 20
Mathew, Gandy, 46
Medical Officer of Health (MOH), 76
metropolitan, 14
Michael, Elias, 19
Michael, Imoudu, 92
migrants, 5, 122–23
migration, 27
Miller Brothers, 19
missionaries, 10, 60, 99
modern currency, 13
modern economy, 9, 13, 61

modern infrastructure, 10
modernization, xii, 3, 9, 20, 27, 44, 54, 71, 125, 136–36
Modern Lagos, 14
monetization, 13, 14, 33, 109, 136
monetized economy, 9, 13, 61
money lender, 90–91
mortality, 16
mosque, 4
Musa, YarAdua, 48
Mushin, 5, 28
music, 102, 124

National Archives, 5
National Bank, 14
National Council of the Nigeria and Cameroon (NCNC), 92
Negroes, 32
neighborhood, 11, 52
neighborhood countries, 99
newspaper, 16
Nguru, 17
Nigeria, xi, 9, 13–14, 30, 56, 82, 115, 140
Nigerian farmers, 14
Nigerian general strike, 92
Nigerian National Democratic Party(NNDP), 79
Nigerian Pioneer (NP), 44–45
Nigerian Railway Corporation (NRC), 5, 20, 136
Nigerian Women's Party(NWP), 80, 82
nineteenth century, 12–13, 15, 30, 33, 50, 101, 121, 135
Nnamdi Azikiwe street, 50
Noise Control Ordinance (NCO), 108

Obafemi, Awolowo, 48
Oba of Lagos, 2
Obasa, Olajumoke, 78, 81
Observer newspaper, 102
Obun Eko market, 2, 72, 121
occupation, 126
Ogi (pap), 78

Ogunfunminire, 2
Ogun River, 12
Oke Aarin, 28
Oke popo, 28, 125
Okesuna, 42
Oko Awo, 28, 43–44, 48
Ollivant, G.B, 19
Olofin, 1, 10
Olowogbowo, 12, 105
Olukoju, Ayodeji, 13, 15, 17, 42
Oluwole, Akinsanya, 35
Onikan, 29
Onitsha, 28, 35, 83
ordinance: ordinance for the better preservation of the town of Lagos from fire, 46
Orogbua's camp, 1
Oshodi, 28, 112
Oshodi Landuji, 124
overcrowding, 44
Oyinkan, Abayomi, 80, 120
Oyo, xi, xv, 13, 123

painters, 30, 33
Pashi, 28, 125
Paterzon Zochonis and company (PZ), 19
Pelewura Alimotu, 79, 85–87, 137
Peter, Marris, 50, 57, 59
Pickering and Bethoud, 19
pickpocket, 107–9, 126
polarization, 16
political economy, 5, 27, 45
political structure, 5
Popo Aguda, 12
population, xv, 4, 11, 18, 28, 42, 45, 51, 56, 112–13, 122–23, 135, 139
population explosion, 27
port city, 12
Portuguese, 1–2, 10, 106
Portuguese town, 12
poverty, 32, 136, 139
pre-colonial, xi, 1–2, 5, 21, 30, 43, 71, 102, 106

printers, 30
private sector, 34
prostitution, 107, 116–19, 121, 126, 140
Public Corporations, 34
Public Works Department (PWD), 31, 33
Pullen Price Control Scheme (PPCS), 82

quarters, 110

race course, 29, 46, 125
railway, 12–13, 20
railway pensioners, 5
railway workers, 137
Raji, Risikat, 34
rent profiteering, 87, 88
residential, 10
residents, xiv, 5, 36, 41, 49, 50, 52, 53, 78, 104, 126
River Niger, 13
River Nun, 1
Robert, Chambers, xvi
Robert, Smith, 10
Royal Navy, 10
Rylands and Sons Ltd, 19

Salami, Bello Jaguda, 105, 108
sanitation, 74, 139
Saro, 18, 28, 100, 103, 123
seamstress, 30
seaport, 13
Secretary of State (SOS), 15
settlement, 1
shipping, 14
shoemakers, 30
Sierra Leonians, xvi, 11, 28, 29, 34, 42, 100, 103, 105, 123
Sikiru, Akanni, 50, 110
slave port, 2
slavery, 32
slum clearance, xiv, 5, 27, 45, 47, 50–51, 53–54, 136, 140
social capital, 5, 27, 55, 135, 138

social change, 27, 54
social infrastructures, 11
social institution, 5
social structure, 5
social values, 99
society, 4
spatial segregation, 12, 28, 33
spencer, 34
strategy, 36, 41, 72, 82, 91, 119
street hawking, 81
street trading, 76–77
subaltern, 4, 60, 122
Superintendent of Police, 38
Surulere, 5, 28, 50–53
survey, 36, 38, 44, 52, 77
swampy, 42, 44, 135
Syrians, 18–19, 29, 89

Tappa, 124
taxation, 74–75, 137
Thomas, Hodgkin, xii
Tinubu Square, 29
Togoland, 28
Town Council, 43, 45, 76, 77, 137
township ordinance, 38–39
trade, 18
trading, 5, 34, 74, 77, 79, 122, 125, 138
transformation, 5, 10, 16, 135
transport, 10, 88
tuberculosis, 44
twentieth century, 15, 20, 78, 101, 107, 135

unemployment, 5, 33, 36, 114
United African Company (UAC), 83
United Kingdom (UK), 15
urban, xi, xiv
urban centers, 4
urban civilization, xi
urban culture, 21, 27, 54
urban experience, 71
urban facilities, 11
urbanization, xi–xiv, xvi, 5–6, 11, 45, 55–56, 59, 61, 71, 125, 135, 139

urbanization policies, 9
urban life, 6, 99
urban poor, 33
urban poverty, 27, 32, 138

Victorial Island, 1

wage employment, 20, 27, 60–61, 136
Walter, Egerton, 13, 75
Walter, Rodney, 14
Warri, 28, 35
water rate, 16, 75
water supply, 15–16
wealth, 32
West Africa, 1, 11, 28, 45, 123, 125, 135
West African Pilot (WAP), 83
West African Review (WAR), 48
Western Region, 14, 32, 48
Williams, Macgregor, 46
Witt and Busch, 19
women, 71, 74–75, 78–79
World War I, 19, 29
World War II, 6, 33, 35–36, 40, 78, 82–83, 107

Yaba, 28
Yoruba, xiv, 3, 11, 34, 37, 56, 58, 72, 81, 100, 101, 106, 113–15, 123

Zabaruma (Migrants from Northern Nigeria), 123
Zeynep, Celik, 47

About the Author

Monsuru Muritala is a senior lecturer at the Department of History, University of Ibadan, Ibadan, Nigeria. He is a 2018 British Academy visiting research fellow at Queen Mary University of London. He is also a recipient of the Cadbury fellowship, and a visiting research fellow at the Department of African Studies and Anthropology, University of Birmingham, United Kingdom in 2015. He also holds the African Humanities Programme (AHP) fellowship of the American Council of Learned Societies (ACLS). He has published extensively in learned journals, books and chapters in books. He specializes in Nigerian history with special bias for Economic and Urban History.

CPSIA information can be obtained
at www.ICGtesting.com
Printed in the USA
BVHW032114101019
560453BV00010B/11/P

9 781498 582148